JUMP START
❧ Your ❧

MARKETING
★ B R A I N ★

SCIENTIFIC ADVICE & PRACTICAL IDEAS
FOR REVOLUTIONIZING YOUR MARKETING SUCCESS

Jump Start Your MARKETING Brain demystifies advanced marketing wisdom. It allows every business owner, salesperson, and marketing manager to have at his or her fingertips the same expert marketing advice and ideas that the Eureka! Ranch provides to leading companies such as Procter & Gamble, Ford Motor Company, Bank of America, Nike, and Walt Disney.

OVERT BENEFIT: This book will show you how to IMMEDIATELY DOUBLE your Marketing Success Rate. From Scotland to Canada to the United States, marketing managers of MEGA-BRANDS and even small businesses have realized near-instant results using this Scientific Advice. The following quotes from small businesses, from people who attended a Jump Start Your Business workshop, give you a sense of the speed of results that are possible.

*"We sent out a trial mail shot on our new product (developed at Jump Start) on Thursday to eighteen customers and received three orders this morning (Monday)—definitely the **fastest response** to any marketing we have ever done.*
★ **Douglas Lamb, The Boxshop Ltd**

*"The materials we produced using the Jump Start principles are by far the **most effective** I have ever used. **I've already sent out four quotes to new customers,** with more on my desk to do."*
★ **Martin Bowman, Q-Pulse Software**

REAL REASON TO BELIEVE: Unlike opinion-preaching gurus, the advice and ideas provided are grounded in HARD DATA. Quantitative data, statistically analyzed, ensures that the advice is RELIABLE & REPRODUCIBLE.

This Book Is Based on Research Involving:

2,700	Advertisements
12,693	Brands
4,349	Business-to-Business Customers
5,252	Industrial Customers
298,832	Retail Consumers
3,557	Sales Representatives

Bottom Line: *Jump Start Your MARKETING Brain* is 50,000 volts of ideas and advice designed to guide business owners and managers toward smarter systems of marketing thinking. It will teach you practical ideas for multiplying the impact of every dollar you invest and every hour you spend on sales and marketing.

PRAISE FOR THE FIRST EDITION OF
JUMP START YOUR MARKETING BRAIN

"Doug Hall is one of the most dynamic and intense people I have ever met. Known for his 'Eureka! Ranch,' Doug is regarded as one of America's Top Business Innovation Experts. One of the real treasures of this book is its layout. The left side of the page 'is data-proven truth, distilled into a single sentence at the top of the page.' On the right side of the page are practical ideas. I am talking about the kind of practical ideas that you will wear out at least two highlighters marking the points that apply to you. **Folks, this book is exactly what you are looking for when you need some ideas and you want to sell more with less investment of time, money, and resources.**"

★ **Jack Covert, 800-CEO-READ**

"**Why We Like This Book: Hall has concocted a valuable formula for making marketing more meaningful** by addressing marketing issues head-on with quantifiable research data and turning those numbers into useful ideas that can improve the way marketers sell. While creating a winning marketing plan, the author also delves into the psychology of selling, the wisdom of numerous historical figures inside and outside the industry, and the many techniques that have brought others marketing success."

★ **Soundview Executive Book Summaries**

"**Now you can base your marketing tactic decisions on proven data (instead relying on your gut)**: Data heaven. If you love research data and smack your lips over campaign results metrics just like candy, you're going to eat this book up. (Plus, the footnotes citing each study are useful when trying to convince your boss to let you do great marketing.) According to one study cited in the book, 'purchase interest in a target subject declined from 53 percent to 38 percent when irrelevant information was added to the concept.' So, we'll stop writing what we think about the book here lest we decrease your interest, and let you move on to reviewers' opinions. . . ."

★ **Marketing Sherpa**

"*Jump Start Your MARKETING Brain* is a **superb resource** for anyone considering, studying, or employed in the complex business of commercial marketing regardless of the products or services involved."

"This book does offer a meaningful benefit to its potential customers. It is clearly based on solid research. And it is presented in a format that makes it user-friendly. It presents significant findings and explains the nature of the research from which they are derived. It then shows readers how to apply them to their marketing challenges."

"**The contents of *Jump Start Your MARKETING Brain* are based on a sound premise: Marketing should be guided on hard evidence and not on 'guru opinions.'** While this doesn't sound like such a profound observation, the bulk of marketing books are based on selective case studies, cherry-picked examples, opinions by 'experts' presented as less than bulletproof facts, and based on logic. This is what *Jump Start Your MARKETING Brain* does. **Any book that attempts to build marketing actions on actual data deserves a second look and perhaps a place in any marketer's bookshelf.**"

"When I read books, I fold down the corner of the pages that contain passages I want to review later. Looking at my copy of the book, I am certain that more pages have folded-down corners than pages that don't!"

"**An extraordinary synthesis of the academic and the pragmatic—**making this a Wheel of Marketing for a new generation."

"**This book takes all of the mystery out of marketing** and replaces it with a systematic and logical system. For *anyone* who takes *their* marketing role seriously, this book is a must read."

"This is a blockbuster work which skillfully blends research and practice. It is NOT another Marketing book to leave on a shelf. *Jump Start Your MARKETING Brain* instead, should sit on your desk, engines revving, until you pick it up and rocket down the road toward profit! The competition will eat your dust."

★ **Andy VanGundy, Ph.D., University of Oklahoma**

"Doug Hall builds on his legacy as the hardest working, most passionate author touring America today. *Jump Start Your MARKETING Brain* features **the richest research and deepest thinking on marketing ever found in a business book**. Doug's tireless commitment to helping independent booksellers survive and thrive is unmatched by any business author."

★ **Neil J. Van Uum, owner, Joseph-Beth Booksellers**

"**This is the most complete and comprehensive book on what it takes to market your business.** It's insightful about human behavior, pragmatic, and powerful. The concepts are simple yet provide the answers to the many brain-torquing questions challenging managers today. This work is provocative; one reading is hardly enough. I view it as a handbook I will be walking around with for many years to come with many pages dogeared and scribbled on."

★ **Ann-Marie Stephens, VP of Marketing, Circuit City**

"**For those of us with a short attention span,** *Jump Start Your MARKETING Brain* **is a tremendous resource.** You can pick it up for a few minutes and read a couple of pages. However, what I have found is that once I pick it up, I end up reading for an hour. Great stuff! I'm planning on using a couple of pages as an icebreaker and conversation starter for our weekly marketing meetings."

★ **David Uible, owner, Vista Grand Ranch**

"*Jump Start Your MARKETING Brain* **is the new and ultimate marketing reference book on how to create, develop, market, and manage brands strategically for the twenty-first century.** It details how to make a real difference in the marketplace and how to actively nurture brands for permanent growth. It's a masterpiece!"

★ **Ilene Quilty, Group Director, Johnson & Johnson**

PRAISE FOR DOUG HALL & THE EUREKA! RANCH

"Eureka! Ranch's unconventional approach has won raves from some of the biggest corporations in the country."

★ **CNN**

"America's #1 Idea Guru."

★ **A&E Top 10**

"Eureka! Ranch … has developed more new products (or offshoots of existing ones) than any other organization in America."

★ **New York Magazine**

"Eureka! Ranch goes to any length to encourage a fresh perspective . . . clients say it works."

★ **Wall Street Journal**

"An entrepreneur who just might have what we've all been looking for . . . the happy secret to success."

★ **Dateline NBC**

"When Doug meets Disney, creativity ne'er wanes;
Our team explodes when he jump starts our brains!"

★ **Ellen Guidera, VP, The Walt Disney Company**

"America's Top New Product Idea Man."

★ **Inc. magazine**

"Doug Hall has a method to his madness, a rigorous, quantifiable process for inventing breakthrough ideas for clients. Unlike many creative gurus hustling ideation wares in the corporate marketplace, Doug makes it imperative that his Eureka! Inventing processes are quantified every step of the way."

★ **CIO magazine**

"Hall has a habit of thinking big. His credentials are impeccable."

★ **Unlimited magazine, Scotland**

JUMP START
✑ Your ✑

MARKETING
★ BRAIN ★

SCIENTIFIC ADVICE & PRACTICAL IDEAS
for Revolutionizing Your Marketing Success

Doug Hall

Portions of this book were originally
published as *Meaningful Marketing*,
Jeffrey Stamp provided technical and
promotional assistance with that edition.

BRAIN
BREW
BOOKS

Cincinnati, Ohio
www.BrainBrewBooks.com
An Imprint of Emmis Books

Eureka! Institute
3849 Edwards Road
Cincinnati, Ohio 45244 USA
(513) 271-9911

The following are trademarks of the Eureka! Institute, Inc.: Meaningful Marketing, Eureka!, Eureka! Ranch, Brain Brew, Brain Brew Books, Measurably Smarter, The Three Dimensions of Creativity, Jump Start Your Business, Merwyn, Marketing Physics, and Capitalist Creativity.

To contact Doug Hall:
  E-mail: Doug@DougHall.com
  Web site: www.DougHall.com
  Call: (513) 271-9911

Library of Congress Control Number: 2005923091

ISBN 157860205X

Cover Design: Stephen Sullivan
Interior Design: Matthew DeRhodes
Editor: Jack Heffron

This book is dedicated

to the Revolutionaries!

To Dr. W. Edwards Deming

and

to Tom Peters—who JOLTED my thinking
—and sparked this edition.

The spirit of adventure is the fuel that drives the creative engine.
It awakens the imagination, fires up the adrenaline,
and ignites the willingness to learn!

★ Doug Hall

TABLE OF CONTENTS

MARKETING BRAIN IQ TEST

At the Eureka! Ranch we believe in measurement. We've found that it's only by measuring our systems of thinking and operations that we can identify where we are and how to make meaningful improvements. To that end, **this Marketing Brain IQ Test is designed to help you benchmark where you are**.

All of the answers have validity in certain situations. Your job is to find the answer that is the most right most of the time. Specifically, of the options provided for each question, choose the one that offers the higher "odds of success." The correct answers are provided in the back of the book on page 298.

NOTE: As I say during lectures and workshops, I ask that there be NO WHINING during the test. Having tested thousands of sales and marketing executives, I know that when you get an answer right, you'll consider it validation of your brilliance. However, when you get one wrong, you might be inclined to whine. Please don't. **Consider your wrong answer to be validation of how smart you were to purchase this book.**

**To take the test, use a PEN and mark ON THE PAGE.
Pencils are for wimps!**

1. <u>The smartest way to significantly grow sales is ...</u>
   a. Build loyalty
   b. Find new customers

2. <u>To build greater annual loyalty, it's smarter to ...</u>
   a. Increase dollars purchased per purchase occasion
   b. Increase frequency of purchase

3. <u>Most new products or services fail because of ...</u>
   a. Poor execution of sales and marketing
   b. Poor product or service performance
   c. Not being a very good idea in the first place

4. <u>When creating ideas for new products or services, the smartest strategy is ...</u>
   a. To create ideas based on listening to the "voice of the customer"
   b. Create ideas that customers are not necessarily asking for

5. **When presenting data to a customer, you will be most effective if …**
      a. You provide a clear and simple chart
      b. You explain the data in clear and simple words

6. **A customer letter or a print ad has the best chances of success if …**
      a. You respect their intelligence and write at a high-school level
      b. You dumb it down and write so a ten-year-old can understand it

7. **Significant overall sales growth can be realized if …**
      a. You cut your product line by as much as 50 percent
      b. You expand your product line to service all customers

8. **When selling a customer it is best to …**
      a. Be blunt and direct about what you offer
      b. Use a softer, relationship-focused approach

9. **Building customer credibility is most effective if you offer …**
      a. A product demonstration
      b. Testimonials from satisfied customers

10. **Forced to choose, buyers prefer salespeople who are …**
      a. Highly dependable
      b. Highly competent

11. **The smartest way to introduce a new consumer product or service is to …**
      a. Introduce it at a lower price to generate trial
      b. Keep your price at list price from the beginning

12. **In industrial marketing it's nine times more important to focus on …**
      a. Price advantages
      b. Performance and quality advantages

13. **With a major breakthrough product or service, you can usually tell …**
      a. You have a winner within twelve months
      b. It usually takes as much as six years before you can tell

FOREWORD
{by Sergio Zyman}

Jump Start Your MARKETING Brain is a proven playbook for surviving in the current world and for growing your business in general.

In place of mindless gimmicks and tricks, it delivers rock-solid data, insightful truths, and **market-altering ideas that will help you get to your business destination**.

This book shows you how to quantitatively tilt the odds of success in your favor. The book also documents practical ideas for making a measurable difference in your sales and marketing results.

In a nutshell, the book teaches what I preach: "How to sell more, to more people, for more money, more efficiently." It also does something that I like to do over and over again, which is to blow up the black box of marketing and to replace it with proven principles. It proves clearly that marketing can and should be considered a hard science, not an artistic mystery.

Like a business anthropologist, Doug Hall has sifted through mounds of academic research and real-world marketplace data so you don't have to. He's dug deep to quantify what really matters—what really works in today's marketplace.

Jump Start Your MARKETING Brain directly challenges conventional marketing wisdom. It backs up its challenges with hard data. Huge chunks of the book are counterintuitive. And at the end of the day, you might think that this is just a trick to get your attention, but it's not. The counterintuitive insights are proven principles that you need to understand if you want to make a real difference for your business.

In today's world, it's time for a revolution in how we market and sell every branded product and service. It's time to start fresh. It's time to lay the policies and principles of failure aside. It's time to embrace a more scientific, data-driven approach where we "play with the odds" instead of "praying for long shots."

Jump Start Your MARKETING Brain is a blueprint for how I see marketing in the future and how I've been seeing it for the last few years. It's the marketing that made me successful. It's a back-to-basics marketing focused on what really matters. It's about connecting customers and consumers with meaningful brands, products, and services in order to get them to give us their hard-earned dollars, yen, pounds, pesos, and euros in return.

The data mining, statistical analysis and insight that *Jump Start Your MARKETING Brain* delivers are impressive. But the monumental aspect of the book is how the Scientific Advice has been translated into Practical Ideas, the kind of actionable, practical ideas that have made the Eureka! Ranch legendary in the corporate world.

Never in business history has there been a greater need for revolution in how we approach sales and marketing. I've been talking about it now for years and practiced it for many more years when I worked for the Coca-Cola Company. Now is the time for a more disciplined, factual, and measured approach. The discipline starts with a fundamental focus on meaningfully serving the real needs of our customers and our consumers. The time for creative geniuses comes after that. You have to have a strategy and a destination before you can start applying creativity to that strategy and destination.

Jump Start Your MARKETING Brain is a book that, beyond any doubts, confirms what I have long believed: **Marketing-centered thinking is and should be the engine of growth for your entire company, not just for your brands.** Marketing thinking is too important to keep hidden in the sales and marketing department. Marketing is the fundamental promise of your organization. It is the glue that guides the direction and inter-relationships between all departments from finance to manufacturing to every other silo that you have on your organizational chart.

When I wrote *The End of Marketing as We Know It*, people wrote me and said, "Oh, wow! Now I get it. I understand what marketing is, and now I want to start practicing it in a more scientific way." The two-page format of *Jump Start Your MARKETING Brain* screams at you to take action—to get up, get out, and do something to make a clear difference for your company; a measurable difference for your company. **The time for excuses is over. The time for action is now**, and I'm sure that after reading *Jump Start Your MARKETING Brain*, many people will write to Hall as they wrote to me, and they'll say, "Now I get it, and I'm going to get it done."

Sergio Zyman
CEO, Zyman Marketing
Former Chief Marketing Officer
The Coca-Cola Company

Sergio Zyman's books include:
The End of Marketing as We Know It
The End of Advertising as We Know It
Renovate Before You Innovate:
Why Doing the New Thing Might Not
Be the Right Thing

INTRODUCTION

Learning is not compulsory … neither is survival.
★ **W. Edwards Deming**

Wake up, Marketers!
    It's time for a revolution.
    Most marketing programs are WORTHLESS!

AND if something doesn't change, most marketing people will soon become cost-savings opportunities!

By most marketing programs, I mean 75 to 95 percent. That's the numeric estimate of the failure rate of marketing initiatives according to academic researchers, it's the forecast based on interviews with CEOs, and it's the conclusion of my own independent research on more than 10,000 ideas.

It's time for a revolution in marketing. It's time for marketing managers and senior managers at companies small and large to change their approach.

The world of sales and marketing faces a crisis of confidence. Senior management of large corporations, as well as many who finance small and medium-sized businesses, has lost faith in the abilities of sales and marketing to grow top-line sales. Instead, management is turning to the more disciplined purchasing, production, and manufacturing groups as they are reliably delivering lower costs and finding new ways to improve bottom-line profits.

The only way we are going to change this negative momentum— and yes, I'm a ZEALOT for the HONORABLE CRAFTS of SALES & MARKETING—is by changing our THINKING SYSTEMS. It's through changing our systems of thinking that we can achieve meaningful, measurable top-line growth and rightfully restore the confidence of senior management and those who finance small and medium-sized enterprises.

Even the biggest of the big need to change their approach. A study by Emergence in 2003 found that of twenty-two advertisers in the "$100 million advertising spending club," only six had marketing slogans recognized by more than 10 percent of the adult population!

And I thought that "stupid" marketing ended with the thankful death of the "dot-con" marketers at the turn of the century. Apparently not.

Since this book was first published, thousands of executives from Singapore to New York to London have taken the Marketing Brain IQ Test on the previous pages. The results have been EMBARRASSING!

When given the multiple-choice test, marketing HOT SHOTS get an average of 30 percent correct. Heck, given that there are only two options for most of the questions, flipping a coin should get them a 50 percent success rate. **Marketing Managers laugh when they get basic questions wrong. I cry.**

Tom Peters is a kindred spirit. He was kind enough to write the foreword to the first book in the Jump Start series, *Jump Start Your BUSINESS Brain*. An e-mail from him, written from his New Delhi hotel room in the fall of 2004, gave me a wake-up call. Here's an excerpt:

Tom Peters's **Re-Imagine Manifesto**

They say I'm extreme.
I say I'm a realist.

They say "We need an Initiative."
I say "We need a Dream, and Dreamers.

They say "We can't handle this much change."
I say "Your job and career are in jeopardy; what other options
*   do you have?"*

They say "Take a deep breath. Be calm."
I say "Tell it to Wal-Mart. Tell it to China. Tell it to India.
*   Tell it to Dell. Tell it to Microsoft."*

They say, "Sure we need 'Change.'"
I say we need "REVOLUTION NOW."

They say "Conglomerate & Imitate!"
I say "Create & Innovate!"

They say "Market share."
I say "Market CREATION."

They say *"Globalization is a bumpy road."*
I say India and China and Asia in general are within two
 decades of running the show: Get ready or get trounced.

They say *"It's a fright."*
I say *"It's a Helluva Ride."*

They say it's *"daunting."*
I say it's *"a hoot."*

They say *"Install cost controls with teeth."*
I say *"Grow the Top Line."*

They say *"Wait your turn, honor those who have marched
 these corridors before you."*
I say Get Off Your Butt & Go for the Gold … TODAY …
 or sign the transfer papers
willing your job in perpetuity to a Chinese or Indian who
Gives a Shit and Gets Up
(VERY) Early and works Saturdays & Sundays.

They say I *"overplay"* the *"women's thing."*
I say the share of Women in Senior Leadership Positions is a
 Waste and a Disgrace and a
Strategic Marketing Error.

They say we need a *"project"* to exploit the women-boomer-
 geezer market.
I say we need Total Strategic Realignment to exploit the
Women-Boomer-Geezer
Opportunity.

They say *"We can't all be Revolutionaries."*
I say *"Why not?"*

They say this is just a Rant.
I say this is just Reality.

They say *"The man is not nice."*
I say *"The times are not forgiving."*

HELPING TO STOP THE MADNESS

Jump Start Your MARKETING Brain is my small contribution to stopping the marketing madness. **It's 50,000 volts of ideas and advice designed to guide business owners and managers toward smarter systems of marketing thinking.**

This book was originally published as *Meaningful Marketing*. It was a proper book. An adult book. A mature book. The result was impressive reviews from such lofty publications as *Marketing Research Magazine*, *Midwest Book Review*, and *Soundview Executive Book Summaries* and from the longtime "sage" of business book reviews himself, Jack Covert, founder of 800-CEO-READ.

The problem was that while the academics and reviewers loved the book's rich amount of data, the real-world folks weren't getting it. Therefore, I decided to "blow up the book." As Picasso once said, "Sometimes the first act of creation is one of destruction."

This revised edition has greater urgency—higher energy—and more bluntness than the first because, as Tom Peters says, **"These times are not forgiving."** I've torn the book apart, reworked, revised, and rewritten it. I've made changes to virtually every page. I've also reorganized the content into sections that better reflect the needs of readers—marketing strategy, marketing message, persuasion, selling, leadership, and teamwork.

Lastly, given the scope of the changes, I figured it was appropriate to give the book a new title and look. Given the disappointing results of the Marketing Brain IQ test, I almost named the book **A First Course in Marketing Literacy**, because frankly, most marketing managers are virtually ILLITERATE when it comes to understanding the fundamentals of marketing. But alas, cooler heads at my publisher prevailed.

THE OVERT BENEFIT OF THIS BOOK TO YOU

The ideas and advice in this book will help you IMMEDIATELY DOUBLE your Marketing Success Rate. Said another way, this book will show you How to Sell More with Less Effort. By following the advice, you will multiply the impact of every dollar you invest and every hour you spend on sales and marketing.

When I say IMMEDIATELY, I mean it. From Scotland to Canada to the United States, I have seen marketers from small, medium, and mega-sized companies realize a doubling of their success rate in just an eight-hour workshop. The following quotes from small businesses

in Scotland, from people who attended a Jump Start Your Business workshop, give you a sense of the speed of results that are possible.

*"We sent out a trial mail shot on our new product (developed at Jump Start) on Thursday to eighteen customers and received three orders this morning (Monday)—definitely the **fastest response** to any marketing we have ever done."*

★ **Douglas Lamb, The Boxshop Ltd**

*"The materials we produced using the Jump Start principles are by far the **most effective** I have ever used. **I've already sent out four quotes to new customers**, with more on my desk to do."*

★ **Martin Bowman, Q-Pulse Software**

THE REAL REASON TO BELIEVE THAT YOU WILL IMMEDIATELY DOUBLE YOUR SUCCESS RATE

Unlike the statements of opinion-preaching gurus, the advice and ideas in this book are grounded in HARD DATA. Quantitative data statistically analyzed ensures that the advice provided is RELIABLE & REPRODUCIBLE. The data behind this book range from a "mind-numbing" review of more than 2,000 academic articles to thousands of hours of original statistical research of data sets provided by Eureka! Ranch clients.

<u>This Book Is Based on Research Involving:</u>

2,700	Advertisements
12,693	Brands
4,349	Business-to-Business Customers
5,252	Industrial Customers
298,832	Retail Consumers
3,557	Sales Representatives

ONE STEP FURTHER THAN EVEN STATISTICAL SIGNIFICANCE

After studying the academic research, it became clear to me that statistical significance or size of study would not be a sufficient standard. I found research on large base sizes that I just didn't find convincing and studies using smaller samples that were convincing. To resolve this dilemma, I decided to review the data sources based on the more challenging legal standard of "truth beyond a reasonable doubt." Specifically, I used the Web site www.lectlaw.com's definition of it:

> BEYOND A REASONABLE DOUBT: The level of certainty a juror must have to find a defendant guilty of a crime. A real doubt, based upon reason and common sense after careful and impartial consideration of all the evidence, or lack of evidence, in a case.

> Proof beyond a reasonable doubt, therefore, is proof of such a convincing character that you would be willing to rely and act upon it without hesitation in the most important of your own affairs. However, it does not mean an absolute certainty.

For every piece of Scientific Advice offered in this book, I asked myself, "Is this advice of such a convincing character that I would be willing to rely and act upon it without hesitation in the most important of my own affairs?"

I realize that it's always possible that new data may contradict what I've written. I look upon potential future contradictions with anticipation, not fear. I love to learn. I welcome the submission of additional data and/or arguments that contradict my findings.

WHAT YOU'LL ACTUALLY REALIZE FROM APPLYING THIS BOOK'S ADVICE

In truth, you will probably do better than double your odds of success, but I figured that you wouldn't believe me if I told you. Studies of Eureka! Ranch clients (mega-brands and small businesses) indicate that through EXTREMELY DISCIPLINED application of the Scientific Advice on these pages, most clients move from 15 percent odds of success with their marketing message to 45 to 60 percent—**in effect TRIPLING to QUADRUPLING their odds.** How much improvement you realize depends on your DEDICATION to learning and your DISCIPLINE in applying the learning to your situation.

NO STATISTICAL KNOWLEDGE REQUIRED

I've translated all statistical terms into common English. The result is that even if you suffered from allergic reactions to high school math, you will easily grasp all advice on these pages.

The Technical Appendix provides specific details on my research sources. I realize that not everyone is as much of a data geek as I am. However, I strongly recommend that you read some of the technical references cited.

HINT: When you find yourself becoming DEFENSIVE—fighting or rejecting the advice I've articulated—you have a responsibility to yourself and your company to seek deeper understanding. With the Internet, accessing the academic articles is easy. If it's a proprietary Eureka! Ranch study, e-mail me at **Doug@DougHall.com**, and I'll provide more details.

THE ADVICE YOU REJECT OFFERS THE GREATEST OPPORTUNITY FOR HELPING YOU MEASURABLY IMPROVE YOUR MARKETING SUCCESS RATE!

IT'S SYSTEMS—THINKING SYSTEMS— THAT CAUSE MARKETING FAILURE

Dr. W. Edwards Deming is considered one of the "fathers" of modern management methods. His work on Total Quality has spawned 6-Sigma, Lean Engineering, and countless other variations. He was instrumental in helping Japan become a world economic power. If you've ever been in awe of the quality of a Japanese car, you've experienced Dr. Deming's legacy.

I have a small personal connection to Dr. Deming that no doubt influences my opinions. The first company in the United States to work with Dr. Deming was Nashua Corporation, where my father was director of Central Engineering. At the time, I was a chemical engineering student at the University of Maine. I'll never forget my father's excitement as he spoke of Dr. Deming's principles and processes. He spoke in wonder at the near-miraculous results he witnessed.

Eventually NBC did a story on what was happening at Nashua Corporation, leading to a team from the Ford Motor Company and others traveling to the company's headquarters in Nashua, New Hampshire.

My dad's excitement infected me. Over the years I've sought to apply Deming's Scientific Method to sales, marketing, and innovation. This book is my learning to date; however, there is much to be done.

Dr. Deming found that most failures were failures of the system. He estimated that 94 percent of a worker's performance is determined by the system they work within, and the remaining 6 percent by their individual effort. The conclusion was clear: **To measurably improve success rates, we must focus on improving the SYSTEM.**

94 percent of failures are caused by the SYSTEM. 6 percent are due to worker error.

Most work on quality has been focused on the factory floor. It's been focused on the reduction of mistakes. In the revised edition of his last book, *The New Economics*, Dr. Deming argued that this was just the start. He estimated that improvements in production quality were 3 percent of the potential for improvement. He felt that fully 97 percent of the big gains were waiting in areas such as business strategy, planning, personnel, marketing, sales, etc.

Deming reported that most energy spent on quality had been focused on the factory floor on eliminating defects. And, though this is important, he warned, **"Absence of defects does not necessarily build business, does not keep the plant open. Something more is required."**

The "more" he then described is, in my opinion, the JOB OF MARKETING. It's the job of marketing to lead the development process. **It's up to marketing to provide a vision for the engineers and scientists. Customers don't invent new products or services.** As Deming said,

> The customer generates nothing. No customer asked
> for electric lights. There was gas and gas mantles, which
> gave good light. No customer asked for photography.
> No customer asked for the telegraph, nor for a telephone.
> No customer asked for an automobile. We have horses:
> What could be better? No customer asked for pneumatic tires.
> Tires are made of rubber. It is silly to think of riding on air.

It's marketing's responsibility to imagine the future. It's marketing's job to blend knowledge of customers, consumers,

manufacturing, engineering, finance, and even legal, and to boldly, bravely invent BIG IDEAS for revolutionizing their industry.

Deming said that management and leaders must "govern their own future, not be merely victims of circumstance." He went on to say that preparation for the future includes "constant scanning of the environment (technical, social, economic) to perceive need for innovation, new products, new service, or innovation of method. A company can to some extent govern its own future."

In recent years, quality efforts, and in particular 6-Sigma efforts by Motorola, GE, and others, have become popular tools for improving competitiveness. Sadly, the sales and marketing departments have resisted involvement. I recall a visit with a senior vice president of marketing at one of the United States' hundred biggest companies. As we stood near the elevator at their New York City headquarters, I commented on a sign advertising the company's 6-Sigma program. In response to my question regarding how the quality program was going she replied, "It's not a marketing thing—it's for production and operations."

Wrong! In today's marketplace, everyone must improve quality. For sales and marketing, quality is measured by the effectiveness and efficiency of marketing and sales programs.

The primary "systems" that are relevant to sales and marketing quality are THINKING SYSTEMS. With continuous improvement in thinking systems, you realize continuous improvement in your marketing response rates, trial rates, and sales success.

When thinking systems are faulty, then no matter how hard you work or how much money you invest, failure is a reproducible certainty. In my thirty years of experience, I've concluded that Deming's observations on quality also apply to marketing:

94 percent of MARKETING Failures are caused by faulty THINKING SYSTEMS. 6 percent are due to worker error

The aim of the Eureka! Ranch is to translate the wisdom of Deming to the world of Sales, Marketing, and Innovation. It's not easy. The first challenge is finding what metric to measure. With our Innovation efforts, it took us nearly a year to create and validate a system for measuring the quality of ideas on a real-time basis during group brainstorming. **This measurement tool has allowed us to transform** our system—resulting in a 10X STEP CHANGE IMPROVEMENT in the quantity and quality of ideas we invent. But that's not the subject of this book—that's the subject of the upcoming *Jump Start Your CREATIVE Brain*.

The measurement of marketing effectiveness is just as difficult. Short-term sales increases due to promotional gimmicks are often matched with equivalent declines in sales in the next time period.

Marketing managers commonly confuse coincidence with cause and effect. They get "lucky" once in their career with a strategy or tactic and seek to repeat it. The result is a career of frustration in not being able to relive the "lucky moment."

The science of statistics provides methods for identifying whether what we are observing is a random event or a statistically reproducible finding. Through disciplined analysis, we can identify scientific principles to guide our everyday thinking and decision-making.

MEANINGFUL MARKETING VS. MINDLESS MARKETING

At the Eureka! Ranch, our "religion" is something we call Meaningful Marketing. Meaningful Marketing is about honest storytelling. **It's about telling with absolute accuracy how your offering will make a meaningful difference in customers' lives**.

Sadly, a quick review of modern advertising finds that Meaningfulness in communications is a rarity. Instead of respecting a customer's intelligence through communicating real news, most advertising attempts to coerce customers using what we at the Eureka! Ranch call Mindless Marketing.

Mindless Marketing is about using persuasion trickery to sell your offering. It's about encouraging customers to make a purchase without conscious thought or consideration.

When a celebrity is paid to use a product to persuade gullible youth to buy, that's Mindless Marketing. When a credit card company offers no interest for 90 days, then raises its rates to loan shark-like levels, that's Mindless Marketing. When a company pays to have its brand shown in a television show, that's Mindless Marketing. When a company gives free gifts to consumers to get them to create "buzz" about their product, that's Mindless Marketing.

The search for "Persuasion Tricks" is nothing new. In 1983 advertising legend David Ogilvy wrote in *Ogilvy on Advertising* of the never-ending desire of the media and the advertising community to find the latest "hot marketing trend."

> There have always been noisy lunatics on the fringes of the advertising business. Their stock-in-trade includes ethnic humor, eccentric art direction, contempt for research, and their self-proclaimed genius. They are seldom found out, because they gravitate to the kind of clients who, bamboozled by their rhetoric, do not hold them responsible for sales results. Their campaigns find favor at cocktail parties. . . . In the days when I specialized in posh campaigns for *The New Yorker*, I was the hero of this coterie, but when I graduated to advertising in mass media and wrote a book which extolled the value of research, I became its devil. I comfort myself with the reflection that I have sold more merchandise than all of them put together.

Both Meaningful Marketing and Mindless Marketing can be successful in the short term. The difference between the two lies in longer-term success rates and profitability. **Research shows that Meaningful Marketing initiatives are twice as likely to succeed in the marketplace long term and five times less likely to be vulnerable to pricing pressures.**

In short, Meaningful Marketing enables you to sell more with less investment of your time and money. Mindless Marketing requires that you sell your product at a lower price, spend more on promotion and advertising repetitions, and hope for a Pavlovian response from customers.

A comprehensive discussion of the differences between Meaningful Marketing and Mindless Marketing can be found in Chapter 6. I've placed it near the back of the book, as the discussion is somewhat theoretical, and I wanted the Scientific Advice and Practical Ideas to be up front. In today's overstressed world, many marketers just don't have the time to read theory. They want ANSWERS, and THEY WANT THEM NOW. Feel free to read this chapter out of order if you're interested in having a deeper understanding of the theory before exploring the tactics.

HOW THIS BOOK IS ORGANIZED

Jump Start Your MARKETING Brain uses a unique two-page format. The left-hand page details a piece of Scientific Advice, its essence distilled into a single sentence at the top of the page. Dr. Deming said, **"A goal without a method is nonsense."** So to reduce my chances of writing a book of nonsense, I've placed a collection of Practical Ideas on the right-hand page, specific ideas for applying the Scientific Advice to your sales and marketing challenges. I've purposely provided an overabundance of suggestions to guarantee that you'll find ideas to help you no matter what your situation.

The advice and ideas are clustered into chapters.

Chapter 1: Marketing Strategy: Marketing Strategy myths and misconceptions are exposed and NEW SYSTEMS of strategic thinking are detailed in this extensive review of what really drives marketing success.

Chapter 2: Marketing Message: The focus here is on how to create more Meaningful Marketing Messages—the kinds of marketing messages that generate significant, sustained success in the marketplace.

Chapter 3: Mindless Marketing: Here you will find a collection of Persuasion Tricks that are very effective at persuading customers to do that which they don't consciously choose to do. Just understand that customers who come to you mindlessly will also leave just as mindlessly. In effect, you are basically renting customers. This chapter comes between the "Marketing Message" and "Selling" chapters as the advice and ideas apply to both disciplines.

Chapter 4: Selling: This chapter provides advice, ideas, and ammunition to help the front-line warriors increase their return on every hour they spend. In the case of small- and medium-sized businesses, the same person often does both marketing and sales. That said, I recommend that even when you do hold both roles, you think of them as distinct

tasks. The thinking systems that drive success in marketing are separate from those that drive selling success.

Chapter 5: Leadership & Teamwork: Advice and ideas to inspire you and your team.

Chapter 6: Meaningful Marketing vs. Mindless Marketing: The last chapter defines the differences between Meaningful Marketing Messages and Mindless Marketing Persuasion Tricks.

Technical Appendix: For those who get as excited as I do about data, here's an overload of technical references, discussion, and documentation.

WARNING: This book could OVERWHELM YOU. It's a DEEP DIVE into the complex world of sales and marketing. It's for those with a genuine commitment to measurably improving their success rate.

If you're not really passionate about marketing or are not truly committed, then you should stop here and take the book back to where you got it. The first book in this series, *Jump Start Your BUSINESS Brain*, provides a simpler, bigger-picture view of how to measurably improve your marketing and innovation success rates.

YOU ARE GUARANTEED TO WIN MORE THAN YOU LOSE

As Ben Franklin once said, "**In this world nothing can be said to be certain, except death and taxes.**" The truths detailed on these pages are proven probabilities. They are not black-and-white certainties. They have been proven statistically and, to me, beyond a reasonable doubt. However, while they are widely applicable, they are not *universally* applicable. There will be situations in which they are irrelevant or just don't apply.

Then, too, even truths with high statistical odds are not certainties. For a weather forecast of 80 percent chance of rain to be statistically correct, it must *not* rain about 20 percent of the time, or one out of five times.

With any individual event, there is a chance that a truth may not apply. However, with repeated application, statistical forecasts become reality. Thus, **if you apply the advice as articulated in this book, you will WIN MORE than you will lose.**

My goal on these pages is to translate scientific findings into written advice. It's advice; it's not THE LAW. You are free to not follow the advice. **You are free to bet on long shots. Just don't complain** when you lose more than you win.

EXTRA DOSES

If you are a true Marketing Revolutionary, SIGN UP for Eureka! Espresso at **www.DougHall.com**. Eureka! Espresso is my occasional e-newsletter and audio PodCast of intense ideas, musing, and rants on marketing and innovation.

The Espresso name is more than an alliteration. I'm such a coffee fanatic that at the Eureka! Ranch we have our own brand called Brain Brew. It's an intense brew stoked with caffeine and the flavor of four of the world's most prized coffee beans. **A test found that after chugging three cups of Brain Brew, participants invented 40 percent more ideas than the decaffeinated control group.**

I believe in following in the footsteps of such noted coffee lovers as Franklin, Twain, Voltaire, Bach, Beethoven, and Brahms. I believe that the power of one's mind is directly proportional to the quantity and quality of coffee one drinks.

I understand that the impact of coffee on health is richly debated. Myself, I'm on the side of Voltaire, who reportedly drank some fifty cups of coffee a day. When told that drinking coffee was a "slow poison," the philosopher replied that it must be very slow indeed, as he had been drinking that much coffee every day for more than eighty years!

THE WHITE SPACE IS YOUR SPACE

Throughout this book I've purposely left WHITE SPACE. This is your space for thinking. This is your space for "connecting the dots" between the scientific advice and your world. **PLEASE BE BOLD—read and write with a PEN**. Write, scribble, think, jot, create, and challenge yourself to find smarter and more creative ways to revolutionize your marketing success.

Doug Hall
January 17, 2005
Cincinnati, Ohio

CHAPTER ONE

MARKETING
STRATEGY

In the spring of 2004, I debated Sergio Zyman, author of the foreword to this book. We conducted a debate in Boston entitled Marketing Mayhem on the importance of smart strategy vs. big ideas. It was billed as Sergio Zyman "the Armani-wearing Mexican" versus Doug Hall, "the Jimmy Buffet–wearing Canadian."

I defended the power of big ideas and stated that when "gurus" like Sergio bring their strategic tablets down from their lofty mountains, nothing happens until they're translated—if they can be translated at all—into a customer-relevant big idea.

Sergio defended the power of marketing strategy and argued that without strategic discipline, "touchy-feely" creativity is a waste of time.

Following numerous jabs and pokes, including a healthy discussion on Sergio's strategic misfortune introducing "New Coke," we came to the conclusion that no matter how hard we tried to defend our singular positions, **STRATEGY and the IDEA are of EQUAL importance**.

Great strategy not translated into a compelling marketing message is just as ineffective as a great message that lacks strategic discipline.

In effect, **great marketing is about "whole-brain" thinking**. It's a blend of left-brained strategic discipline with a right-brained big idea.

The Scientific Advice and Practical Ideas on the following pages will cause you some anxiety. They will challenge your established beliefs. That's GREAT! It means I'm making progress on my mission to incite a revolution in your marketing thinking.

With respect to my friend Sergio Zyman, this first chapter focuses on Marketing Strategy.

In this chapter you will find Scientific Advice and Practical Ideas on 1.) the fundamentals of smart strategic thinking, 2.) selecting target audiences, 3.) naming—the single most important decision you make as a marketer, and 4.) advice and ideas on marketing plans.

{ 1 }
SCIENTIFIC
ADVICE

WHEN IT COMES TO DRIVING NEW PRODUCT TRIAL RATES AND CORRESPONDING SUCCESS RATES, YOU HAVE THREE DISTINCT STRATEGIC OPTIONS

A monumental study involving 239 new products and 3,500 consumers tracked over 52 weeks identified three distinct strategies for achieving success in generating trial of new initiatives. As the leader of your organization, you need to make a commitment to one and focus your organization's energy.

1. Be Bold and Brave!: New products offering a major point of difference generate above-average trial rates. Interestingly, the research finds a U-shaped distribution. You can succeed with a low price and little uniqueness or by being Dramatically Different. Moderate levels of uniqueness are the least successful. At this level of uniqueness, customers are asked to make a change in their behavior for no good reason. **To be successful with a uniqueness strategy, the uniqueness must be big enough and bold enough to be worth the hassle of changing.**

2. Spend! Spend! Spend!: Spending MORE MONEY does work. The research found direct relationships between new product trial rates and 1.) higher average advertising spending, 2.) higher levels of feature, display, and distribution, and 3.) lower average price. The challenge with this strategy is to balance the investment relative to the longer-term return.

3. The Original Wal-Mart Strategy: The third approach is to attack the market where there is little competition. New products generated greater trial when introduced into 1.) categories with fewer existing brands, 2.) less existing advertising spending, and 3.) less intense competitive reactions. This is the Wal-Mart strategy. Wal-Mart focused their initial expansion in small towns to avoid strong competition. And as Sam Walton said, "There was much, much more business out there in small-town America than anybody, including me, had ever dreamed of." When they achieved skill and scale in distribution and merchandising they were then ready to compete in the major metro markets.

PRACTICAL **IDEAS**

Leverage Courage: Dramatic Differences in products and services can occur only when management has the courage to direct resources on the discovery and development of true new-to-the-world inventions. **Courage is a necessity** because with real R&D, there is a risk of failure. Fortunately the rewards are also spectacular. To the courageous go higher trial rates, sales, profit margins, and government-granted monopolies in the form of patents.

Combine Resources to Create a SURGE in Spending: American distance runner Frank Shorter used a SURGE strategy to win the 1972 Olympic Marathon. "At nine miles, the front pack slowed going around a hairpin turn," he explained. "My momentum carried me to the front. I put down my head and ran to get away just as I had on the playgrounds of my youth. In track races, if you're willing to take the risk, you can throw in surprise surges. If you train to do this, you can recover more quickly than the opposition. You keep doing it until no one covers the next surprise surge and you win. The surge lasted almost eight miles. At 17 miles I slowed down to let my body recover, but I didn't look behind." Shorter destroyed his opponents through the use of a SURGE of energy. Think: **How can you create a SURGE in spending that will break the "will" of your competition?** Can you "borrow" marketing money from other divisions within your company or partner with other small businesses for a joint marketing effort to create a SURGE in spending?

Have Patience: Unlike Target and others who went to small towns only after having saturated the big cities, Wal-Mart took the opposite approach. It entered the small markets—the low-potential markets—first, then went to the BIGGEST MARKETS. Can you do the same? Can you first enter a more minor channel of distribution, sell some, learn a lot, and make improvements in your offering, your marketing, and your plan?

{ 2 }
SCIENTIFIC
ADVICE

THE EASIEST WAY FOR YOU TO IMMEDIATELY IMPROVE YOUR MARKETING RESULTS IS BY MAKING DECISIONS BASED ON A 60/40 WEIGHTING OF PURCHASE INTEREST AND UNIQUENESS

The value of uniqueness as a driver of marketing success is well known. Uniqueness sets off a chain reaction of benefits. When your offering is unique, it's easier to get distribution and awareness. Your trade customers have a real reason to stock products that are genuinely new, as opposed to simply another variation of the same old stuff. When you're really new and different, it's easier to make a profit, as customers have no viable alternative. And with no direct competitor, you don't have the downward pricing pressure that commodity markets experience.

To dramatically improve your ability to select between two new product options, consider BOTH customer purchase interest and uniqueness.

Research comparing customers' initial purchase intentions and perceptions of uniqueness with actual marketplace behavior found that a weighting of 60 percent of customers' purchase intention score and 40 percent of uniqueness perception score is most predictive of actual marketplace behavior.

This approach can be challenging to execute. The vice president of a major beauty care company had two new products to decide between. Concept A had strong purchase interest and horrible uniqueness scores. Concept B had very good purchase interest scores with exceptional uniqueness scores. Despite my pleading to take uniqueness into account when making the decision, the vice president selected New Product A because, as he said, "It's the safest choice to go with the idea liked by the most consumers." Fast-forward twelve months: New Product A is introduced and fails. Without a unique product, the trade is reluctant to take the item, and because the product isn't inherently newsworthy, the brand has trouble generating awareness.

The need to maintain a healthy tension between uniqueness and meaningfulness was shown in a study of 312 project managers. The research found that "meaningfulness" of uniqueness in new products and marketing plans was twice as predictive as "uniqueness" alone in explaining new product sales, market share, relative profitability, and return on investment.

PRACTICAL IDEAS

Get Data Fast and Cheap: If you don't usually collect this kind of data, here's the fast way to gather it: Prepare written descriptions of each of your ideas for new products or services. Ask thirty or more potential customers (the more the better) the following questions for each of the new ideas:

1. On a scale of 0 to 10, how likely is it that you would purchase this product/service if it were offered?

   Definitely Not Buy   Definitely Buy

0	1	2	3	4	5	6	7	8	9	10

2. On a scale of 0 to 10, how unique do you believe this product/service is?

   Not Very Unique   Extremely Unique

0	1	2	3	4	5	6	7	8	9	10

Calculate the average value for each question, then multiply the first question's value by 60 percent. Multiply the second question's average by 40 percent, and add the two figures together. Finally, compare the weighted scores for each of the written descriptions.

Mine Archives: If you already have lots of past concepts that you've tested, review the results from a fresh perspective. Apply a 60/40 weighting to the purchase intent and uniqueness questions and look for potential big ideas that you might have overlooked in the past.

{ 3 }
SCIENTIFIC
ADVICE

WHEN YOUR STRATEGY IS FOCUSED ON INNOVATIONS THAT CREATE NEW MARKETS OR INDUSTRIES, YOU'RE 9.6 TIMES MORE LIKELY TO REALIZE PROFITABLE SUCCESS THAN YOU ARE BY "PLAYING IT SAFE" AND FOCUSING ON INCREMENTAL INNOVATIONS

Be bold! Be brave! Strategies focused on close-in ideas or "low-hanging fruit," as they're called, are for losers. There is no such thing as easy profits. The smart path, the only reliable path to big SUCCESS, is BEING BOLD!

A study of 108 companies found that 86 percent of new offerings were "safe ideas" (line extensions or other variations of current offerings) and these safe ideas collectively delivered 62 percent of sales and 39 percent of the average company's profits from innovation. Alternatively, the 14 percent of innovation offerings focused on creating new markets or industries delivered 38 percent of sales and some 61 percent of innovation profits. Comparing the ratios of percentage of profits with the percentage of initiatives, we find that **products or services focused on creating NEW MARKETS generated 3.8 times more sales and 9.6 times more profit**.

Automobile visionary Henry Ford rejected the prevailing view that cars were for "rich people" and saw a future where everyone could afford a car. He described the importance of a focusing on new markets and ideas this way: **"Businessmen go down with their businesses because they like the old way so well they cannot bring themselves to change. One sees them all about—men who do not know that yesterday is past, and who woke up this morning with their last year's ideas."**

Sadly, the depth and breadth of the challenge is huge. Research of 120 brands across 13 different countries found that only 1 in 10 users felt their brand was even modestly different from others. And the perceptions of those who are not brand buyers was only half as strong.

The Harley-Davidson motorcycle company is in business today because of its early focus on new markets. It looked for sales opportunities beyond consumers. It convinced the U.S. Postal Service to move from bicycles to motorcycles. It also found great success with sheriffs, state patrols, and the military. By the end of World War I, all of Harley-Davidson's production was going to the military.

PRACTICAL IDEAS

How NOT to find unique ideas: Focus groups are the worst way to find big, bold ideas. Customers can only tell you the world as they know it. Quality guru W. Edwards Deming once said, "Customers can't say what new product or service would be desirable three years from today. New ideas are generated by imagination, risk, innovation, trial and error by the producer."

How TO FIND unique ideas: Take personal responsibility for the challenge. Get personally involved in your category and in categories near your category. Seek out the "thought leaders" in your industry. Who are the retailers, salespeople, consumers, customers, or even members of the media who are most aware of where categories are going? Seek them out and ask about tomorrow. Ask them what they anticipate the future looking like in three years, five years, and ten years. Don't be bashful. Just ask those involved in your industry for their ideas and insights. Listen especially closely to those ideas that contradict your established thinking. Radical ideas, different ideas offer the greatest potential for helping you realize meaningful growth.

Think NEW TO THE WORLD, Not New to You. It's common to confuse "new to our company" with new to the world. Customers don't care whether you've never offered a certain type of product or service before. They're interested only in what you can do that NO ONE ELSE CAN DO.

{ 4 }
SCIENTIFIC
ADVICE

A STRATEGY THAT ANTICIPATES CUSTOMERS' FUTURE NEEDS IS TEN TIMES MORE PREDICTIVE OF SUCCESS THAN ONE FOCUSED ON CUSTOMER SATISFACTION

GET IT? Read it again! Innovation strategies focused on "serving customers" are for losers. **To win big, you must find the courage to be a true LEADER! You must ANTICIPATE the future.**

Here's the research: Leaders of 120 different business units were asked a series of questions to determine their innovation strategy. Their orientation toward a CUSTOMER SATISFACTION strategy was determined based on agreement with such statements as: *We are more customer-focused than our competitors, We measure customer satisfaction systematically and frequently, and Our business exists primarily to serve customers.*

Their orientation toward a FUTURE FOCUS was determined based on agreement with such statements as, "We help our customers anticipate developments in their markets," "We continuously try to discover additional needs of our customers **of which they are unaware**," and "We innovate even at the risk of making our own products obsolete."

The results of the two orientations were then correlated with each business unit's innovation success versus competitors. Modeling found that a **FUTURE FOCUS beat a Customer Satisfaction focus by a factor of TEN!**

Another study of 312 project managers found that a "customer-focused" orientation significantly reduced the uniqueness of new products created by a company. Finally, research has found that a customer-satisfaction focus often results in major pressure on profits. John Naver of the University of Washington Business School described it this way: "Customers' expressed needs and benefits can be known readily by all competitors—a situation that leads typically to competitors offering the same benefits to a given set of customers and then having to engage in aggressive price competition in the attempt to create superior value for the subject customers."

PRACTICAL **IDEAS**

Follow the Questions: Take the questions from the research and use them as stimulus for new ideas.

> *How can we help customers anticipate developments in their markets?*
> *How can we discover additional needs of our customers of which they are unaware?*
> *What could we do that would make our own products obsolete?*

Unlearn the Past: Dominant firms in disk drives, copiers, minicomputers and mainframe computers stayed in their existing businesses too long. Stop asking current customers for ideas. Akio Morita, co-founder of Sony said, "Our plan is to lead the public with new products rather than ask them what kind of products they want. The public does not know what is possible, but we do." Rather, focus some energy on the fringes. Spend time with customers who NEVER EVER buy your category. Look into the future for your industry. What would you do if you were starting your business all over again right now?

Exceed Customers' Expressed Needs: To win customer loyalty, set a standard of exceeding customers' expressed needs. When you exceed customers' expectations, you will reduce your need to offer price discounts in order to create a value perception.

Anticipate the Future: Clayton Christensen of Harvard, author of *The Innovator's Dilemma*, described the problem this way: "An excessive customer focus prevents firms from creating new markets and finding new customers for the products of the future. They unwittingly bypass opportunities and allow entrepreneurial companies to catch the next great wave of industry growth." Instead of discovering the one right answer, challenge yourself and your staff to create three "future-focused scenarios": If X happens, then what will customers want? Translate your thoughts into writing, and step back and assess the probability of each scenario. Then TAKE ACTION.

{ 5 }
SCIENTIFIC
ADVICE

HAVING THE COURAGE TO BE THE FIRST TO MARKET NEARLY DOUBLES YOUR SALES VERSUS BEING THE FOURTH TO MARKET

When you are the first, you win a chain reaction of advantages. When you are the first to discover a new technology, the government gives you a government-guaranteed monopoly. **When you are the first with a new idea, you generate real NEWS—positive publicity and "buzz."**

When you have the courage to take a stand, stick your neck out and be a pioneer, you gain a laserlike focus on your development efforts. Your packaging, pricing, positioning, and product or service development efforts are more efficient as a result of a common alignment.

Research on the impact of order of entry for new brands quantifies the advantage of being first versus being a follower. On average, brands that are second to market generate 71 percent of the sales of the pioneer. Those that are third generate 58 percent, and those that are fourth some 51 percent of the sales of the brand that is first to market.

By definition, the first to market is news. When you have news, then you have information to communicate, and as the first, you command a customer's conscious attention.

When you have a copycat offering, you are more likely to have to resort to low prices and other Mindless gimmicks to get customers' attention.

IMMEDIATE FIVEFOLD IMPROVEMENT IN EFFECTIVENESS: When you offer "real news," the impact of your sales and marketing efforts is multiplied. A study found that **advertising for products offering REAL NEWS was FIVE TIMES more effective at growing sales** than advertising for more familiar or less novel, established brands.

NOTE TO SKEPTICS: There are studies indicating that pioneers fail. Truth be known, pioneers, followers, and followers of followers all fail. However, if you read ALL the studies—and I have—the lesson is clear. When you're a true pioneer, you measurably increase your odds of success.

PRACTICAL **IDEAS**

Define Yourself from the Point of View of First: Look within your offering and find something that you are the first to offer. Ideally, this is a simple and dramatic statement: the first computer repair service that does house calls, the first beer with zero calories (we can dream, can't we?). Don't be surprised if you don't have something simple to claim. Most products and services don't. Don't despair. You have other options.

Define First as a Limited Category: Define what you're the first at based on a limited subset. For example, we're the first in our town to offer in-home repair of consumer computers. Or we're the first in our industry to offer 24/7 customer service.

Define First as a Combination: Define what you're the first at based on a unique combination. For example, we're the first to offer French cuisine dining in thirty minutes. Or we're the first industrial lubricant company to offer twenty-four-hour delivery and credits for recycled oils.

Repeatedly Articulate What Makes You the First: Articulate your point of difference everywhere—at the start of every sales presentation, on every advertisement, on every brochure, on your voice mail message, on your business cards, on your letterhead, and on every T-shirt, mouse pad, and coffee cup that you print.

Meaningful Difference Affects Development Success: The lack of a Meaningful difference is a common reason why many managers have a hard time generating momentum on "small" ideas within their organizations. When you seek the support of fellow employees on an idea that is not meaningfully different, you are in effect asking them to make an operational change or disruption for no good reason.

THE SECRETS TO SUCCESS ARE SIMPLE!

First, be Bold and Brave.

Second, add Uniqueness to innovation-decision metrics.

Third, seeking new markets is ten times more successful than pursuing incremental innovations.

Fourth, a FUTURE-FOCUS strategy is ten times more valuable than a "Voice-of-the-Customer" approach.

Finally, PIONEERING results in DOUBLE the sales volume over being fourth to market.

The bottom line is simple:

$$\textbf{S.O.S. = S.O.L.}$$

If you offer the S.O.S. (Same Old Stuff)
you are S.O.L. (---- Out of Luck).

GROW OR DIE!

THERE IS NO OTHER OPTION!

Become a FANATIC for uniqueness! Be so distinct you're perceived to be a MONOPOLY, or don't whine when you become a price-driven COMMODITY. The only thing that holds back most companies from success is the lack of courage in the executive suite. **Instead of boldly blazing new trails and anticipating the future, most executives play not to lose.**

There are two ways to fight the fear that comes with change:

1. <u>Focus on SERVING OTHERS</u>: The most effective way to gain the courage to change is to focus on SERVING others. The soul of heroic acts, be they storming the beaches of Normandy, discovering a life-saving drug, or defending your children from harm, is sacrificing oneself for others. When you are on the right side of "RIGHT," you will have the courage necessary to win over those who are WRONG.

2. <u>Evoke the only emotion more powerful than fear—GREED</u>: If your organization or banker lacks a soul that can become truly committed to serving others, then evoke greed. When the opportunity for financial gain exceeds the fear of failure, then you will win support from even the most heartless of financial plunderers.

{ 6 }
SCIENTIFIC
ADVICE

PLAN PATIENCE INTO YOUR MARKETING PLANNING TO ENSURE THAT YOU HAVE THE ENERGY TO ENDURE THE JOURNEY TO BIG SUCCESS

Research indicates that it takes thirteen months of research and development to make a 20 percent change in a product, it takes 20 months for a 40 percent change, and 41 months for a 100 percent change.

Research also indicates you need to have PATIENCE with your introductory marketing plan when you're introducing a new product or service that represents a GENUINE REVOLUTION.

This advice comes from a long-term study of thirty-one mega innovations such as automobiles, color TVs, camcorders, compact disc players, cellular phones, direct broadcast satellite TV, and home VCRs. On average, it took six years before volume grew rapidly. Volume in the early years was pathetic. In fact, just before the takeoff point, only 1.7 percent of customers had made a purchase of items that today are multi-billion-dollar industries.

Really big ideas take time to educate the marketplace and to gain customer trust. It's possible that with a huge advertising budget you can break the cycle of history. However, the probabilities are clearly against you.

The CEO of one of America's largest companies told me that he has come to the same conclusion. The more UNIQUE the company's new product or service, the more it spreads its marketing dollars over a longer period of time. "It's been hard, but we're learning patience," he says. "We now lower our initial volume objectives and spread our marketing investment over as much as four years instead of focusing on twelve to eighteen months."

The message is simple: If you wish to CHANGE THE WORLD—you need PATIENCE with your development and marketing of your BIG IDEA.

PRACTICAL IDEAS

Be Prepared to Survive on Low Volume Levels: There is a good chance that volume will be a fraction of what you anticipate. Plan how you will make adjustments if the initial volume is smaller and growth is slower than expected. In the calm before introduction, you have significantly greater ability to develop smart and effective contingency plans.

Win in Niche Markets to Reduce Discouragement: Focus your sales and marketing efforts in the first few years on niche markets where the point of Meaningful difference you are delivering is most highly valued. These markets will be less price-sensitive to your initial high cost. And by staying focused on a market where you can "win," you will reduce the chances for emotional wreckage and discouragement caused by your mega-meaningfully different idea taking time to generate major volume. The Iams Company initially sold its premium pet foods exclusively through veterinarians, a market it could defend and compete in. Its success was so great that Procter & Gamble paid more than $2 billion for the company. P&G then used its marketing muscle to take the brand into mass-market distribution.

Be Cautious with Early Investments and Forecasts: When your company's development investment has been big, the tendency is to be aggressive with early investments and forecasts. *Be cautious.* Set up a conservative introductory sales and marketing program that you can clearly "win" at. Then separately, conduct investment tests in smaller markets to validate that a bigger investment will deliver a favorable return.

Reassure Customers of Your Staying Power: Reinforce the long-term viability of your company and offering. Research on customers' perceptions of major innovations finds that beyond key benefits, customers are also concerned about long-term viability. Reinforce that your new product, service, or company is here to stay.

{ 7 }
SCIENTIFIC
ADVICE

TWICE AS MANY NEW PRODUCTS OR SERVICES FAIL BECAUSE OF A BAD IDEA AS BECAUSE OF A POOR MARKETING PROGRAM OR POOR PRODUCT/SERVICE PERFORMANCE

New products and services are a three-legged stool consisting of the idea, the product/service, and the marketing program. Mathematically, the three have a direct and multiplicative impact on success.

No matter how great your offering's performance and marketing plan, without an idea that makes a Meaningful difference to customers, few if any will bother to purchase it.

No matter how great your idea and marketing program, no one will make a repeat purchase without a great product, and you will fail.

No matter how great your idea and product performance, no one will know to purchase or be able to purchase your product without a marketing plan that generates awareness and distribution.

Tracking forty-eight new products from entry into the marketplace, a study found that on average they generated 58 percent awareness. Of those aware, 9 percent actually purchased, and of those who purchased, some 38 percent made a repeat purchase. If we subtract each of these results from the theoretical 100 percent that could have been achieved, we find that the idea is the largest source of lost customers.

42 percent did not become aware of the offering—a failure of the marketing plan.

62 percent who tried the product didn't make a repurchase—a failure of the product performance.

91 percent of those who were aware didn't make a purchase—a failure of the IDEA.

NET: Bad Ideas are a 2.2 times greater source of failure than marketing plan and a 1.5 times greater source of failure than the product performance.

When your volume is low versus expectations, look first at improving your core idea. The meaningful benefit difference offered by your brand is the single largest source of lost customers.

PRACTICAL **IDEAS**

It's the Idea, Stupid: Step back and ask yourself what meaningful difference you offer to customers. A classic mistake is to take one idea and spend 99 percent of your money, time, and energy optimizing marketing efficiencies through reviewing media buys, sales-force coverage, or mail-order list selection. At best, you can realize a net efficiency improvement of maybe 2 percent to 5 percent. A smarter strategy is to focus on the message itself. When small-business owners spend a full eight hours improving their marketing MESSAGE, they realize as much as a 10 percent to 50 percent improvement in marketing response rates.

Play "King of the Hill" with Marketing Messages: There is no such thing as a marketing message that can't be made more effective. Challenge yourself and your staff to perpetually discover new and more effective ways to articulate your Meaningful Marketing message.

Develop low-cost test systems, such as direct mail or point-of-purchase testing systems, to quantify improvement. On a regular basis review the collection of tests you've conducted to identify patterns and trends regarding what's working and what's not.

Improve Marketing by Spending More on Product: Most marketing spending is a meaningless, Mindless waste. Challenge yourself to consider what level of product or service improvement you could deliver if you dramatically cut marketing expenses. Short term, the volume may take a hit, but long term, when word of mouth from customers kicks in, you could realize substantial growth.

{ 8 }
SCIENTIFIC
ADVICE

NEW PRODUCTS AND SERVICES THAT ARE CONCEPT EXTENSIONS GROW SALES AND PROFITS, AND CAN HELP GROW YOUR PARENT BRAND

The most obvious reason to pursue new products and services is to grow sales and profits. However, if we're smart about it, we can also use them to grow our existing businesses. Note that concept extensions are not the same as concept variations, which might represent other flavors or sizes. Concept extensions belong in separate categories.

Research shows that the **introduction of new products and services can revitalize customer perceptions of an existing Flagship brand.** Research was conducted on the "halo" effect on the parent brand of introducing line extensions (new flavors or varieties of the same product) as well as new concept extensions (leveraging the Flagship Brand's Overt Benefit in NEW PRODUCT CLASSES).

After just a twenty-five-second exposure to ideas for line extensions or concept extensions, consumers' attitudes toward the parent brand improved significantly. Important, too, is that the attitude improvement remained even a week later to those shown the ideas for concept extensions.

Net: When you introduce concept extensions, i.e., take your trademark and benefit into new categories, you place a sustainable halo over your existing brand.

Research also shows that in the event that the concept extension is a failure, there is less risk of a negative effect on the parent brand's image. Customers don't appear to blame the parent brand for the failure of a concept extension.

Net: With Concept Extensions you gain a positive halo for your Flagship Brand with less risk of damaging that brand in the event of a failure.

PRACTICAL **IDEAS**

Think "could do" not "would expect": A classic mistake when looking for concept extensions is to follow a path of asking consumers or customers what other products or service they would expect the Flagship Brand to offer. It's a mistake because you'll be sent chasing variations that are not true CONCEPT EXTENSIONS but rather minor, micro-niche line extensions. Instead, take responsibility and think "COULD DO" not "WOULD EXPECT."

List the OVERT BENEFIT you deliver to customers. Then challenge yourself to think of categories beyond your current category, your current channel of distribution, your current knowledge base. Challenge yourself to think of categories by focusing on your loyal and your occasional customers. Where else do they shop? What do they do? What are their interests?

Having identified potential category extensions, now get customers to react to the ideas YOU'VE DEVELOPED. Check out the research article based on this advice ("The Dynamic Effect of Innovation on Market Structure") in the Technical Appendix. Conduct a study similar to the one described, and quantify for yourself the impact of the Concept Extension on your Flagship Brand.

Don't Forget Licensing or Acquisitions: If you're adventurous in your thinking, you will create ideas that make NO SENSE to develop and market. No problem. If the idea is big enough, it might justify your purchasing another company that has skills in the new category. Alternatively, if your Flagship Brand is well respected, it might be that you can license the idea and your trademark to another company to execute. Remember that the research indicates Concept Extensions offer significant opportunities and little risk.

{ 9 }
SCIENTIFIC
ADVICE

IF YOU WISH TO GROW BIG, FINDING NEW CUSTOMERS IS 2.8 TIMES MORE IMPORTANT THAN BUILDING CUSTOMER LOYALTY

A common debate when attempting to grow sales is, Should the primary emphasis be on increasing the number of customers or on increasing loyalty by selling more to existing customers?

Common wisdom is that it's easier to build sales through increasing loyalty than it is by cultivating new customers. For small growth—1 to 20 percent—this might be true. But for mega growth—25 to 400 percent—the common wisdom is flawed.

This truth is based on analysis of 9,804 brands scanned by UPC (universal product code) numbers in grocery, mass merchant, and drug stores. A statistical model was created to explain total annual sales relative to the number of customers the brand had and dollars spent per customer over the year. Analysis found that the **number of customers was 2.8 times more important in explaining big brand success than loyalty was**.

As a secondary check, the 9,000-plus brands were divided into three equal-size groups based on total annual sales, and the relative importance of the number of customers versus loyalty was compared. Again, the number of customers was found to be about three times more important than the amount purchased per customer.

Specifically, versus small brands, big brands had 978 percent more customers who purchased on average 331 percent more per year. Clearly both factors are important. However, if your resources are limited, the data indicate that your first priority should be on increasing your total number of customers.

Research also indicates that the smaller your brand, the more likely you are to lose customers—"churn." Research shows that small brands have nearly twice as many customers switching to another brand as big brands do. In category after category, research shows that brands with the greatest number of customers also have the greatest loyalty.

I recognize that many will resist this learning. That's fine. As Dr. Deming said, "Learning is not compulsory . . . neither is survival."

PRACTICAL **IDEAS**

Quantify Your Customer Count: Quantify how many customers you currently serve and determine whether that customer base is growing or declining. Identify where they are coming from or where they are going. Set a numeric and specific goal for growth. With data, you can make quantitative progress.

Perpetually Focus on Finding New Customers: As part of every sales and marketing plan, devise an overt and specific program for bringing in new customers. Regularly seek referrals from existing customers. Hold educational seminars that demonstrate the virtues of your product or service.

Relentlessly Seek New Customers, Occasions You Can Serve, and Problems You Can Solve: Think beyond people. Think of occasions when your product or service is used. How can you modify it to broaden appeal? Think of target problems that you can solve with your current offering or a modified offering. Be bold in your thinking.

Remember the Goal Is *Total* Customer Growth: Becoming *really* big requires more net customers. If you add 1,000 and lose 1,200, you're not going to grow. As you focus on growth, be sure that you've committed the necessary resources to maintain vitality among existing customers.

Redefine Your Benefit to Broaden Your Audience: By redefining your benefit, you open yourself to new customers. Classical music concerts are usually thought of as entertainment for classical music lovers. The Indian River Festival of Classical Music doubled attendance by redefining events more broadly as experiences for nurturing romance—"Music You Can Hear with Your Heart."

{ 10 }
SCIENTIFIC
ADVICE

INCREASING THE AMOUNT BOUGHT PER PURCHASE IS 3.5 TIMES MORE IMPORTANT THAN THE NUMBER OF TIMES A CUSTOMER PURCHASES

As stated before, increasing your number of customers is the MOST IMPORTANT strategic area for growth. However, that alone will not ensure success. In addition to bringing in new customers, you must be sure to keep current ones. You must ALSO build and maintain loyalty. Obviously, **the most effective way to generate loyalty is to offer a GREAT SERVICE OR PRODUCT**.

Annual purchase volume is made up of the amount of times customers buy *and* the amount they buy at each purchase. In the marketplace both strategies are pursued with brands offering frequent-buyer clubs as well as supersizes. But from a marketing strategy standpoint, it's most important to increase the amount bought per purchase.

Statistical modeling of household purchasing data from more than 9,000 consumer products found that **volume per purchase is 3.5 times more important than frequency of purchase in explaining the total amount that a customer purchases each year**.

Conceptually this makes sense. Competition is not static. Your competitors are perpetually making offers to entice your most loyal customers to experience what they have to offer.

Think of customer loyalty as a giant roulette wheel. With more loyal customers, you have a larger proportion of the wheel dedicated to your brand. When customers make purchase decisions, they spin the wheel. With each spin of the wheel, there is a defined opportunity to win or lose your customer's next purchase. When a customer purchases twice as much as normal, you receive 100 percent of both the current purchase and the next purchase.

PRACTICAL IDEAS

Design Tangible Incentives for Volume Purchasing: When customers are prepared to purchase, give them overt incentives to purchase more. Don't harass buyers. Rather, delight them with a tangible opportunity to make a larger investment in your brand through a discount on larger-volume purchases.

Repackage—Supersize!: Repackage your product or service into larger sizes. If you market services, offer long-term contracts. If you sell products, create supersized versions. Increasing product package size increases both customer value and your profitability, as it rarely causes a proportional increase in your costs. The same is true for services.

Use Customer Service to Rewrite Purchase Orders: Use customer-service visits, calls, e-mail, or direct mail to upsell. Give customers a special opportunity to "rewrite the purchase order" and extend their product or service usage. This has multiple benefits to you: 1.) It provides you with direct customer feedback on quality; 2.) it enhances customer perception of your commitment to them; and 3.) it offers the opportunity to expand the customer's initial purchase.

Design Complete Solutions: Think hard about what else a customer needs to purchase in order to more fully experience and enjoy your product or service. Challenge yourself to create a complete-solution package so customers don't have to make a separate purchase.

Bundle Your Company's Brands: Bundle a collection of your company's products and/or services to increase your share of the customer spending. This is a way to realize genuine synergy from owning multiple brands.

{ 11 }
SCIENTIFIC
ADVICE

THE SIMPLEST WAY FOR YOU TO GROW TOP-LINE SALES IS TO CUT YOUR NUMBER OF VARIATIONS

The easiest way to increase sales and profits may be to discontinue 50 percent of your variations. Classic thinking is that offering a multitude of product and service options will help you increase sales because you'll reach a broader range of customers. (As mentioned earlier, variations and extensions are not the same. This strategy applies to variations of the same concept—extra service plans, flavors, or sizes. Concept Extensions grow the brand in a different product class or category.)

Three separate studies indicate that reducing the number of variations you offer can have a dramatic positive impact on sales. It appears that more variations result in more customer uncertainty and consequential delay of decision making and purchasing.

> *Study 1:* Retail stores eliminated 10 percent of the least popular items in eight categories from their shelves. This alone resulted in a 4 percent increase in category sales.

> *Study 2:* The bottom 54 percent of products were discontinued across forty-two categories of an Internet-based retailer. This resulted in an average 11 percent increase in sales.

> *Study 3:* Consumers were offered samples of twenty-four or six flavors of jam to taste and purchase. When twenty-four flavors of jam were offered, 2 percent of customers purchased. When six flavors of jam were offered, 12 percent of customers purchased.

Basic production economics tells us that low-selling variations are often a drain on profitability. Yet often we fall into the temptation of offering something for everyone.

PRACTICAL **IDEAS**

Get the Real Numbers: Assess your business situation with mathematical honesty. What are the real sales and real net profit of each and every product variation you offer? Look at the long-term trends and identify those offerings in long-term decline. Examine the bottom 50 percent of your offerings. If you were to eliminate them, what percentage of the volume would shift to other offerings? What cost savings could you realize? Tom Monaghan, founder of Domino's Pizza, simplified his menu by limiting the number of sizes and toppings—and enabled consistent thirty-minute delivery by doing so.

Evaluate for Meaningful Differences: Review your brand's offerings and classify them according to their Meaningful benefit difference to customers. Challenge yourself to document the tangible differences between products. Review your marketing materials for the clarity of your differences. Ask your customers for their understanding of the differences. Having made your evaluations, make courageous cuts in the variations and permutations you offer. Items that offer the same basic benefits are excellent candidates for elimination.

Focus on an Area Where You Can Be Excellent: Leslie Wexner was running a moderately successful women's clothing store. After noticing that sportswear was his biggest seller, he opened THE LIMITED (so named because he had a limited selection of sportswear only). As Wexner explained, "[Sportswear] was our most profitable line, and my feeling was that if you made money in chocolate ice cream, why sell other flavors?"

{ 12 }
SCIENTIFIC
ADVICE

WHEN YOU PURSUE INNOVATIONS THAT CREATE NEW MARKETS YOU REALIZE 9.6 TIMES MORE PROFITS THAN WHEN YOU TRY TO "PLAY IT SAFE" WITH INCRMENTAL INNOVATIONS

Success in sales and marketing is a relative concept. It's relative to how much you've sold versus a predetermined objective. Most managers have an intense personal interest in results relative to the objective because that's usually the basis for personal commissions and bonuses.

Sadly, sales usually fall short of forecasts. **A study of fifty-three new products found that the average sales forecasting error was 65 percent and that the median error (middle value) of sales forecasts was a 26 percent shortfall.** In effect, if you miss your objective by less than 26 percent, you're doing better than half of the researched companies.

A study involving 103 computer software firms was conducted to determine what traits influenced companies' sales forecasting accuracy. The companies with more reliable forecasts conducted more customer interviews before creating their forecasts. The data clearly showed that conducting interviews with a few potential buyers produced better forecasts (a 91 percent confidence level), and interviews with fifty or more potential buyers produced even greater improvement (97 percent confidence level).

Many factors classically assumed to impact forecast accuracy showed no significant impact, including judgment of founder, judgment of industry experts, competitive analysis, and market research concept tests.

Net: To increase forecast accuracy, talk to more customers to gauge their reaction to your new idea.

PRACTICAL IDEAS

Get Out and Talk to Fifty or More Potential Buyers: When it comes to forecasting customer interest, nothing beats the value of face-to-face conversation; the more the better. Instead of debating the merits of your offering in internal conference rooms, go out and talk with real customers face-to-face. As you talk, listen and learn earnestly. Don't try to persuade; rather, listen and understand what customers perceive. Remember, customers are far more likely to act on their perceptions than on your view of truth.

Talk to Customers in Different Ways: You can maximize the reliability of your customer feedback by providing them with multiple perspectives of your offering. Provide customers with the facts and the feelings of your new offering. The more they can honestly analyze, feel, and experience what you have to offer, the greater the accuracy of their feedback. Provide customers with a real demonstration. If that's not possible, provide them with a clear, honestly written description of how your offering will affect their lives or businesses.

Don't Hide Your Negatives: Detail the strengths and weaknesses of your offering. Be honest with your customers. In a straightforward manner, detail every trade-off you've made in your product or service design and why you feel those were the correct decisions. Customers understand that 200 percent greater performance at 20 percent of the cost is rarely reality. Explaining trade-offs in a calm and confident manner removes the chances of emotional overreaction.

Document Your Past to Prevent Repetition: Review what you did to generate your past sales forecasts. Document the methods used and the accuracy of the results. Then estimate the real cost of forecasting errors. This figure provides the necessary data to support additional forecasting research before the next new product or service is shipped.

{ 13 }
SCIENTIFIC
ADVICE

TO INCREASE YOUR LONG-TERM ODDS OF SUCCESS, DON'T CUT YOUR PRICE IN THE SHORT TERM

Customer expectations of value received and cost paid are set when they make a purchase. When customers make initial purchases at a discounted price, they develop a lower value perception than if they purchase at the regular price.

A study was conducted of matched sets of stores for five new products. In one set of stores, during the first few weeks of availability, the initial price was set about 20 to 30 percent below the regular price. In these stores, the price was increased to the regular list price after the trial period. In the other stores, the products were introduced at regular list price.

Across all five of the new products, **long-term volume was higher when the brand was not sold at artificially cheap prices upon introduction**.

I don't have the data available, but if we were able to calculate cumulative profit, it's likely we would find an even more dramatic negative impact on bottom-line profits.

Artificially low prices "rent" customers, and rentals must eventually be returned. When you sell on price, you mindlessly train customers to perceive low price as the primary benefit of your offering.

Meaningful Marketing means customers make a conscious choice for good reasons. It means that they perceive real value. The net result is a deeper, more Meaningful connection with customers and longer-term sales and profits.

PRACTICAL **IDEAS**

Provide Proportional Trial-Size Offerings: Lower price reduces customer risk, but it also creates an artificially low price/value relationship. To prevent this, offer miniature sizes of your product or service. A trial size, a single use or limited supply that is proportionally priced reduces the absolute price while still maintaining the appropriate price/value relationship.

Pursue Exclusive Distribution Arrangements: When your offering has a Meaningful difference, it can become a tool to help retailers build customer traffic by using it as a loss leader. And when one retailer discounts your price, soon all do, resulting in an artificially low price perception by customers. By building exclusive distribution agreements in specific areas, you reduce the chances that competitive forces will unnecessarily depress your pricing.

Market Free Samples or Bonus Discounts with a Partner: Generate sampling yet maintain pricing integrity by jointly promoting your new product or service with another brand. The combination of your product with another will enhance the special one-time-only aspect of the promotion and not allow customers to tie the deal they got on your product to your brand's price. For example, when a customer receives a free one-year subscription to a cooking magazine when they purchase a gourmet cook stove, they don't expect the magazine to be free forever.

Encourage Customers to Use Competitive Discounts: If you're feeling really bold, tell your customers when your competition is offering special discounts. Especially in business-to-business situations, this demonstrates your confidence in your product's Meaningful difference.

{ 14 }
SCIENTIFIC
ADVICE

TO SPEED SUCCESS, TARGET YOUR INITIAL SALES AND MARKETING RESOURCES ON THOSE CUSTOMERS WHO ARE MOST OPEN TO TRYING NEW THINGS

Customers have varying levels of acceptance and interest in Meaningful Marketing messages.

On the cover of their book, *The Influentials*, Ed Keller and Jon Berry wrote, **"One American in ten tells the other nine how to vote, where to eat, and what to buy."** They make a compelling case for the existence of a group of thought leaders who have a disproportionate power to persuade the masses.

A research study on customers' attitudes toward innovative product concepts conducted in Canada, France, and North Africa classified roughly one-third of the population as *innovators*—those very open to new products and services. Two-thirds of the population was classified as *imitators*—those content with following the innovators.

In general, the research indicates that those most likely to try new ideas tend to have higher self-esteem, are better educated, and are more informed than the average customer. The good news, according to Keller and Berry, is that when you make an impression on influentials, they are prone to vigorously spread the word about your product's virtues.

You have limited sales and marketing resources. If you're not careful, you can use them up trying to sell to those who, frankly, no matter how hard you try, are not likely to purchase in the beginning. An important part of sales and marketing effectiveness is knowing when to stop chasing the prospect who asks lots of questions and uses lots of your energy yet is highly unlikely to buy in a reasonable amount of time.

PRACTICAL **IDEAS**

Focus on Whom Your Difference Means the Most To: Step back and consider what type of customer can realize the greatest benefit from your offering. Who will see your difference as the most Meaningful? Identify them and write them a one-page letter proclaiming the good news of how you can make a real difference for them.

Leverage Your Fanatics: All business categories have fanatics. In the case of technology, it's user groups. With celebrities it's fan clubs. With restaurants it's their most frequent diners. Identify and then leverage this group by giving it the first opportunity to experience your newest product or service. Afterwards, seek its help in spreading the word.

Fuel Influentials' Passion for Being Smarter: Influentials, fanatics, and other thought leaders have a natural passion for in-depth understanding. The masses are content with simple understandings of your technological wonder. Influentials love to be seen as smarter. Fuel this passion with detailed test results, technical schematics, and perspective on your development pedigree. Empowered with knowledge, influentials will spread the word to others.

Follow the Historical Thought-Leader Patterns: Research indicates that high-performing salespeople tend to focus their attention on those customers with the ability to influence others. The quickest way to identify the thought leaders among your existing or potential customers is to research when they bought the most recent big innovation in your category. Those who led the last time are the most likely to be the thought leaders with your new offering.

{ 15 }
SCIENTIFIC
ADVICE

FOR FAST PROFIT GROWTH, TARGET FIRST-TIME AND ONE-TIME CUSTOMERS

A common marketing strategy mistake is to focus all energy on loyal customers. Against conventional wisdom, research finds that on average, loyal customers actually pay a lower mean price than do first-time or one-time customers. Loyal customers often represent a healthy percentage of profits because of the volume of their purchasing. However, on a profit-margin basis, they are often the least profitable customers.

If you focus 80 to 90 percent of your energy on your loyal customers, the odds are you'll lose sales and profits. To grow your business, you need to use a portfolio approach to marketing where you invest in the core as well as in helping short-term/one-time customers become loyal customers.

In most cases at least one-third of sales and profits come from non-loyal customers. This finding is confirmed by two separate studies.

The Scanner 9000, a data set of 9,804 brands that have been tracked by UPC numbers in grocery stores, mass merchants, and drug stores, found that 62 percent of the average brand's customers and 34 percent of annual volume came from those who made only *one purchase* during the year.

A two-year tracking study of a mail-order catalog found that 47 percent of its customers and some 38 percent of its profits came from short-term, non-loyal customers.

NET: Not only is growing customers 2.8 times more important than growing loyalty (see Marketing Strategy Advice No. 9), new customers are often MORE PROFITABLE. **And first-time customers are also the source of all future loyal customers.**

Many short-term customers are mindless buyers; they're attracted by a promotional offer or simply an impulse desire to try something else. **Our challenge is to be sure they are aware of our Meaningful difference so that they fully notice and appreciate it**, thus laying the basis for developing a Meaningful connection with our brand.

PRACTICAL IDEAS

Make It Easy for Customers to Impulse Purchase: Make purchasing for new customers as easy as possible. If you have a Web-based business, remove lengthy sign-in processes. If you offer a product or service, streamline paperwork and remove credit checks on small orders. The benefits in increased sales and profits will more than make up for the few losses from fraud.

Continually Test New Customer Segments: Dedicate a portion of your time and resources to discovering unexpected customer segments and business opportunities. When you do direct-mail programs, test new mailing lists. When you work a trade show, focus extra energy on those who don't currently buy from you. Place your products in unexpected retail locations and track the resulting reactions.

Issue Direct Marketing Challenges: Overtly challenge non-buyers to give you a try. Communicate your advantages persuasively through side-by-side demonstrations and testimonials from customers who've recently switched to buying your brand.

Celebrate the Arrival of New Customers: Define special methods for handling new customers' needs. Provide special instructions, guidance, and help with their "rookie" needs. Warmly welcome them to your brand and your people.

Create Special New Customer Follow-Up Systems: Have a defined follow-up process to learn your new customers' satisfactions and dissatisfactions with your product or service experience. Overtly ask for another sale, and if it's not appropriate at that time, define when in the future you should contact the customer again—then do it.

{ 16 }
SCIENTIFIC
ADVICE

STEALING YOUR COMPETITORS' CUSTOMERS OFFERS A GREAT OPPORTUNITY IN HEAVILY PRICE-PROMOTED CATEGORIES

Just as occasional customers represent a significant amount of sales and profits, so too do your competitors' customers. They can be shifted away from their current choice when provided with a Meaningful difference or when presented with an even easier and more mindless option: a discounted price.

Mathematical modeling was undertaken on the source of weekly sales increases for various brands of coffee among one hundred households over a two-year period. The results indicated that more than 84 percent of sales increases were due to brand switching (non-current customers switching to the promoted item), 14 percent from purchase acceleration (current customers repurchasing sooner than normal), and 2 percent from stockpiling (current customers buying more than normal at one time).

Clearly, when an industry is heavily promoted, like the coffee category, a large segment of the population becomes trained to purchase only when the price is reduced.

The Meaningful Marketing challenge is to find ways to convert the price switchers into deeper and more loyal customers. This requires customers to first notice and then value our Meaningful points of difference.

PRACTICAL IDEAS

Be Relentless in Articulating Your Differences: In the face of perpetual discounting, you must become relentless in articulating what makes your product offering unique. Communicate your distinctiveness even when articulating price discounts. Through continuous communication, you will eventually build awareness that your offering delivers value, not just low price. You won't reduce the need for discounts totally. However, even a small shift can create a big improvement in your bottom-line profits.

Leverage Customer Purchase Cycles: Understand the purchasing cycles of your customers. Arrange your follow-up e-mail, direct mail, and personal contacts to maximize your chances of making connections just before a new purchase is required. As you're planning, don't be shy about directly asking your customers when they anticipate making another purchase.

Segment Your Offerings for Extreme Differences: Challenge yourself to strip your offering to the absolute lowest possible cost. Consider the unthinkable: Eliminate packaging, options, variations, and "nice" extras. Focus this stripped-down version on those customers motivated by price alone.

Push your offering to the ultimate in service. Provide added value to those customer segments that value Meaningful differences.

Use Endorsements to Talk of Differences: Use endorsements to articulate the dramatic differences that customers have experienced as a result of switching to your offering. Better yet, leverage testimonials that speak of the value customers have received from repeated use of your product or service.

{ 17 }
SCIENTIFIC
ADVICE

IF MEGA-GROWTH IS YOUR GOAL, TAP THE FOUR CORE FUTURE GROWTH OPPORTUNITIES— WOMEN, GEEZERS, CHINA, AND INDIA

The world economy is changing, and trillions of dollars are at stake.

WOMEN are vastly under-marketed to. Do the math. Women are responsible for 83 percent of consumer purchases, 91 percent of all new homes, 90 percent of cars, and 80 percent of do-it-yourself home projects. Women write 80 percent of all checks and actually own 53 percent of all stock in America!

GEEZERS or Baby Boomers represent a seismic shift. Do the math. Today, geezers control 70 percent of all wealth and account for 50 percent of all discretionary spending. And this is just the beginning. In the future they will be even more important. By 2010, the number of people 18 to 44 will have declined by 1 percent. The number of Americans who are 55-plus will increase by 21 percent. The number between 55 and 66 will increase 64 percent.

CHINA & INDIA. These two markets are about to take over the world. From a human capital standpoint, India has 3.6 times more consumers, and China has 4.4 times more consumers than the United States. Together China and India have a population EIGHT TIMES BIGGER THAN THE UNITED STATES! Most importantly, both countries are making massive investments in education. And education is the fundamental driver of genuine economic growth. For example, Roosevelt's GI Bill of Rights in 1944 made it possible for 8 million World War II veterans to attend college. For the first time, the idea that education was only for the elite was shattered. The rapid growth in students resulted in rapid expansion in the skills and abilities of the workforce. It also made possible dramatic increases in academic research—the kind of fundamental R&D that drives long-term economic growth.

In the United States, the next most promising market is the Hispanic population. After Mandarin (China) and Hindi (India), Spanish is tied with English as the world population's "first language." By 2050, the U.S. Census Bureau projects that 24 percent of the country's population will be of Hispanic origin.

PRACTICAL **IDEAS**

Admit You Don't Know: The first step in tapping into these opportunities is to admit that you don't know. Don't assume that your previous experiences apply to these new customers. Take the seemingly easiest category: women. Since when have men been known to understand women? When we are able to let go of our egos, our experiences, and our preconceived beliefs, we are able to learn and understand.

Create Quotas for GROWTH: I'm against government-mandated quotas. However I'm in favor of capitalism. Quite frankly, the days of the WHITE MEN'S CLUB running American business are done. Given the TRILLIONS IN REVENUE that is at stake, it's irresponsible for any large company not to have an aggressive program of recruiting and promoting women and geezers, as well as managers from China and India. Yes, I did include geezers. As the market shifts, smart companies will need to find ways to attract, retain, and leverage the wisdom of older managers.

If in Doubt, Do ANYTHING: The challenge of marketing to the audiences listed can seem daunting. If we're not careful, we will become mentally constipated. In our effort to get everything "right," we'll end up with analysis paralysis. It's only by venturing into these markets that you will really learn. So if in doubt, get up, get out, and get going!

{ 18 }
SCIENTIFIC
ADVICE

TO ENSURE STRONG TRADE SUPPORT, FOCUS YOUR ATTENTION FIRST AND FOREMOST ON IDEAS THAT GENERATE INCREMENTAL SALES FOR YOUR TRADE CUSTOMERS

There isn't much mystery in how to gain genuine excitement from trade customers: that is, customers who are resellers of our goods or services. Quite simply, offer them an OVERT BENEFIT. Show them how your offering can meaningfully grow their overall business. **If you can't, show how your product will grow your customers' overall sales. Then be prepared to pay for the support you get.**

Research conducted with 145 buyers on their sales priorities shows that their definitions of success are similar to your own for new products. On a ten-point scale (ten being most important), the following are the top three priorities for retail buyers when evaluating new products.

1. *Generate Incremental Sales* (8.6 importance): The new product should generate significant net extra volume, not just cannibalize existing volume.

2. *An Exciting and Unique Consumer Advantage* (8.4 importance): Trade customers look for big ideas that generate big volume. They make their evaluations by looking for evidence that your offering meets an unmet need, provides a unique advantage to consumers, or offers the potential for genuine shopping excitement.

3. *Substantial Marketing Support* (7.9 importance): Your level of marketing support is evidence of your confidence that your new product will generate significant sales. In addition, trade customers know that when one manufacturer makes a significant marketing investment, it causes healthy competition that results in more total category spending and overall category growth.

PRACTICAL IDEAS

Genuinely Grow Retail Sales Volume: Develop the products and/or merchandising concepts that can meaningfully grow the sales of your retail customers. Create higher-value product offerings that spark customers to "trade up" to higher-revenue-producing options. Develop merchandising programs that deliver incremental sales. For example, quantify the incremental category growth that occurs when products are shelved in multiple locations in the store or the customer's catalog.

Prove Your Advantage with Comparisons: Make your difference clear. Develop promotional materials that bring your point of difference to marketing and display materials. Show your advantage boldly. If possible, bring a live taste test, demonstration, or other real-world experience to your meeting with the customer. Don't shy away from demos that take some work. Your willingness to put in the effort is evidence of your personal belief in your offering.

Record Your Customer Excitement: Use video of customers speaking to the wonder and the impact your new product delivers. Don't worry about the fact that the tape is edited. If your testimonials speak with relevance and authenticity, they will be convincing. Alternatively, what do you think it says to a buyer when you don't have testimonials declaring that the new offering is great?

Lead a Revolution toward Smarter Spending: Document the Meaningful impact of your smarter marketing methods. Detail the effectiveness of your approach to sampling, trial generation, and targeted marketing. Estimate the translation of your smarter approach to equivalent dollar spending under older, less efficient marketing approaches.

ALIGNING YOUR NAME WITH YOUR BENEFIT DOUBLES A CUSTOMER'S RECALL OF WHO AND WHAT YOU ARE

Your brand name defines who and what you are. The more it meshes with your sales-and-marketing message to illustrate a Meaningful difference, the more likely customers will remember it. Examples of benefit-suggestive brand names include DieHard batteries, Mop & Glo floor cleaner, and Beautyrest mattresses.

Researchers showed 160 adults a series of marketing messages and brand names. Two days later, they were asked to recall the various messages. Suggestive brand names generated correct recall of the marketing messages 33 percent of the time. Non-suggestive brand names generated only 15 percent correct recall.

Your brand name is an overt declaration of what you offer. The more related and synergistic your name is with your message, the more effective your marketing will be.

A separate analysis of some 901 new products found that the odds of long-term marketplace survival were 34 percent greater when the new product's brand name evoked the benefit instead of using an abstraction or some unrelated name.

When creating a suggestive brand name, be careful not to become merely descriptive. When your name simply describes the product, it's difficult to register and defend your trademark. For example, a coffee called HOT & DARK would be more difficult to protect than the one we use for our Eureka! Ranch coffee: BRAIN BREW. The key thought I keep in mind when creating names is to look for one that is RELEVANT yet UNEXPECTED. I look for names that suggest a relevant benefit in an unexpected way.

Advertising legend David Ogilvy's description of advertising applies equally to the standard for selecting your brand name: "Tell the truth, but make it fascinating."

PRACTICAL **IDEAS**

Think Literally: Remove from your mind anything you think and know about your brand. Look deeply at the literal collection of letters of your brand name. Look in a dictionary and a thesaurus for direct meanings and synonyms. If your name is truly fanciful and not in any dictionary, then explore the meaning of the root components that make up the name.

Challenge yourself to speak of your product or service in terms of the literal meaning of your brand name. Create sales and marketing materials that help customers make direct connections between your name and your benefit.

Articulate Your Trademark's Genealogy: Review your history. Where did your name come from? What did it originally mean? What are its roots? How has it evolved over the years? In an appropriate manner, share this history with your customers. When a customer understands your history, you create deeper connections.

Think Graphically: Repeat the process detailed above with your graphical identity. Review your colors and any icons or symbols for potential connections with your brand's values and/or core benefit. Bring the connection to life for customers through direct education of the history and purpose behind your graphic identity. Once you've "connected the dots" for customers, they will always associate your graphics with your core business message.

How to Value Licensed Names: Another way to find a name is to license one from another company. In effect, create a "concept extension" for the parent brand. For example, whiskey brands are often licensed for use in barbeque sauces. In this case, they provide the barbeque sauce manufacturer a brand name and a key flavor ingredient. Research indicates that the smartest way to quantify the value of a potential licensed trademark is the percentage of your target audience that has personally used the trademarked brand in the past twelve months. A common mistake is to assess the value based on awareness. Don't. With a "borrowed" name, you are looking to enhance trust and credibility, and that is built only through usage.

{ 20 }
SCIENTIFIC
ADVICE

WITH REALLY UNIQUE NEW PRODUCTS OR SERVICES, YOU'LL BE MORE SUCCESSFUL WITH A NEW BRAND NAME THAN WITH AN EXISTING BRAND NAME

After creating a new product or service, you often have a choice between using an existing brand name as part of the name or developing a new brand name.

Using an existing name for a concept extension, line extension, or flanker has the advantage of adding a real "reason to believe" based on the known nature of the parent brand. Using a new brand name has the advantage of creating a new equity.

Research shows that when a new offering has a benefit related to an existing brand, the new offering is twice as likely to be successful if it uses the existing brand name. If Nike were to develop sports medicine centers, its experience working with top athletes would provide some real reason to believe the centers would be of high quality.

Conversely, **if the offering has a benefit very different from the existing brand, research suggests that using a new name is more effective.** For example, if Nike were to invent a breakthrough closet that cleans clothes as they hang on their hangers, it would make more sense to create a new brand name or to license one related to cleaning, such as Tide or Ariel.

The lesson is simple: When your benefit is very different, the established name acts as a negative "drag" on the new brand. If the new benefit is similar to the existing one, the established name provides credibility that it can deliver on the promise.

A separate study of ninety-six brands over thirty-eight years confirmed this finding. During the initial years of really new products, the data revealed that brands with new names were 24 percent more likely to succeed. Later, when the market was more mature, offerings carrying established brand names were 60 percent more likely to succeed.

A new brand name is a public statement that a new and meaningfully different offering is available.

PRACTICAL **IDEAS**

Create a Brand Benefit Ledger: To decide whether you should use your established name or a new name, make a list in two columns of the Overt Benefits that your established brand and the new offering provide to customers. Next, cross out all overlapping benefits and review what's left under the new offering's column. If what's left is a REASON FOR EXISTENCE by itself—not simply a "nice to have" minor bonus—then the NEW NAME is probably the way to go. If there's no MEANINGFULLY UNIQUE benefit left in the column, then using the established brand name makes more sense.

Tell Your Story Line Directly: When your offering leverages existing brand equities, say so directly: "For fifty years we've been your trusted source for X." "As the most popular brand, we know X," or "You know you can trust us for X." Overtly make the direct link between the parent and new item. Don't assume that customers will get it themselves.

When your offering is genuinely new, then be equally overt in your communication: "For the first time ever . . ." "Announcing a revolutionary new . . ." "A patented scientific breakthrough now makes it possible to . . ." Again, be overt about the magnitude of the revolution. Make your sales presentations and marketing materials look and feel as unique as the offering you bring forward.

Use Your Name as a Source Mark When Necessary: When your big brand name is not a good fit with a new product or service for whatever reason, consider using it as a "source mark." In this case, the brand is sold as "From the makers of X." The use of a source mark provides virtually all the credibility benefits of branding the offering with the big brand name with fewer risks.

{ 21 }
SCIENTIFIC
ADVICE

TO MAXIMIZE IMPACT, MINIMIZE THE DECLINE YOUR MARKETING MESSAGE UNDERGOES FROM YOUR OFFICE TO THE REAL WORLD

From your conference room to your customers, a dramatic decline occurs. **Most marketing messages are rarely noticed, seldom comprehended, and almost never acted on.**

The truth is, your customers don't spend significant time pondering your marketing messages. Tracking research on the step-by-step effectiveness of a direct mail marketing campaign documented the decline in effectiveness.

1. *Didn't Notice:* When called later, only 60 percent of those who had received the mailing remembered receiving it.
2. *Didn't Bother:* Only 47 percent of those who noticed the message actually bothered to read it.
3. *Didn't Understand:* Only 25 percent of those who read the marketing piece could accurately state the primary benefit of the new offering.

The total decline is multiplicative. The actual number of customers who were in a position to make a Meaningful decision—that is, were aware of and correctly understood the offer—was only 7 percent of the sample that was sent the mailing.

100 percent (were mailed new product message)
× 60 percent (customers who remembered receiving it)
× 47 percent (customers who read it)
× 25 percent (customers who correctly understood it)
= 7 percent (number in a position to make a MEANINGFUL purchasing decision)

Sadly, in my consulting work I've seen even worse than this.

PRACTICAL IDEAS

Measure the Effectiveness of Each Marketing Step: Quite simply, measure the decline in effectiveness at each stage of your marketing. Conduct phone, mail, or e-mail surveys to measure the effectiveness of each step. With hard data you are now empowered to make MEANINGFUL improvement. Focus your energies on those areas with the greatest opportunities for improvement.

Leverage the Multiplicative Impact of Meaningfulness: Declining effectiveness is yet another reason to focus on making your message as MEANINGFUL as possible. Just as investing time in thinking deeply about architectural plans reduces cost and time of construction, so, too, does adding more meaningfulness to your marketing.

Step back from your business and assess if what you are doing now will be recalled with pride when you're retired. Or will it blend into the mindless blur of life? **If you don't think your current marketing will be a Meaningful memory tomorrow, then it's probably not MEANINGFUL to your customers today.**

Look at Your Materials in Context: When you review your marketing materials, look at them in context. Place twelve direct-mail envelopes in a pile with yours. Watch a collection of commercials with yours in the middle. Flash your billboard on a screen for the seconds it takes to drive past it. When you look at your message in context, you look at it through customers' jaded eyes.

{ 22 }
SCIENTIFIC
ADVICE

YOUR CHANCES OF LONG-TERM PROFIT GROWTH ARE GREATER IF YOU INVEST EFFICIENCY IMPROVEMENTS IN BOLDER, BETTER PRODUCTS AND SERVICES INSTEAD OF SHORT-TERM PROFIT GAIN

Cost-cutting programs are perpetually popular with business leaders. With the financial windfall you have three choices: 1.) You can use the money to improve customer satisfaction; 2.) you can take the savings as bottom-line profits; or 3.) you can do both simultaneously.

Research of 186 companies found that a strategy of investing quality savings on improving customer satisfaction is dramatically more effective than either a profit enhancement or a dual strategy. Only the focused customer-satisfaction quality strategy correlates with overall company financial performance, company return on assets, and long-term stock returns.

Success in business is simple. **To grow, you need to provide customers with a value proposition greater than that offered by your competition.** Fair pricing is a losing strategy. **For customers to purchase your offering, they must believe that the benefit you deliver is worth more to them than the money in their pocket.** And this usually means that you must offer them an overt benefit that is not available anywhere else. Short of this they may buy once because they have to, but they will not return unless you tilt the value equation in their favor by dropping your price.

Cost savings is not a viable strategy for significant growth. We understand that some readers may be getting violent at this stage, saying, "Yes, but you don't understand our category" or, "Yes, but our industry is different."

To you nonbelievers, I say, Get over it. If your life revolves around cost, you've lost the game and just don't know it yet. A study of the commodity price index for grain, milk, steel, plastic, and oil indicates that from 1845 to 1999, commodity prices have dropped an average of 80 percent!

NET: If commodity pricing is your strategy, you can safely assume that over the long term a 1.5 percent decrease in price per year will be the unrelenting average you must beat—and that's just to stay even.

PRACTICAL IDEAS

Think Offense, Not Defense, with Marketing Costs: As you seek to improve your sales and marketing cost-effectiveness, focus energies first on how you can more meaningfully connect with customers' needs. Instead of dwelling on what you can eliminate, focus first on articulating the virtues of your offering more Meaningfully. Instead of mindlessly advertising to millions, send a product sample to a subset of higher-probability customers. Instead of making millions of prospecting calls for your professional service, create a lecture or book that can provide an in-depth display of your wisdom.

Enroll Everyone in Customer Satisfaction: Enroll the entire company in quality improvement. Make satisfaction of customer needs the primary focus of all departments. Create measurement systems that align each department's output with real customer satisfaction. Challenge each department to identify ideas that it can implement to improve customer satisfaction. Milton Hershey, founder of the famous chocolate company, said, "Give them quality. That's the best kind of advertising in the world."

Define What You Would Spend Money On: Challenge your team to define how it would spend an additional 20 percent on your product or service to improve customer satisfaction. What would be the specific impact for customers? Having defined a specific benefit, now find ways to pay for it through quality-improvement programs.

Break the Commodity Cycle: If you're caught in a commodity marketplace, split your brand in two. Maintain the current brand to keep paying the bills. Then develop an alternative, value-added, premium-margin option. Keep the overhead costs on the new initiative low so that you stay in the market long enough to learn, change, adapt, and grow successfully.

{ 23 }
SCIENTIFIC
ADVICE

LEVERAGE YOUR UNIQUE STRENGTHS

There is a natural tendency to view the grass as greener at competitive companies. Having worked for multiple companies in the same industry, I can tell you that this is a giant fallacy. Everyone has advantages. Everyone has disadvantages.

The facts don't matter. What does matter is how you look at the situation. Do you see it as an opportunity and exploit your unique resources or do you sit and whine about what you lack?

This came to light in a study that showed the ADVANTAGE of being SMALL. A study was conducted with a cross-section of some eighty-five types of brands (products and services) over a five-year period. It found that the more successful a brand becomes, the more customers perceive that quality has slipped.

Bigger brands are perceived to offer poorer quality. This perception is often true, as what was once handled with a craftsman's care is now handled by inflexible systems built for mass efficiency. What was also once led by a passionate entrepreneur whose name is on the door is now an efficient and dispassionate corporate system.

NET: If you're small, exploit the perceptions of "uncaring" and "poor quality" that customers link to your bigger competitors.

Interestingly, there was one exception to this perception of poor quality with big brands. The research found that when customers pay a premium, they are less likely to see a growth in sales as a decline in quality. Inherent in a premium price is a core belief of higher quality that mass-market, commodity-priced brands don't enjoy.

PRACTICAL IDEAS

When You're Small, Leverage It as an Asset: Don't apologize for your small size. Rather, use it as an asset. Articulate and deliver customer service that exceeds expectations. Use your nimbleness and responsiveness as a major advantage versus the market leader.

Quantify the differences between you and competition by conducting independent tests of the time it takes for your staff to answer customer-service phone calls versus the competition. Show side by side the fine print and bureaucracy in competitive purchase order systems and/or warranties versus your simpler, more customer-centric approach.

When You're Big, Articulate Continuing Quality Growth: When you're highly successful, don't forget what sparked your success. Don't assume that customers perceive your products to be high quality. Knowing your name and trusting your quality are two different things.

Make continuous improvement in your customers' experience with your goods or services a cornerstone of continuing growth. If competition is weak, compete with yourself; proclaim proudly the Meaningful improvements you've made in the past one, three, or five years.

Articulate How Higher Price Allows Greater Quality: In a portion of your communications, define the measurable differences inherent in your product or service. Quantify the technology and the higher quality of raw materials built into your offering.

{ 24 }
SCIENTIFIC
ADVICE

IF YOU WANT TO DRIVE SUCCESS WITH YOUR WEB SITE OR PRINT ADVERTISING, FOCUS YOUR ATTENTION MORE ON THE WORDS. THEY ARE TWICE AS IMPORTANT AS THE PICTURE WHEN IT COMES TO GETTING CUSTOMERS TO STOP AND TAKE NOTICE

Said bluntly, "It's the idea, stupid!"

Pictures are a valuable way to visualize your benefit. However, **when it comes to marketing effectiveness, ideas matter most, and nothing communicates ideas like words**.

This advice is not new. Advertising legend David Ogilvy proved it repeatedly in a famous series of marketing tests years ago. He once said, "The wickedest of all sins is to run an advertisement without a headline. It's your introduction, your entrance to your message."

Sadly, many advertising people don't like to follow this advice, preferring instead to employ clever photos, montages and visual gimmicks. They argue that customers don't have any time to read words. They're right, and they're wrong. They're right in that customers have NO TIME for reading mindless hype. They're wrong, however, when it comes to providing customers with MEANINGFUL news and information on what the offering will do for them.

The basis for this advice is a massive study involving 1,365 ads and some 3,600 consumers. It used an infrared signal to track where participants' eyes looked as they paged through a magazine. The research found that **when it came to getting customers to stop and take notice of an ad, text was twice as important as pictures**.

A couple of other interesting findings from the research: If you place your ad earlier in the magazine, you increase the probability that customers will notice your message. Also, familiarity reduces customer interest. In effect, the longer you've been around, the more you must dedicate yourself to discovering and communicating NEW NEWS about what you'll do for your customers.

(NOTE: I've included this advice in the chapter on Strategy as opposed to Marketing Message because a true commitment to "messages that matter" is a strategic decision. A MEANINGFUL marketing message is designed into the strategy, not "created in execution.")

PRACTICAL IDEAS

Create the Storyline First: When creating your print advertising or Web site, first create your storyline. Where is the news? Where is the point of drama? Having agreed on your storyline, write the headline and think of it as your "introduction or entrance" to your message. Then, with simple words, tell the story of what you're going to do for your customers if they give you their time, energy, and money. Lastly, figure out a photo that visualizes the benefit and/or your point of difference.

What if you don't have a story to tell? What if you don't have any news? What should you do then? Simple. DON'T ADVERTISE. Dedicate your energies to reinventing your offering so that it represents a true leap forward versus your competition. This advice may sound severe; it's not. The research clearly shows that without real news, your chances of actually realizing any—and I mean ANY—return on your marketing investment is virtually nil. The Frito-Lay company uses this strategy. It runs advertising for Lay's Potato Chips, Doritos Tortilla Chips or Frito Corn Chips only when it has new product news to communicate.

Learn from the Print Masters: Infomercial and direct-mail companies are great at headlines and storylines. Print journalists at the great papers—the *Los Angeles Times, Chicago Tribune, New York Times,* and *Toronto Globe and Mail*—write great headlines and stories. Observe how the experts use headlines to bring you the reader into the story. Observe how they communicate complicated concepts with ease and efficiency. Compare and contrast publications. Buy four different newspapers on the same day. Compare and contrast how each writer and each paper covers the same major news story. After reading, apply your learning to the creation of a message for your offering.

{ 25 }
SCIENTIFIC
ADVICE

SMART STRATEGIC THINKING CAN HELP YOU REDUCE YOUR CHANCES OF FACING A STRONG COMPETITIVE ATTACK

A study of 249 managers' experiences with competitive reactions to new products identified four strategies that can help you reduce the speed and scope of reaction from competition. By thinking through various competitive scenarios and using one or more of these four strategies, you can reduce your chances of being attacked and losing.

Pursue Major Product Innovations: When you pursue Meaningful product differences, it takes significantly longer for the competition to react. **The more unique your new offering, the more time and skill it takes your competition to design, develop, and produce a comparative offering.**

Attack Larger Companies: **The larger your key competitor, the slower their response will be.** Quite simply, very large companies tend to face inertia and inflexibility. Additionally, they often have large investments in established ways of production and are reluctant to self-cannibalize.

Pursue Markets with a Few Strong Competitors: **Markets that have only a few strong competitors are significantly slower to respond to competitive introductions.** It appears that when there are only a few strong competitors, each reacts slowly to avoid sparking an all-out war within the category.

Avoid Fast-Growing Markets: The faster a marketplace is growing, the more likely that competitors will view it as being of major strategic importance. **Markets that are old and growing slowly are more likely to be ignored by major competitors.**

PRACTICAL **IDEAS**

Pursue Meaningfully Different Ideas: The more dramatically different your idea is compared with established practices, the less likely you'll be copied quickly. Find the courage to do the unthinkable. Identify your competition's greatest source of manufacturing or production skill. Then create ideas that make this asset irrelevant to customers.

Attack the Biggest Competitors: Orient your competitive and comparative marketing against the largest competitors. If you can't find one giant to attack, focus your energies where there are a few giants that display low levels of direct conflict and price discounting. The bigger the company, the more likely they are to ignore smaller competitors and the longer it will take them to copy you.

Focus with Exclusive Distribution: Cosmetics entrepreneur Estée Lauder decided early on to focus exclusively on upscale department stores. Focusing on this class of stores only, she created a product that they could make a profit on, as it wouldn't be discounted. The relatively small number of potential customers also allowed her to personally make most of the sales calls. She was known for never giving up. When a manager of the prestigious Galleries Lafayette account in Paris refused her, she "accidentally" spilled her perfume on the floor of the store. The reaction from passing customers to the scent was so positive that she made the sale.

Pursue Markets that No One Wants: Who are the customers that no one wants? What are the most "boring" categories and industries? Who are the most difficult customers to service? The less interesting the opportunity looks on the surface, the less likely it is that the competition will defend, copy, or attack your introduction. Charles Schwab did this with his discount brokerage service. While all other stock brokers focused on the large institutional investors, Schwab vigorously targeted the individual investor.

{ 26 }
SCIENTIFIC
ADVICE

THINK SMARTER THAN OTHERS. BASE YOUR LOYALTY PROGRAM ON SOMETHING OTHER THAN DISCOUNTS

In 1981, American Airlines invented the world's first frequent-flyer program. Within seven days, United Airlines introduced a program of its own. Before long, it became the cost of doing business, and all airlines had some form of a frequent-flyer program. Today it's one of many reasons why most if not all of the major airlines have filed for bankruptcy. **Selling CHEAP (giving discounts) to your best customers makes you feel good at the start, but long term it's the road to ruin.**

Industry experts point to data that indicate once customers join a loyalty program, they increase spending on that brand by an average of 27 percent. Further, 43 percent of members say that loyalty programs lead to more frequent purchases, and 16 percent said a loyalty program causes them to choose one option exclusively. Heck, anyone would take a deal that's offered. The real question is does the program generate INCREMENTAL PROFITS? I don't think it does, and Exhibit A is the unfunded liabilities of the airlines and credit card companies. At the end of 2001, the world's airlines had given out an estimated 12 trillion frequent-flyers miles, with two-thirds of those miles as yet unredeemed. They're making money short term, but long term—just like Social Security for the government—someone has to pay the costs.

Jump-start your company's thinking and find ways to make your program about connecting with other users, sourcing new information, advanced information and exclusive offers.

PRACTICAL IDEAS

Leverage Special-Access Loyalty Programs: The simplest and maybe the least expensive benefit you can offer to loyal customers is special access and priority service. The travel industry does this well. Car rental agencies and airlines offer express services for check-in and free upgrades when available. The offer of special access is the ultimate thank-you to customers for their loyalty. Explore opportunities to provide preferred shipping, ordering, or delivery to your most loyal customers.

Leverage Special-Knowledge Loyalty Programs: Loyal customers have an advanced understanding of your product or service. Open a system of dialogue with loyal customers. Encourage advanced discussions on a two-way basis using e-mail and Web sites. Give them access to the leading edge of your company's thinking. And listen to their ideas. The greater the interaction between your company and your customers, the tighter the loyalty bond.

Leverage Collector-Loyalty Programs: Collector-loyalty programs can be very powerful. Collectors exist for everything from dolls to stamps to antiques. To encourage collecting, empower secondary markets like fan clubs and auction houses. Jump-start collectibility by offering limited or exclusive editions of your product.

Your Approach Is as Important as What You Give: Maybe the most important thing to consider regarding loyal customers is how you treat them. A simple thank you and remembering their names are at least as important as what you give them. This is not always easy, as loyal customers are also the ones most likely to voice their suggestions for improvement. Over time, their suggestions can sound like complaints, and you can start consciously or subconsciously treating your loyal customers badly.

{ 27 }
SCIENTIFIC
ADVICE

THE MORE YOU MEASURE, THE MORE YOU'LL MAKE MEASURABLE PROGRESS

The late Bob Goldstein, former vice president of advertising for Procter & Gamble, once said, **"In many fields of human endeavor, improved measurement has been a precursor and a necessary requirement for improved solutions."** So, too, improved measurement may well be a precursor for improved solutions with your marketing effectiveness.

Everything that can be a potential cause, effect, or result can be quantified. The most fundamental measurement is a standard for your own results. The beneficial effect of goal setting for task performance is one of the most robust and replicable findings in psychological literature. By goals, I mean challenging, tough-to-reach, specific goals. Not easy, see-what-happens, give-it-a-try goals.

The very act of writing down a challenging goal has a near magical ability to make it a possibility.

A study was conducted of 491 independent salespeople who had recently started a new job. The salespeople were surveyed on their personal, self-set sales goal for their first year:

- ★ 60 percent reported setting no goal of any kind.
- ★ 32 percent reported setting a general earnings goal.
- ★ 8 percent reported setting a specific annual dollar earnings goal.

The level of goal setting had a direct correlation with earnings. In contrast to those salespeople who set no earnings goal, those who set a general goal earned twice as much, and those who set a specific goal earned nearly three times as much.

When you define on paper your clear and concrete objective, you fuel your internal motivation. You are in essence challenging yourself to grow and achieve your own standards.

PRACTICAL **IDEAS**

Develop a Plan for Meaningful Growth: What is your past six-month, twelve-month, or two-year trend? This is your natural momentum. Next, calculate what a doubling or tripling of your growth trend looks like. What will it take to deliver this kind of growth? If your sales are declining, what will it take to turn your sales around?

Working harder is unlikely to be the answer. Rather, you will need to make a significant change in your sales and marketing. You will need to change your message, how you deliver your message, or the frequency of your message delivery.

Always Quantify Advertising Effectiveness: Measure every new piece of advertising and every media vehicle. Include a toll-free phone number or Web site for more information or special offers. *Always* collect and analyze your response rates. Great advertising immediately generates customer interest. Identify a specific customer mailing list or television, radio, or print advertising vehicle to conduct your tests with. The more tests you run, the greater your understanding.

Always Quantify Media Efficiency: The cost of space in print media or airtime on television or radio varies according to the quality and quantity of impressions delivered. The choice of media vehicle should be based on cost efficiency. By researching the relative response rates of various media options, you gain leverage in negotiations. If one vehicle generates half the response rate, then you can push hard for a significantly lower price.

Stay Honest about Milestones: Develop a "shipping" mentality whereby your organizational culture prides itself on *not* missing key milestones no matter what. When a salesperson gives his word to the customer that a new product or service will be delivered, he's speaking for everyone.

CHAPTER TWO

MARKETING MESSAGE

Entrepreneurs who are having difficulties with marketing often ask me WHERE TO ADVERTISE. Is it better to use print, radio, Internet, direct mail, or television? Pushing further, they'll ask what magazine, what direct-mail list, what search engine is most effective.

In most cases they're focused on the wrong issue. **Their REAL PROBLEM is that they don't have an effective marketing message.**

From a big-picture standpoint, your marketing success is determined by a simple equation:

**Marketing Message Effectiveness x
Advertising Media Reach = Sales**

If your marketing message's selling effectiveness is "ZERO," it doesn't make any difference where you advertise or how much you spend.

It is true that some media vehicles offer greater cost efficiencies than others. For example, if you're selling home repair products or services, mailing to a list of those who subscribe to a home repair magazine could be more efficient.

I said *could be* because you need to do the math. Assuming that you have a great marketing message, you need to figure out your net cost per response, per inquiry, or per sale. In today's marketplace, targeted media vehicles are often so overpriced that what started as an increase in efficiency is actually more costly PER RESPONSE than the "less hip" mass media vehicles.

It's important to note, however, that you can test media vehicles only when you have a very effective message. When your message is weak, it's difficult to quantify meaningful differences in media effectiveness. I learned this from an interview with two-time Olympic archery gold medalist and world-record holder Darrell Pace. Darrell explained his approach to testing new equipment: "I only test new equipment when I'm shooting well. That's the only time I can really tell if an equipment change makes a real difference."

At the Eureka! Ranch, we've quantitatively tested more than 10,000 marketing messages. And the conclusion is clear—in most cases the messages are just not very meaningful. Charting of the data indicates that Dr. Deming's observations regarding the source of quality errors in manufacturing holds true in marketing.

94 percent of Marketing failures are due to POOR MESSAGES.
6 percent are due to poor Advertising Methods or Vehicles

The fact is that EVERY MEDIA METHOD WORKS if you have a MEANINGFUL MESSAGE. And by Meaningful Message, I mean specifically a message that articulates a MEANINGFUL DIFFERENCE.

The challenge is in the second word: DIFFERENCE. The courage to BE BOLD and UNIQUE is rare. That's why this book is dedicated to the REVOLUTIONARIES, folks like you who have the courage to learn new ideas and take action on them.

Chapter 2 starts with Marketing Message Fundamentals, the fundamental drivers of success no matter what your product, your service, or your industry. The chapter ends with a set of "Secret Weapons"–specific advice and ideas for more specialty methods to drive success.

The first three pieces of scientific advice in this section summarize the Three Laws of Marketing Physics from *Jump Start Your BUSINESS Brain*.

YOU WILL NEARLY TRIPLE YOUR ODDS OF SUCCESS WHEN YOU ARE OVERT ABOUT WHAT BENEFIT YOUR CUSTOMERS WILL RECEIVE AS A RESULT OF PURCHASING YOUR OFFERING

Customers have little time to compare, contrast, and consider your product or service offerings. The never-ending flood of voice mail, e-mail, and junk mail has caused customers to develop a protective barrier against new marketing messages. To break through the barrier, you need to be OVERT about the customer benefit you offer.

The classic mistake that managers make is to communicate the FEATURES of their offering instead of the BENEFITS. They make the ASSUMPTION that customers will be able to translate your feature to their benefit.

Features are the facts, the components, the technologies of your offering. Benefits are what the features will do for the customer. **Benefits are what the customer will receive, experience, and enjoy as a result of the features.**

When you communicate an Overt Benefit instead of features, you increase your odds of success by 290 percent.

Research shows that the more work required of your customers to translate your "features" into "benefits," the less likely they are to notice, consider, and purchase what you have to offer. The following visuals show the interrelationships we're talking about.

PRACTICAL **IDEAS**

TARGET
Audience
Occasion
Problem

Overt Benefit
"What's In It For Me?"

Step 1: The first step to SUCCESS is to articulate your TARGET Audience, Occasion, or Problem. This is the point of focus for your marketing message. Then articulate the OVERT BENEFIT that you will deliver to this target. Your consumers or industrial customers would phrase it differently—"What's in it for me?"

Transform Features into Benefits: Features are not benefits. It requires work on the customers' part to translate your features into what benefits they will receive. To improve marketing effectiveness, take the work out. Review all your marketing messages and ask, "Why should customers care?" Transform every feature statement into an *overt* benefit promise.

For a step-by-step process for finding your OVERT Benefit, see *Jump Start Your BUSINESS Brain.*

YOU WILL MORE THAN DOUBLE YOUR ODDS OF SUCCESS BY COMMUNICATING A REAL REASON TO BELIEVE YOUR OVERT BENEFIT WILL BE DELIVERED

Customer trust is at an all-time low. The public opinion pollster Yankelovich found that 93 percent of customers have no confidence in the advertising messages of major corporations. Being overt and obvious about your unique and Meaningful benefit will get customers to notice you. Providing a *real* reason to believe will help you increase their confidence and close the sale.

When you offer a REAL Reason to Believe, you increase your odds of success by 233 percent.

Today's customers are media savvy. They've learned to discern the difference between real substance and the usual smoke and mirrors. Presenting proof that the Meaningful difference you are promising will be genuinely delivered is critically important.

Proof can take many forms, from demonstrations to clinical test results to common-sense explanations: faster service because we have service locations in all parts of the region, for example. If you're a salesperson, you're part of your brand's Real Reason to Believe. In fact, **the overt benefit to a company of a human sales force is the enhanced credibility that develops from their relationships with customers**.

In an ideal world, your Overt Benefit would be so daring and bold that it DEMANDS your reason to believe in order to be taken seriously.

The amount of reason to believe needed to satisfy customer apprehensions is directly proportional to your level of boldness. The bigger your promise, the more reason to believe you need to provide.

PRACTICAL IDEAS

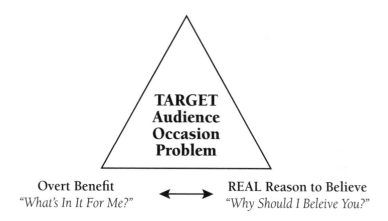

TARGET
Audience
Occasion
Problem

Overt Benefit   ⟷   REAL Reason to Believe
"What's In It For Me?"   *"Why Should I Beleive You?"*

Step 2: In an ideal world, the benefit will have caused some tension and anxiety in customer's minds. It will require you to resolve the tension by offering a REAL REASON to believe.

Use Overt Honesty to FIND Your Credibility: Your credibility is built from honesty. When an offering is not right for your customers, tell them so. When you don't know the answer, don't bluff; tell them you'll research it and find the answer.

Plan to Exceed Customer Expectations: Credibility is built when the customers' experiences exceed their expectations. Design pleasant surprises into your brand experiences, like personally showing up to help with their installation of new products—even though it's not in the contract. Give free upgrades, extended warranties, or personal phone calls after purchase to check on satisfaction and answer any questions. To measure the true health of your brand, ask customers, "Did the product/service experience meet or exceed your expectations?" With one question, you'll know where you stand.

For a step-by-step process for articulating your REAL Reason to Believe, see *Jump Start Your BUSINESS Brain*.

YOU WILL MORE THAN TRIPLE YOUR ODDS OF SUCCESS IF YOU COMMUNICATE A DRAMATIC DIFFERENCE IN YOUR OVERT BENEFIT AND/OR YOUR REAL REASON TO BELIEVE

Your job is to create a MONOPOLY.

Every product or service that is sold lies somewhere on the continuum from MONOPOLY to COMMODITY. At the extremes, your offering is either one-of-a-kind—in effect a MONOPOLY—or it's the S.O.S. (Same Old Stuff)—a COMMODITY. In the case of the latter, the only way you can enhance customer value is by lowering your price.

Most brands start out as something approaching a monopoly. They capture a unique piece of the market by bravely offering something that no one else offers. Then competitors without brains enough to be original copy and clone the pioneer. In time, if the originator doesn't recharge the offering with breakthrough improvements, it becomes perceived as a commodity.

When you offer a DRAMATIC DIFFERENCE, you increase your odds of success by 353 percent.

The key word is DRAMATIC. Dramatic as in BOLD, OBVIOUS, SIGNIFICANT. Not small, minor, or "hair-splittingly unique."

Your DRAMATIC Difference usually comes from the offering of a DRAMATICALLY Different OVERT BENEFIT. It comes from satisfying your customer's needs like no other offering can do. However, having a unique REAL Reason to Believe can generate customer relevant news as well.

In some categories, such as weight-loss products, beauty-care products or regulated products such as Vodka, the Overt Benefit is virtually identical between brands. In these cases, Dramatic Difference can come from REAL Reason to Believe, e.g., *This time you'll really lose weight because* . . .

PRACTICAL **IDEAS**

Dramatic Difference
"Why Should I Care?"
The First or Only...

**TARGET
Audience
Occasion
Problem**

Overt Benefit
"What's In It For Me?"

REAL Reason to Believe
"Why Should I Beleive You?"

Step 3: Now with clarity—evaluate how MEANINGFULLY Unique your offering is.

> Is it THE FIRST or ONLY to offer the **benefit**?
> Is it THE FIRST or ONLY to solve this **specific problem**?
> Is it THE FIRST or ONLY to offer a **COMBINATION of Benefits**?
> Is it THE FIRST or ONLY to offer **TRUE REASON TO BELIEVE**?
> Is it THE FIRST or ONLY to offer customers this **level of VALUE**?

If it's not one of these, then you must think hard about the viability of your offering.

For a step-by-step process for finding your DRAMATIC Difference, see *Jump Start Your BUSINESS Brain.*

{ 4 }
SCIENTIFIC
ADVICE

WHEN YOU ARE SPECIFIC ABOUT YOUR POINT OF DIFFERENCE, YOU INCREASE YOUR ODDS OF SUSTAINED SUCCESS BY 52 PERCENT

Customers are creatures of habit. Breaking their buying habits requires you to overtly, specifically, and directly articulate the benefit of your offering.

To get customers to listen, you must give them a dramatic reason. A study of 901 marketing messages for new products found that when the sales messages specifically stated the product's point of difference, those brands were 52 percent more likely to survive for five years or more than those that were less overt.

Customers are overwhelmed. It's estimated that they have more than a million different purchasing options or SKUs (stock-keeping units) to choose from. The average large grocery store carries some 5,000 SKUs. Contrast this with the fact that the average family buys 80 to 85 percent of their needs from just 150 SKUs. **Customers simply don't have the time to seriously study every marketing message for every new product or service.**

To cope with the marketing chaos they face, customers have learned how to rapidly sort and categorize marketing messages as Meaningful or simply Mindless Marketing Trickery. Through thousands of purchase and usage experiences, they've learned how to identify the difference between a smoke-and-mirrors claim ("unsurpassed performance") and a specifically Meaningful one ("cuts your time in half").

Large corporations have trouble being specific about what they offer because of their highly conservative legal departments. Small businesses have trouble being specific because of their natural tendency to be humble rather than boastful. In both cases, **the answer is not to overhype. Rather, it's to tell the genuine truth about what the customer will receive.**

PRACTICAL **IDEAS**

Quantify Your Benefit: Factually and measurably determine what your benefit advantage is over the competition. Is your product 50 percent more durable? Can it be installed in 30 percent less time? Do you have a customer-service response time that is twice as fast? Is your service system three times more reliable?

If you can't quantify your advantage, then don't complain when customers go to a lower-cost competitor. Lower cost is a benefit that is specific and numeric. The only way to confront a specific price disadvantage is to offer your customers a specific and measurable value advantage.

Miracle-Gro has become the No. 1 brand of specialty plant fertilizer behind a promise to "GROW PLANTS TWICE AS BIG." The marketing manager told me that they can support a claim of nearly five times bigger but that it's too unbelievable for customers so they only promise a doubling.

Be SPECIFIC with Your Message: L. L. Bean sold his boots with a brilliant articulation of benefit. "Outside of your gun, nothing is so important to your outfit as your footwear. You cannot expect success hunting deer or moose if your feet are not properly dressed. The Maine Hunting Shoe is designed by a hunter who has tramped Maine woods for the past eighteen years. **They are light as a pair of moccasins with the protection of a heavy hunting boot.**"

Speak of Your Uniqueness from the Viewpoint of New and Existing Customers: Use the words your existing customers use to speak about your advantages. Existing customers of your product or service have integrity and an honesty of perspective. Ask both long-established and new customers what makes you different. Ask them to quantify the difference. Ask them to compare and contrast their experiences before and after purchasing your brand.

{ 5 }
SCIENTIFIC
ADVICE

BY BEING OBVIOUS ABOUT WHAT OVERT BENEFIT YOUR CUSTOMERS WILL RECEIVE, YOU WILL INCREASE YOUR SUCCESS RATE BY 75 PERCENT

The more work required of your customers to translate your message into how it affects them and their lives, the less likely they are to notice, consider, and purchase what you have to offer.

Analysis of more than 901 new products found that those with a benefit message that was overt and obvious were 75 percent more likely to succeed in the marketplace than those whose message was broad and indirect.

Challenge yourself to create messages that are SELF EVIDENT. Peter Lynch, the famous mutual fund manager at Fidelity Investments, once said, "Go for a business that any idiot can run because sooner or later any idiot probably is going to be running it." The marketing message equivalent would be, "**Develop a marketing message that any idiot can execute because sooner or later, any idiot probably is going to be executing it.**"

Don't promise that your dog food has patented dental crystals. Be *obvious*: Say that your patented dog food guarantees fresh breath for twelve hours after your dog eats it.

Don't promise that your industrial lubricant is technically advanced. Be *obvious*: Say that your advanced lubricant reduces breakdowns, even in 700-degree heat.

Don't promise that your running shoe features rebound technology in the sole. Be *obvious*: Say that the rebound sole in your footwear reduces fatigue by 50 percent, meaning you can walk and run longer without getting tired.

Let a customer say no because they're not interested in what you offer. But *never* let a customer say no because they don't understand what you offer.

PRACTICAL IDEAS

Use Your Voice Mail Messages as a Test Market: Articulate what's in it for the customer in an obvious fashion, and then script the voice mail messages you leave for customers. State clearly, "I'm calling about the new [product or service] we have that can help you [save 30 percent, increase quality by 20 percent, improve your direct mail response rates by 40 percent, create the most romantic Valentine's dinner, etc.]."

Make twenty-five calls and measure the number of callbacks. Then script another message and try again. When you get the right benefit and state it in an obvious fashion, you'll know it, because response rates will increase by 50 to 100 percent.

Model Your Message Based on the Great Masters: Direct-response marketers (print, direct mail, Internet, infomercials) leverage *overt* and *obvious* benefit communication to drive response rates. To learn from these masters, gather a collection of great junk mail and/or set your VCR to record infomercials. Take a morning to tell your sales-and-marketing story in the format that the direct-mail pieces or infomercials use. When they claim a benefit, make a claim; when they give a testimonial, give yours. At the Eureka! Ranch, this technique has become a staple in our marketing invention tool kit.

{ 6 }
SCIENTIFIC
ADVICE

YOU WILL INCREASE YOUR ODDS OF SUCCESS BY 74 PERCENT IF YOU OVERTLY LINK YOUR REAL REASON TO BELIEVE WITH YOUR OVERT BENEFIT

Marketing is about storytelling. It's about telling how your Meaningful benefit difference will enhance customers' lives in some way. **Your Meaningful benefit difference is *what* customers will receive. Your credibility is *how* you will deliver on that promise. Your ultimate success is based on the synergy between *what* and *how*.**

Analysis of 901 new product-marketing messages found a 74 percent greater chance of success when there was strong synergy between the overt benefit and credibility.

Great marketing tells the whole story and tightly links the benefit with credibility: "We're the first brand to offer [*overt benefit*] because we [*real reason to believe*]."

When you catch your customers' attentions with a Meaningful benefit difference, a natural anticipation builds of how you will make their lives better. That soon gives way to a fear of once again being disappointed. Customers have been disappointed so many times that, while they are excited about your product's potential, they are simultaneously suspicious.

The simplest way to ensure linkage between Overt Benefit and Real Reason to Believe is to tell a friend your Overt Benefit and have him ask "WHY?" questions repeatedly:

- ★ "Why should I believe you?"
- ★ "Why are you able to deliver what you promise?"
- ★ "Why can you do what none of your competitors can do?"

Your answers to the direct question will help you find reasons to believe that truly, directly link to your benefit promise.

PRACTICAL IDEAS

Audit Your Meaningful Benefit Claims for Honesty: Don't overhype. Most sales and marketing credibility problems are self-inflicted. Overstating what you really can do is a sure way to hurt credibility. Remember, trust in you declines every time a customer makes a purchase and is disappointed.

Look carefully at all your selling claims and ask yourself, "How do I know that this claim is absolutely true?" If you can't defend a claim easily and without question, consider modifying it or eliminating it altogether.

Focus on Simple Storytelling: After reviewing all printed materials, step back and tell a trusted friend, an innocent child, or a wise elder the story of your offering. Record what you say, and then review the recording and edit until it's a comfortable story.

Speak Directly to Your Meaningful Benefit Difference: Challenge yourself to find simple, solid, natural, credibility-building factors that link directly to the benefit. If you have a collection of customer testimonials, use the ones that speak directly to your Meaningful difference. For example, if your benefit is about reliable, speedy service, use testimonials that show how, even during a major snowstorm, you still delivered the work on time.

Preemptively Confront Customer Skepticism: Left to themselves, customers can imagine all sorts of reasons not to believe you. Preempt this negative spiral by candidly confronting the skepticism. Say without hesitation, "We can do this because . . ." or "What makes this possible is . . ." By candidly confronting the issue, you help turn skeptics into converts. If they then have to sell others within their company or family, you've given them the ammunition they need to convert others.

{ 7 }
SCIENTIFIC
ADVICE

BY FOCUSING YOUR MARKETING ON DOING ONE THING GREAT, YOU INCREASE YOUR ODDS OF LONG-TERM SUCCESS BY 60 PERCENT

When you FOCUS on Doing One Thing Great, you make a commitment to excellence. It immediately tells customers that you have a passion for excellence and understanding.

Analysis of more than 901 new products found that when the marketing message was highly focused on one benefit, the brand was 60 percent more likely to succeed in the marketplace than when the message was unfocused.

When you promise ALL THINGS, you're perceived as a MASTER OF NONE. All brands have many dimensions. Most dimensions are simply the cost of getting in the game—not dramatic differences.

Think hard about your offering. What is the one element that, above all others, defines why someone should become your customer? **What is the one Meaningful difference that is most Meaningful to your customers?**

When your offering is highly focused, your word-of-mouth advertising is turbocharged: It's simply easier for customers to tell others about your virtues.

Today's customers have an overwhelming amount of information available to them. With focusing, you increase the odds that today's overwhelmed customers will detect and take action on what you really offer.

In the world of retailing, examples of FOCUSING are everywhere: Staples focuses on making it easy for small businesses to get office supplies, Victora's Secret focuses on romantic lingerie, and Wal-Mart focuses on low prices.

PRACTICAL **IDEAS**

Make Defining Your Brand an Urgent Priority: If you don't know what your brand stands for, there's little chance that your customers do.

Sadly, it is rare to find a brand that has a clear definition. We know this because when we conduct invention projects, we ask various members of management what their brands stands for. Usually not even 30 percent of the responses are the same. When we give lectures, we often ask for business cards and are shocked to see how few of them feature any articulation of what the brand stands for.

To define your brand, you must learn how to say no. We suggest the following process: Videotape old customers, new customers, non-customers, new employees, and old employees. Have the interviewees explain their relationship with the brand and then answer three quick questions:

- ★ When you hear [*your trademark*] what comes to mind?
- ★ What is the one thing that [*your trademark*] is best at?
- ★ What is the one thing that [*your trademark*] does that no one else does?

Edit the videotape and then, with a team of managers, review the tape and write down what is said and what is not. Play the tape three times. Then have your management team members write down their own responses to the questions. Use all the responses as the basis for defining clearly what you want your brand to stand for in customers' minds.

Publish Your Focused Brand Vision on Everything: Once you've clearly defined what your brand stands for, publish it everywhere. It should be on your business cards, your letterhead, and every other sales and marketing piece that you distribute.

{ 8 }
SCIENTIFIC
ADVICE

TO ENSURE THAT YOUR MARKETING MESSAGE IS UNDERSTOOD, CRAFT IT SO THAT A TEN-YEAR-OLD CAN UNDERSTAND IT

The KISS Principle (Keep It Simple, Stupid) is more than a slogan; it's the truth.

The more complex your marketing message, the less likely customers are to take the time to stop, read, or listen and understand.

When a group of people creates sales and marketing messages, complexity increases exponentially. Everyone has a little idea here, a small suggestion there. When all the "help" is added together, it's no wonder that the resultant message is confusing to potential customers. Two studies quantify the virtue of keeping your messages simple.

Both studies followed a set of 901 new products from introduction for at least five years. The original marketing message was evaluated and the results compared in terms of long-term success or failure. **Analysis found a 70 percent increase in success probability when a marketing message was clear and easy to understand.**

Additionally, the marketing messages were evaluated using the Flesch-Kincaid reading complexity measure. Brands with messages written at a fifth-grade reading level or lower were 25 percent more likely to survive than those with messages written at a higher level of complexity. This does not indicate that customers are functionally illiterate. Rather, it proves the effect today's overstressed world has on potential customers' ability to focus.

The need for simplicity is true even when selling sophisticated technology. In the corporate buying world, you will find both technically literate and technically illiterate managers. To succeed, you must translate your technological wonder so that even the most technically illiterate manager can understand it.

PRACTICAL **IDEAS**

Choose Nouns and Verbs over Adverbs and Adjectives: Tell customers what you will do for them.

Speak the truth.

Use adverbs and adjectives sparingly.

Use nouns and verbs to tell the action you will apply to a person, place, or thing.

Ruthlessly edit hype, hyperbole, and harangues out of sales letters, advertising, and presentations. Avoid sweeping or global generalizations that cannot be readily supported.

Explain Your Idea to a Fifth-Grader: Tell a child your sales and marketing story. Then ask him to repeat what he heard. Correct the difference between what you said and what he said to sell more with less effort.

Focus on Exactly What Will Be Different: When customers purchase your product or service, what will be different? How will their lives be better? What exactly will they now experience that they didn't before?

Do the same with your annual sales and marketing plans. Ask your team, "What exactly are we going to do differently this year?" "We're going to work harder" is not an acceptable answer. Remember, to change results, actions need to change. If you can't define what will be meaningfully different at the start, chances are, nothing will be meaningfully different at the end of the year.

{ 9 }
SCIENTIFIC
ADVICE

YOU WILL TURBOCHARGE YOUR MARKETING COMMUNICATION BY VISUALIZING YOUR MARKETING STORYLINE

After you've defined your marketing "storyline" in words, visuals can help communicate to your target audience your Overt Benefit and Real Reason to Believe.

Pictures and images used with strategic discipline can help customers speed their understanding.

In a research study consumers were shown advertisements for the same brand of frozen meals. The only variation was the photographs used to represent them. Consumers' interpretations of the product varied widely depending on the visual.

* When a close-up of the food was shown, consumers viewed the brand as "appetizing and delicious."
* When a collection of six dishes was shown, the brand was seen as "having larger variety."
* When a variety of people was shown, the brand was perceived as "everyone likes."
* Simply changing the visual could double consumer ratings on key attributes such as "good for families" and "good for everyday meals."

This advice does not mean you don't need words. The photos in this research simply set the stage for purchasing by helping customers identify whether the offering was for their target audience or needs. It is through the words that you tell the story of the meaningful difference you offer and what makes it possible.

PRACTICAL **IDEAS**

Be Sure that What You Show Is Most Important: When you show your product front and center, that communicates that your product is what is most important. When you show your service people, it says that service is your most important asset. Stop now and look at what you see in your brochure, on your Web site, or behind the counter of your retail store. Do you see the most important dimension for customers to know? If not, then change it. Show the story of your offering.

Tell Your Story without Words: With digital cameras there is no excuse for not having high-quality images. When you snap a photo, you can check the photo quality immediately. If the lighting or the framing is not right, you can take it again and again until you get it right.

Bring your ease-of-use benefits to life by showing customers how to use your product through a sequence of visuals. Bring your emotional benefit to life by showing the excitement, pleasure, or joy through descriptively dramatic images. Use your Web site as a storyboard to educate your customers.

Ask Customers What Images They Recall: When you don't know what to show, ask your customers. Visual image recall is often a powerful means to identify what is most Meaningful to customers.

To gain insight into consumers' habits and practices, have them e-mail you images or take pictures with a disposable camera of when and where they would use your product.

{ 10 }
SCIENTIFIC
ADVICE

THE MOST SUCCESSFUL MARKETING MESSAGE YOU CAN CREATE IS ONE THAT STATES WITH PRECISION WHAT CUSTOMERS WILL ACTUALLY EXPERIENCE FROM YOUR OFFERING

Great Marketing tells the story of the product or service with precision. It doesn't understate or overstate the virtues of the offering.

A professor provided study participants with a marketing message that either 1.) accurately articulated performance, 2.) understated product performance, or 3.) highly overstated performance. A control group was provided with no marketing message. Based on the marketing description, participants rated their expectations of the product. After viewing and sampling the item, participants rated the product again.

The group receiving an accurate marketing description had similar ratings before and after product experience, 8.9 and 9.1 respectively.

The group receiving a marketing message that badly understated the product's performance provided an initial low rating of 3.2. After use, the rating rose to 6.6. However, this is still below what was independently determined as the accurate rating of around 9.0. Understating your marketing message leads to customers perceiving your product—even after use—at less than its full value.

Having no marketing message generated a product rating after use of 7.7. This is better than the poor message, but still below the 9.0 that is considered truth.

Participants who were presented with an overstatement of the product gave a high initial rating of 16.7. However, after use, the rating declined to the truthful rating of 9.0. Note: Overhyping the offering did not create an enhanced perception of the product. Instead, it resulted in a customer who clearly understood that he had been tricked by marketing. This is not the path to a Meaningful customer connection.

PRACTICAL IDEAS

Use Customers to Enhance Marketing Accuracy: When you understate your offering's performance in your sales and marketing message, you run the risk of having customers understate its performance even after they've experienced it.

When you overstate your offering's performance in your sales and marketing message, you run the risk of having customers feel they've been tricked. This has the potential to create a negative impact on their perception.

Involve customers in marketing evaluation. Present a set of customers with your message. Have them use your product in a real-world setting. Then ask them to evaluate your marketing message based on their experiences. Seek their help in precisely articulating your message by listening to how they talk about it.

Involve Technology Experts in Marketing Development: Those who invented, designed, and developed your product or service often have a deep understanding of your offering's true strengths and weaknesses. The challenge is that they might speak in a technical language that is not customer friendly. Teach them to speak in simple, friendly terms, and you will have a valuable resource to use.

Quantify Your Offering Versus Expectations: Ask customers to rate how interested they are in purchasing your product or service on a scale from zero to ten (zero equaling definitely not buy, ten equaling definitely would buy) based on reviewing your marketing message. After use, have them rate it again. Average the pre- and post-use ratings across fifty to one hundred customers. Compare the pre- versus post-use ratings. When your scores are within one point of each other, you have achieved balance between your marketing promise and actual performance. Note, as a general rule, when using a scale like this, average scores should be above five and ideally above six.

{ 11 }
SCIENTIFIC
ADVICE

TO WIN BIG WITH INDUSTRIAL MARKETING, YOU SHOULD FOCUS ON THE FUNDAMENTALS OF BENEFIT, UNIQUENESS, AND EASE OF UNDERSTANDING

Within the world of marketing, consumer marketing tends to dominate the academic literature and popular press books.

This truth shows how the basic principles of Meaningful Marketing also hold true in industrial product marketing. A study was conducted of 103 new industrial products in the United States, Canada, and Europe. For each initiative, a total of 298 variables were measured. The four most important measures for predicting success were:

> Important Customer Benefit
> Unique Performance
> Easy-to-Communicate Benefits
> Good Value for the Money

Unsuccessful products in the study had significantly lower values on each of these top success variables.

The road to industrial marketing success is not hard: Provide your customers with a Meaningful benefit difference, keep it easy to understand, and provide your customers a lot of value for their money.

It's easy to delude ourselves into thinking that we are delivering against these dimensions, when in fact we are not. The natural tendency is to exaggerate benefits, points of difference, and value perceptions. Don't. In the world of industrial marketing, the community of buyers is small. A charlatan is quickly identified.

PRACTICAL **IDEAS**

Focus on What Excites Your Customer: Learn how to sell new customers by listening closely to your current ones. Ask those customers most familiar with your offering what excites them the most about your product or service. Compare what *they* say with what you say in your marketing messages. Listen closely to how they explain what is important to them. The language of customers often has a level of genuineness that no brochure from the home office can ever match.

Find Your True Difference: On one sheet of paper, list the overt benefits of your new offering. Then cross out all those that can be found from another broadly available competitor's alternative. What are left are your Meaningful benefits.

Tell Your Story to the Uneducated: In industrial markets, our education can often be a barrier to our marketing communication skills. If we need a technical briefing, marketplace survey, and/or industry dictionary to understand your point of difference, then your odds of success are poor. Also, your customer's management team likely has significantly lower understanding of technical details. Define and refine your message until you can explain it clearly to someone who is not in your industry. It will then be ready for customer presentation.

Define Why Your Value Proposition Is Great: Stress what customers receive for their money. Make sure that customers fully understand the depth and breadth of your quality. In today's competitive marketplace, costs are rarely random. If your offering costs more than others, there is often a real reason. Higher absolute cost can be due to the use of better-quality ingredients, a higher commitment to customer service, or a greater research and development investment for creating more effective product or service designs.

{ 12 }
SCIENTIFIC
ADVICE

BY REVERSING YOUR BENEFIT AND PROMISING PREVENTION OF A LOSS, YOU CAN OFTEN REALIZE DRAMATIC GAINS

Most marketing managers subscribe to the power of positive thinking. However, research finds that often "avoiding a negative" can be more motivating than the promise of something positive. Politicians are experts at this tactic. They usually focus their advertising more on "preventing the negatives associated with their opponent" than on their personal virtues.

A broad collection of academic studies supports the power of "prevention of a loss" as a strategy.

Prevention of a loss as the motivation force even applies to business managers themselves. An academic study found that when it came to making the decision to invest in new Internet technologies, managers were more motivated by the fear of obsolescence than by the opportunity for enhancement.

In another example, a study was conducted with college-age women who were encouraged to follow the American Cancer Society's recommendations for breast self-exams.

Those who were presented with the positive message received the following kind of message: *By doing breast self-exam now, you can learn what your normal, healthy breasts feel like so that you will be better prepared to notice any small, abnormal changes that might occur as you get older.*

Those who were presented with the loss-prevention message received the following kind of message: *By not doing breast self-exam now, you will not learn what your normal, healthy breasts feel like and you will be ill-prepared to notice any small, abnormal changes that might occur as you get older.*

The research found that those who read the loss-prevention message had significantly higher attitudes and intentions toward doing breast self-exams. And a four-month follow-up study found they were also significantly more likely to actually perform breast self-exams.

When you overtly discuss how your offering reduces the chance of loss, you amplify the customer's focus and attention on your Meaningful difference.

PRACTICAL IDEAS

Define Your Benefit as Preventing a Loss: Define what you offer first as a positive benefit to your customers. Then define your offer as a means of preventing a loss of freedom, money, health, or whatever your primary marketing dimension is.

Once you've defined your benefit as both a positive and as a method for preventing a loss, test both methods in market research, in voice mails you leave for potential customers, or as part of your next direct-mail campaign. Quantify the difference and act accordingly.

Quantify the Long-Term Costs of Inaction: Document the cost to a customer of not using your product or service. Quantify the tangible loss they will suffer if they continue using your competitor's offering instead of yours. Dimensionalize the long-term impact by multiplying the effect over many usage experiences and/or years.

Articulate Fears and Doubts: Identify the "soft cost" losses that customers will experience if they don't purchase your offering. Articulate the lack of peace of mind, the uncertainty, and the lack of confidence that can develop as a result of poorer quality and poorer performance.

Put a Face on the Loss: Make the loss that a customer could experience as real as possible by telling the personal story of one or more customers who have suffered it. The more you can help customers see, feel, and relate to someone who has suffered the loss, the more motivating the preventive power of your offering will be.

{ 13 }
SCIENTIFIC
ADVICE

BEING HONEST ABOUT YOUR WEAKNESSES
WILL OFTEN GAIN MORE CUSTOMER SUPPORT

When you are honest about a weakness, you increase your credibility. **When you admit that "No, we don't," you actually increase customers' desire to purchase from you.**

Customers understand that everyone, every product and every service, offers strengths and weaknesses. They realize that the creation of a great skill in one area results in trade-offs in others.

A research study was conducted on five products' ads that claimed either excellence in five different product dimensions or superiority in three areas and lack of superiority in two. The advertisements that disclaimed superiority for two dimensions were found to be significantly more persuasive than those that claimed perfection.

Another study found that trust was the primary driver of increased persuasion when features were disclaimed. A set of consumers was shown advertisements for two products containing either claims of excellence in all areas, or claims of excellence in most areas and statements that the competition was superior in two areas. Research found that the advertisements that disclaimed performance in two areas were perceived by potential customers to be significantly more truthful.

Customers have become numb to marketing that promises miracle cures. When you're forthright about not being the ideal provider for a certain product or service, you increase your credibility for the next buying cycle when customers might truly need something for which you can supply a Meaningful difference.

When you honestly articulate your weakness, you are in effect helping customers' decision processes. You help relieve them of needing to discover your flaw—which past experience tells them is present in all brands.

PRACTICAL **IDEAS**

Be Open about Your Weakness: Research has found that customers actually trust more when you honestly and openly state what you're not the best at. Think about your offering. What are your strengths and weaknesses? When you add them together, do you still win? If your combination of traits is superior, why not make the differences open and easy for customers to see for themselves?

Pursue a Philosophy of Underpromising: Develop a reputation for delivering more than you promised with regards to delivery timing, customer-service response time, quality, etc. Get known as a sales or marketing person who exceeds expectations as opposed to one who regularly exaggerates.

Make Sales Contingent on Your Evaluation: When there is even the smallest doubt in your mind about the appropriateness of a certain product or service for your customer, say so. Offer to make the sale contingent on your personally checking to make sure that your product works right and/or that the customer is happy with the purchase.

Tell Your Offering's History of Success and Failure: With experience you will learn the strengths and weaknesses of your product or service. Without telling competitive secrets, relate your experience with when your offering has been most effective and least effective. The mere fact that you admit to less than spectacular results in any situation or condition at all will dramatically increase customers' trust.

{ 14 }
SCIENTIFIC
ADVICE

IF YOU CUT IRRELEVANT WORDS FROM YOUR MARKETING MESSAGE, YOU'LL MAKE IT AS MUCH AS 40 PERCENT MORE PERSUASIVE

Ernest Hemingway said, "**The most essential gift for a good writer is a built-in, shockproof shit detector. This is the writer's radar and all great writers have had it.**" The same is true for marketing messages.

When customers are making a purchase decision, they are motivated by a desire to learn what makes you great. They are also motivated by a desire to not make a mistake—to prevent a loss.

When your marketing message has IRRELEVANT JUNK (B.S., Marketing Hype, Smoke and Mirrors) it's harder for customers to discern what the true message is. Research indicates that when irrelevant information is added to communications, customer interest declines.

Marketing information can be directly related to the task. For example, in looking for a fast computer, a customer could evaluate the speed of the computer's processor and the amount of RAM (random-access memory), features that can improve speed.

Marketing information can also be irrelevant to the task. In the fast-computer example, irrelevant information could include "as seen in a recent movie," "as advertised on television," or "made in the U.S.A." Each of these detracts from the main message of speed you want to communicate.

Ten separate experiments have shown that when irrelevant information was stripped away to leave a highly relevant marketing message, customer interest increased significantly. As an example, in one study, purchase interest in the target concept increased some 40 percent (from 38 percent to 53 percent purchase intent).

Irrelevant information reduces customers' beliefs in the ability of your product or services to deliver on the promised benefit. It causes confusion and distraction, reducing focus and faith in your true Meaningful difference.

PRACTICAL **IDEAS**

Follow the Advice of Stephen King: Best-selling novelist Stephen King recommends that second drafts of manuscripts should be 10 percent shorter than the first. You can do the same with your marketing. Cut the least relevant 10 percent of the ideas from your marketing message.

Even more powerfully, put aside your marketing materials and with a fresh computer screen rewrite them in a natural voice. When we talk to customers, we tend to naturally synthesize our message so as not to bore our customers and to get to the point more quickly.

Eliminate Advertising Gimmicks and Smoke and Mirrors: Focus your advertising message on providing relevant yet unexpected news about your brand. Mindless humor, video gimmicks, outrageous shock, and esoteric philosophy is for Hollywood movies, not capitalist advertising.

Great advertising is easy. It starts with a simple Meaningful benefit difference that resolves a real customer problem or enables a genuine customer desire. Ultimately, it provides real reason to believe that the promise truly will be delivered.

Ignore Options: Many products and services come in a multitude of customized options. Rarely are these options a reason for purchase. The core brand offering is usually the real driver of persuasion. Options of form or format are simply executional details. Eliminate discussion of them to simplify your message. Focus your marketing communications on the one thing that you do really great.

{ 15 }
SCIENTIFIC
ADVICE

WHEN YOU TALK DATA INSTEAD OF SHOWING DATA, YOU DOUBLE YOUR PERSUASIVE ABILITY

Just as it takes a customer effort to translate your features into benefits, it also takes effort to turn your chart of data into benefits that motivate them.

Plus, frankly, most adults are scared of data. Numbers, charts, and statistics cause them great mental pain. When you talk findings instead of displaying raw data, you dramatically increase your persuasiveness. Researchers showed 250 consumers various forms of nutritional information on two food products. One test cell used a chart of hard data on the percentage of the recommended daily allowance of various nutrients the food had. The other test cell was given the same information but in simple storytelling language.

The results indicated that the storytelling approach was more than twice as effective as the numerical chart in communicating the food was more nutritious (37 percent versus 18 percent). It also prompted nearly three times more customers to say they intended to purchase (16.8 percent versus 5.8 percent). Lastly, the storytelling format also generated significantly more accurate recall of the information presented.

When you tell your story with simple words, you make it easier for customers to understand and comprehend your Meaningful difference. Telling customers you have 40 percent of the recommended daily allowance of protein requires customer processing for relevance. Alternatively, a description of excellent protein content relative to the competition provides an actionable frame of reference.

Opportunities exist for combining the two techniques. By explaining that your product offers nearly twice as much as the competition does of the body-building protein your child needs, you have translated the hard data into a Meaningful benefit difference.

PRACTICAL **IDEAS**

Transform Data Charts into Words: Translate data charts into simple words. Explain your core benefit to customers using simple language. Record yourself talking through the data chart as part of a presentation to identify the best words. The words you use could well be what you need to make the point. If you must provide a chart, place your verbal description below the chart itself to add clarity to your message.

Transform Technology into Words: We appreciate the fact that your technological wonder is considerable. However, you will increase your odds of success if you can tell it in a simple story. Translate your "techno-speak" into a simple explanation, using analogies where necessary. The benefit to you is customers who understand and better recall your Meaningful difference.

Be a Storyteller: Turn your marketing message into storytelling. Tell the story of what led you to develop your offering as it is. Create drama through the tension of the challenge; that is, the problem you addressed and the discovery of your solution. Ron Popeil, founder of Ronco and inventor of the infomercial, required that every product he offered SOLVE A PROBLEM. Problems also motivate Richard Branson, founder of The Virgin Group. He said, "I don't go into ventures to make a fortune. I do it because I'm not satisfied with the way others are doing business."

Synthesize to Simplify: Today's customer has no shortage of data, information, and knowledge. The challenge is to discern the Meaningful versus the meaningless information. Seek ways to condense masses of information into simple analogies.

{ 16 }
SCIENTIFIC
ADVICE

IF YOU THINK SMART, YOU CAN LEVERAGE CUSTOMER STEREOTYPES OF YOUR CATEGORY TO YOUR ADVANTAGE IN YOUR COMMUNICATIONS

Consumers have preexisting stereotypes about their ability to understand and comprehend various categories of new products and services. You can leverage this stereotyped thinking to your advantage.

When a category is perceived to be complex and hard to understand, customers give up before they even begin considering new information. It's not that they don't want or need advanced technology; it's just that they feel incapable of accessing it.

Alternatively, **when customers feel that they understand a category of products or services, they are more likely to believe they have the capability of understanding Meaningful differences.** This empowers their ability to become more consciously involved in the decision process.

A study was conducted among 140 adults who were shown alternatives for low-complexity products (refrigerators and washing machines) and high-complexity products (personal computers and digital cameras).

When novel benefits and features were added to the low-complexity products, they caused a statistically significant *increase* in customer appeal.

When novel benefits and features were added to the high-complexity products, they caused a significant *decline* in appeal.

The implications are that when you have a low-complexity product or service, you should celebrate your uniqueness and wow customers. When you have a high-complexity product or service, don't avoid celebrating your advantages, but be conscious of how you teach customers your wow!

PRACTICAL IDEAS

With High-Tech Help, Customers Believe They Can: When your offering is in an advanced technology category, be sympathetic to customers' lack of technological self-esteem. A friendly, educational approach to your marketing will win you their understanding and trust. Avoid the fancy jargon and instead use simple analogies to shine a spotlight on your Meaningful difference. Tell customers that your new artificial intelligence system is like having a 24/7 expert assistant. Use photos and illustrations to show differences so that customers can see it as they read it.

Proclaim How Your Technology Simplifies Everything: Make ease of understanding and operation an overt and Meaningful benefit. Design into your offering ease of operation. Quantify how much easier it is to use your offering. A research study found that when customers were told that a new technology was automatic versus manually operated, they were significantly more interested. This finding reinforces the earlier truth that reported on the importance of reducing customer stresses.

Be Daring in Old and Stable Categories: When your category is old, be bold and brash about your technological innovation. Customers fully understand what your core product is about; now push the news. Don't allow yourself to be held back by naysayers who don't believe that change is possible; old categories can and must reinvent themselves.

Focus on Advanced Customers in Tech Categories: When your category is technologically complex and your improvement or product is complex, target initial marketing efforts on leading-edge customers. Customers with advanced understanding and technical experience will most appreciate and applaud your technological advancements.

{ 17 }
SCIENTIFIC
ADVICE

IF YOU THINK SMART, YOU CAN LEVERAGE THE CUSTOMER TENSION OF DESIRING BOTH NEWS AND LACK OF CONFUSION

Success comes to marketers who communicate BREAKTHROUGH NEWS! However, with breakthroughs comes change. And change causes CHAOS and CONFUSION.

Smart marketing is about finding ways to maximize NEWS while minimizing confusion.

The dual nature of these forces was found in a research study explaining customers' recall of a sales and marketing presentation's details. The two most important dimensions, each with equal and significant correlations, were news and lack of confusion.

There is little doubt of the value of news. The greater the new information that is presented, the more likely customers are to meaningfully remember your offering's genuine value.

Equally, the more confusing your message, and thus the more mental effort it takes customers to comprehend and follow your description, the less likely they are to take the time to process it.

Clearly, there is an inherent tension between uniqueness and confusion. The more dimensions of news—uniqueness of product, uniqueness of packaging, uniqueness of performance attributes— the greater the probability of confusion from customers.

In today's high-tech world, this is even more challenging. Few customers really understand or wish to learn how the automatic pilot in an airplane works or the physics behind how our car achieves better road handling.

However, at the same time, if they can't understand it, they are left with a lack of trust and acceptance of what is promised.

Our challenge is to provide a relevant yet simple story of what's in it for the customer and how it works, yet maintain an unexpected dimension that supplies uniqueness.

PRACTICAL **IDEAS**

Use Analogies: When your technology is genuinely complex, find ways to use analogies to help the uneducated understand your approach. Step back from your product or service and draw examples from other industries, Mother Nature, or other simple comparisons to make the complex appear to be simple.

Go over the Edges: To describe the complex in a simple way, force yourself to put in writing what your product is and does. Having completed this, rewrite it twice, each time forcing yourself to use fresh language and to avoid repetition. Do this once a day for five days. At the end of the fifth writing, give a friend five versions to review and edit into one concise and high-impact message.

Shorten the Benefit Feedback Loop: Find ways to accelerate the realization of your Meaningful benefit. Shorten the amount of time it takes to install and understand your offering before a significant portion of your benefit, if not all of it, is realized by the customer.

Describe the Magic Moment: Focus your marketing on the magic moment that defines your benefit. If you're selling tutoring to help with college entrance exams, talk about the pride a parent felt when a previous client successfully graduated from college. If you're selling a goof-proof cooking system, leverage the excitement the customer will feel as they bring the food to the table. If you're selling insurance, articulate the peace of mind customers would experience were the unthinkable to happen. By powerfully articulating the magic moment of benefit you offer, the customer will find it easier to accept complexity in delivery.

{ 18 }
SCIENTIFIC
ADVICE

YOU WILL KICK UP YOUR CREDIBILITY BY BEING RELENTLESS WITH RELEVANCE

Customers are intelligent. When you get their attention, they evaluate the relevance of your messages more than you may think. And when what you say doesn't make sense, they are significantly less likely to make a purchase.

A study was conducted on the importance of relevant expertise. A print ad of a new sports energy bar was designed that featured a photo of a man described as either a former U.S. Olympic track and field athlete or as a leading Broadway actor who has starred in two movies.

Consumers were significantly more likely to indicate they would purchase the new sports energy bar when an athlete was used versus an actor.

It just makes sense. An athlete has relevant expertise for a sports bar. An actor is irrelevant noise.

So too, when you offer a GUARANTEE with conditions, exceptions, and other fine print, you reduce the relevance of the guarantee. A series of five experiments was conducted to determine the relative impact of various factors on a customer's perception of financial risk with certain warranty options.

The research found that a no-excuses, top-quality warranty significantly reduced a customer's perception of financial risk. Alternatively, a moderate warranty had the same effect as a poor warranty or no warranty at all. Limited warranties, warranties requiring the customer to pay a portion, or even having the warranty come from a leading company with a long-established reputation did nothing to assuage a customer's financial fears.

Customers have become highly educated in their understanding of marketing tricks. They know the difference between RELEVANT Credibility and marketing smoke and mirrors being used to trick them into making a purchase.

PRACTICAL IDEAS

Testimonial Relevance: Use testimonials that speak directly to your Meaningful benefit and that are by an independent or expert authority who is credible. The point of drama in the testimonial should link directly to your Meaningful Marketing message. For example, an award-winning chef can speak to the ability of your wine to enhance the taste of food. A production supervisor can speak to the improvement in production efficiency he's noticed from your industrial lubricant.

Demonstration Relevance: Use demonstrations that speak to the moment of drama inherent in your Meaningful Marketing message. Even exaggerated demonstrations can be effective if they speak to the challenge. For example, when a floor cleaner cleans Grand Central Station in New York City, it gives you confidence that it can really clean stubborn dirt in your kitchen.

Stand Behind Your Offering: Take a personal stand for integrity and honesty. Be overt in all sales and marketing claims. Check that your statements are honest both literally and in what perceptions they evoke. Go beyond legal definitions of truth to the standard of "beyond a reasonable doubt" as we've outlined in the opening of this book. By taking a stand that transcends your competitors, you build your trust account with customers.

Guarantee Your Offering: Boldly guarantee that you will deliver what you promise. Guarantee your product or service without any fine print. If you have concerns about offering such a guarantee, then you have bigger problems to address than sales and marketing.

Respect Your Customers' Intelligence: Today's customers understand the games marketers play when it comes to product and service claims. They understand when you are hyping, tricking, and misrepresenting your claims. Rework your advertising and sales presentations to be "literally" credible, even to yourself.

{ 19 }
SCIENTIFIC
ADVICE

SOME QUICK THOUGHT STARTERS TO HELP YOU CREATE NEW MARKETING MESSAGES:

A. Leverage COMPARISONS When You Are Offering a DRAMATIC Difference.

Research shows that when you have a new offering that is OBVIOUSLY UNIQUE versus your current offering or your competition's offering, OVERT COMPARISION increases purchase interest and the number of POSITIVE THOUGHTS customers have about your offering. Conversely, when you are offering a difference that is EXPECTED for your category of products, the use of a comparison appears to backfire, i.e., it causes more NEGATIVE THOUGHTS.

> **Thought-starting example:**
> YOUR BRAND NAME
> The SUPERIOR Alternative to *Your* CATEGORY

Unlike with others in [THE CATEGORY], with [YOUR BRAND NAME] you will experience . . .

B. When Your Difference Is NOT SELF-EVIDENT, Provide a SIDE-BY-SIDE Overt Benefit Explanation.

Research shows that you can make comparison work even if it's not self-evident as long as you articulate the OVERT AND SPECIFIC Benefits of your new approach. A literal side-by-side chart listing the benefit advantages of your new approach can be very effective.

> **Thought-starting example:**
> YOUR BRAND NAME
> Providing more BENEFIT versus Your Competition

Competition	Your Brand Name
Feature	Your New Benefit
Feature	Your New Benefit

C. When You LACK HARD CLAIMS, Inspire Customers to Focus on the IDEAL.
Research shows that brands that lack hard claims can increase their marketing effectiveness if they challenge customers to focus on the IDEAL end state. This can be a valuable way to revitalize an established brand that customers have misperceptions about.

> **Thought-starting example:**
> What if you could . . .
> What if you could . . .

Today, your dreams can be a reality with YOUR BRAND. . . . (Then explain how.)

D. When You HAVE HARD CLAIMS, Challenge Customers to Focus on Their Responsibilities.
Research shows that when you have hard claims of superiority, you can increase your marketing effectiveness if you challenge customers to focus on their duties, responsibilities, and obligations.

> **Thought-starting example:**
> You're responsible for . . .
> It's your duty to . . .

With one phone call, you can get help with your responsibilities. YOUR BRAND is the first . . .

CHAPTER THREE

MINDLESS MARKETING

★ ★ ★

Unlike the Marketing Message chapter that focused on the MERITS of your MEANINGFUL Difference, the Mindless Marketing persuasion tools in this chapter are designed to "trick" customers into making a purchase.

I have a LOVE-HATE feeling toward this chapter. I love the HARD DATA THAT BACK UP THE ADVICE. However, I dislike encouraging marketing trickery.

I guess I'm just old-fashioned. I believe that great advertising tells the TRUTH in a persuasive and memorable manner. I believe that advertising agency McCann Erickson's corporate slogan, **"Truth Well Told"** is the definition of great marketing.

I've included a detailed listing of the most effective Mindless Marketing tricks because in the chaotic marketplace of today, it's becoming harder and harder to get customers to listen to even meaningful messages.

Like Lucille Ball in the famous "Candy Factory" episode, **buyers are often too stressed to stop, look up, and take notice of new products and services. In today's world we need a little KICK to get our messages noticed**.

While I've included these Mindless Marketing tricks for you to use, I've reserved the LAST WORD on them for myself. You'll read in Chapter 6 why for SUSTAINED SUCCESS **I believe that you should use them only. . . as a "spice" to get your Meaningful Marketing message noticed**.

Mindless Marketing should be used "in addition to" as opposed to "in place of" Meaningful Marketing. Meaningful Marketing should be the foundation of your marketing message. Mindless Marketing should be used as a promotional tool to help you gain the attention of your customers.

Meaningful Marketing + Mindless Marketing = Smart Marketing
(Foundation)   (Promotional Tricks)

When crafting ideas for new products and services it's smartest to evaluate options based on which offers the most Meaningful Marketing difference. After defining clearly what you can do for customers, then add some Mindless Marketing promotional spin to ensure that customers stop and take notice of what you have to say.

BEWARE: If your offering is not GENUINELY GREAT, then a reliance on Mindless Marketing tricks can actually backfire. A customer tricked into making a bad purchase fights back. The Internet offers a sound platform for SCREAMING LOUDLY. Some years ago the automotive magazine *Car and Driver* found that when a customer has a great experience with a new car, he or she tells eight other people. After a bad experience, however, he or she tells sixteen people.

The more Mindless Marketing tricks are used, the less effective they become. Take a magician as an example. During the first presentation of a magic trick, the audience is easily distracted through misdirection. However, few magic tricks are strong enough to survive a repeat performance. With repeat viewings, the audience is more aware and observant of truth. So it is with Mindless Marketing tricks. You may fool customers once, or maybe even twice, but rarely can Mindless Marketing overcome a sustained lack of meaningful value in your product or service offering.

Recently, Grass Roots Marketing has become the hip thing for marketers to explore. Sadly, many don't get it. Marketing gimmicks DO NOT drive Grass Roots Marketing. Rather, it's great Product Development and Customer Service that drives true Grass Roots "world of mouth."

I've inserted this chapter between MARKETING MESSAGE and SELLING as the advice and ideas presented are really the intersection of marketing and sales. They can be used in marketing messages or promotion campaigns as well as in direct-sales situations.

These Mindless Marketing persuasion methods are scientifically proven to be effective. In fact, in your own life you've probably been on the receiving end of many of them.

If you wish to learn more about Mindless Marketing persuasion, you should get the book *Influence: Science and Practice* by Robert B. Cialdini. Professor Cialdini is the world's master of persuasion magic. His research on ways to influence and persuade others is rich and broad.

{ 1 }
SCIENTIFIC
ADVICE

YOU CAN PERSUADE OTHERS BY SIMPLY GETTING THEM TO SAY YES ... YES ... YES

There is real value in the momentum of getting a customer to say yes, yes, yes. Humans have a need for personal consistency. Once they say yes to a path of action, they are much more likely to feel good about the decision and to continue to say yes to additional requests.

In the field of persuasion research, this is known as the *foot-in-the-door* or the *low-ball* technique. The strategy is simple: Get a customer to say yes to a small and harmless request, and he is much more likely to say yes to additional, larger requests.

This truth has been validated hundreds of times by academic researchers. A study found that when participants were asked to answer five research questions (small request), they were 28 percent more likely to answer a second twenty-question survey (larger request) than if they were asked to answer only the twenty-question survey.

In another study, conducted on fundraising for the American Heart Association, participants were asked to answer four questions (small favor), then asked to make a donation. Of those asked to do the favor first, 34 percent made a donation versus 19 percent of those who were asked just to donate.

Positive momentum creates positive momentum. Even seemingly harmless concessions by customers can dramatically improve your odds of sales success. Simply getting customers to make a positive statement about themselves, their work, or their life has an impact on selling. Researchers phoned consumers asking for permission to visit their house to sell cookies for charity. When directly asked if they could visit, only 10 percent of the respondents said yes. When asked how they were feeling before being asked to visit, 25 percent said yes!

PRACTICAL **IDEAS**

Use the Franklin-in-France Selling System: When Benjamin Franklin was ambassador to France, he gained influence with a key thought leader by first asking to borrow a book from his library (small request). He returned the book promptly and borrowed another. Having proven his reliability, he then initiated discussions on larger requests.

Seek an opportunity to gain knowledge and wisdom—through sharing a book, suggesting a good training program, asking customers' opinions. A customer who has shared his mind with you will be more willing to share his wallet.

Even a Penny Will Help: In the American Heart Association survey detailed earlier, the simple phrase "even a penny will help" was added to the small-request then big-request test sequence. The result was a 50 percent donation rate versus 19 percent for the donation-only request. Think about your business. What is the smallest, tiniest thing a customer can do—"just take a test drive," "just taste our new beer," "just answer a few questions," "just put down a $5 deposit." The smallest commitment will generate the largest persuasion impacts.

Get It in Writing—Any Writing: When students filled out a form after volunteering to help a charity, they were three times more likely to actually show up than those who simply gave a verbal commitment. Seek ways to get your customers to send you e-mail or letters, fill out questionnaires—anything. The simple act of putting words to paper can be the start of a continuing relationship.

{ 2 }
SCIENTIFIC
ADVICE

WHEN YOU GET CUSTOMERS INVOLVED, THEY ARE MORE LIKELY TO STAY INVOLVED AND MAKE A PURCHASE

The most powerful application of the foot-in-the-door customer concession trick is when customers become physically and mentally involved with your offering.

For example, when customers go through a great deal of trouble to find or buy something, they develop an enhanced sense of its value. The greater the intensity of stress and effort required to acquire something, the more positive the attitudes toward the end result. Marine boot camp and college fraternities both leverage this fundamental human dynamic. **The more a person "owns the effort," the greater the commitment that will develop.**

In a similar manner, after we have spent a lot of time learning how to operate high-technology hardware or software, we are reluctant to throw away that investment. Or after we've spent significant time learning a trade, a craft, a hobby, or a system of any kind, we are reluctant to leave it.

Research studies have shown the impact of varying intensities of initiation rites on commitment to a group. College students were put through varying levels of personal embarrassment to become part of a group. The research found that those who endured the greatest initiation stress had the most favorable attitudes toward the eventual group and group members.

The key to leveraging the power of initiation is that there must be a Meaningful payoff from the pain. The end result—be it a product, a service, or a new vendor—must offer something that is Meaningful to the participant. If the end result offers nothing special, then it is unlikely that many will endure the initiation stress.

Initiation doesn't have to always be a singular pain. A series of small, incremental initiations can get customers to mindlessly commit their time and energy so that they are less likely to walk away from their "investment."

PRACTICAL **IDEAS**

Tour and Educate: Get your customers involved in learning and studying about your product. Engage them in the process of understanding deeply what makes you uniquely valuable. Do whatever it takes to get them to tour your production facility. Ideally, get them to visit in person. If you get them to physically visit your factory for a day, they will be mentally with you forever.

Purposely Leave Information out of Materials: When you have a Meaningful difference, make it overtly clear. But avoid the temptation to detail all information—terms, pricing, etc. Rather, require customers to call you for details. The simple act of making a phone call to you to gain additional information tilts your odds of sales success significantly.

Aggressively Pursue Customer Inquiries: Customers who make even a small investment of their time on your business have dramatically greater chances of becoming a customer than those who you cold call on. This is why it's important to promptly follow up on every customer inquiry.

Leverage Longtime Members: Seek out those who are long-term members of your trade association. Leverage their commitment to the industry. This can be especially helpful if what you are offering has the potential to improve, enhance, or grow the industry.

Seek Those with the Biggest Problems: Those customers who have the greatest problems offer a special opportunity for you to create a Meaningful connection. The greater the pain they feel, the greater the bond they'll have when they realize relief with your solution.

{ 3 }
SCIENTIFIC
ADVICE

WHEN YOU SET A SPECIFIC DEADLINE, YOU MORE THAN DOUBLE YOUR ABILITY TO "CLOSE THE SALE"

We've all experienced the anxiety of a deadline: "This sale ends tonight." "This is a limited-time offer." "If you don't act now, I can't guarantee the price or availability."

Anytime we give a deadline or restriction, we speed action. A study was conducted where students were paid a few dollars to complete a questionnaire with varying requests of completion time. When they were given no deadline, 25 percent completed the questionnaire; with a three-week deadline 42 percent completed it; and with a five-day deadline some 60 percent completed the questionnaire. Net: The more flexibility in timing, the less likely customers are to take action.

From a personal perspective, it's the "prevention of a loss" that drives customers to take action. In order to avoid the regret of not having made a decision customers will often make a quick decision.

Often the reason why customers are not making a decision is because they are confused. This is the case when we're not focused and when more than one option is available and each offers a distinct set of Meaningful benefits. For example, technology Product A might be ultra-easy to operate, while Product B is more complicated but with higher performance characteristics. When we have a clear vision of our needs, the energy to resolve the conflict is minimal and we simply decide.

However, in many cases the "right answer" is not self-evident. In these cases Option C, to delay the decision and seek more information, becomes the preferred choice. A test of 121 college students found that 46 percent chose to wait until they learned more about the various models when presented with a conflicting choice. To avoid getting into a perpetual cycle of delay, FOCUS on articulating the MEANINGFUL virtues of your offering.

PRACTICAL IDEAS

Be Specific in Your Requests: When seeking to persuade, use a deadline in decision making to influence the customer's direction. Be direct and specific about your request. And define clearly the costs of delaying a decision.

The Power of Silence: Silence in a meeting is a form of deadline. When you don't speak, you create a need for customers to talk. One of the most common mistakes that salespeople make is to talk too much. When you stop speaking, you put pressure on the customer to make a decision or to share information with you that could be of help.

Deadline Reinforcement and Reminders: Deadlines can easily be forgotten. When you take a stance on a deadline, make it clear. Then hold to the deadline. Reinforce and warn of consequences. And when the time's up, it's up. Be firm in following through on your deadlines or you lose all future credibility.

Crossing the Cost Threshold: Use deadlines to quantify the cost/value relationship in a transaction. Illustrate how a missed deadline affects the bottom line, and you have a clear leverage tool when dealing with a rational, focused customer. Use the sense of emotional loss or fear with a customer with a more emotional personality.

When Customers Are Confused, Give Them Information and a Deadline: When customers are simply overwhelmed at the choices before them, it can sometimes be effective to provide "new data" in the form of a summary of the virtues of each option, thus showing them how your offering fits their needs best. A little "kicker" of a deadline for a special bonus offer can also help break the stalemate and get a decision.

{ 4 }
SCIENTIFIC
ADVICE

WHEN YOU GET CUSTOMERS TO PERCEIVE YOUR OFFERING AS SCARCE, YOU INCREASE THEIR PERCEPTION OF ITS VALUE

The scarcer an item, the more valuable it feels. Marketers of collectibles from baseball cards to coins to antiques understand the profit potential in marketing items that are rare.

Numerous studies have found that just as deadlines create purchasing motivation, scarcity creates a greater perception of value. One study found that ratings of a college cafeteria's food quality increased significantly when students were told that a fire had occurred in the kitchen, causing the cafeteria to be closed for several weeks. Another study found that when students were given a jar containing just two cookies instead of ten, they rated the quality and value of the cookies significantly higher.

Scarcity is yet another component that customers use to simplify their decision making. When something is sold out, they make the simplistic assumption that it is because other customers have found it to be of high quality.

In addition, when we lose access to something, we perceive the loss as a loss of freedom. This causes a passion for restoring our freedom by purchasing or acquiring the restricted item.

Basic economics tells us that when demand exceeds supply for goods or services, the result is upward pressure on pricing. When more people are interested in purchasing than there is availability, the net impact is an increased sense of worth.

In effect, the marketplace is one giant auction. **When supply exceeds demand, buyers retain control over pricing. When demand exceeds supply, sellers have control over pricing.**

PRACTICAL **IDEAS**

Expand Demand Beyond Supply: If your offering provides a Meaningful difference, you have a simple means for increasing profitability—overmarket. Marketing more than you can supply. Ideally, aim for 20 percent more demand than you can supply to maintain or increase pricing.

The challenge with increasing demand is greed. Manufacturers feel that the loss of even one sale because of a lack of availability is a loss of revenue. Stop and reassess the reality of the situation. If you dramatically increase your supply, you will end up losing profit margin.

Be *Genuine* with Scarcity: In today's world of instant communication, customers are far more savvy at discovering false claims of scarcity. The Internet makes it easier for them to discover when you're lying. Make sure your claims of scarcity are true. Otherwise, you will be labeled a cheat.

Create a Buzz about Demand: Don't let product-supply issues stop the momentum caused by the very consumer demand that sparked the scarcity to begin with. Fuel the buzz by "apologizing" publicly for the lack of supply. Long after supply catches up with your demand, you will have set in customers' minds the clear understanding that your company creates "wow" demand. This can be of great help the next time you introduce something new.

Remember Supply vs. Demand Determines Profitability: An aggressive marketing campaign can be a profitable way to increase demand and thus your ability to raise your price—or at least reduce your price discounting. In this case, marketing serves two purposes: It generates sales and provides protection against discounting through increased customer demand.

{ 5 }
SCIENTIFIC
ADVICE

WHEN YOU MAKE A MEANINGFUL CONCESSION TO A CUSTOMER, HE OR SHE WILL OFTEN RETURN THE FAVOR AND MAKE A PURCHASE

Giving something to get something in return is one of the oldest and most reliable of persuasion tactics. Giving something to get something can be seen in client dinners at gourmet restaurants, donations to political campaigns, and even aid to the leaders of foreign countries.

The success of this tactic has been quantified in dozens of academic studies. The most classic form of the concession tactic is called the *door-in-the-face* persuasion tactic. The salesperson makes an extreme demand and upon receiving a negative response, gives up on the extreme request and makes a smaller demand. The smaller demand is seen as a concession to the customer. The customer then feels obligated to reciprocate by saying yes.

A study of the effectiveness of fund-raising tactics confirmed the power of making a concession. When potential donors who had said no to the extreme request of becoming part of a long-term monthly donor program were then asked to simply make one donation, some 34 percent said yes compared to 19 percent of those who were asked only to make one donation.

In another study, college students were first asked an extreme request—to donate their time, two hours a day per week for two years, helping younger children. When they said no, they were then asked the smaller request, to help chaperone one two-hour trip to the zoo. Of those asked the extreme request followed by the small request, 50 percent agreed to chaperone versus only 17 percent when asked only the small request.

When you make a Meaningful concession, it can cause a potential buyer to feel a responsibility to give something back to you by responding positively.

PRACTICAL IDEAS

Move from Pushing for the Sale to Gaining Leads: When a customer can't buy or won't buy, fall back and ask for names of those who might have an interest. By releasing sales pressure, you can create an environment where the potential customer voluntarily gives you names and phone numbers of quality leads. Then you can approach the sales leads with a personal recommendation: "Bill suggested that I call."

Give Something Away: A mail-order catalog company mailed its customers overstock items that they would normally sell at warehouse sales. The free gifts had an average value of fifteen dollars. Response rates from those receiving the free gift rose from 5 percent to 25 percent and their average purchase from $100 to $300. Think about your business. What can you give away to hook customers?

Sell from High to Low: Present your most expensive option first, then move to lower-cost options. A study by a manufacturer of expensive billiards tables found that when customers were first shown low-cost then higher-cost tables, the average sale was for $550. When they were shown the $3,000 tables before lower-cost options, the average price of the billiards table purchased was more than $1,000!

Give Price Discounts or Free Bonuses to Close Sales: Persuade uncertain customers through introduction of special offers or free bonuses if they make an immediate decision. The momentum of your concession can tip customers toward making a commitment.

Make a Concession to Get Customers to Trade Up: After a customer has made a purchase decision, offer a special deal on the higher-grade model or service option.

{ 6 }
SCIENTIFIC
ADVICE

WHEN YOU GET CUSTOMERS TO PERCEIVE YOU AS AN EXPERT OR AUTHORITY, THEY ARE MUCH MORE LIKELY TO PURCHASE

Customers are inclined to follow the directions and advice of authorities. An authority can be a specific person or the perception of a company's or brand's expertise. Authority can come from perception of power or prestige.

In one classic study a man walked on the "wait" light at a city intersection. More than 3.5 times more people went with him—against the instructions of the light—when he wore a high-status suit and tie than when he was dressed in lower-class clothing. Other studies have found overt stereotypical responses to those dressed as doctors, ministers, and members of the military.

Similar behavioral changes have been seen in reaction to automobiles. In one study, a high-priced black sedan or a beat-up station wagon drove up and stopped at a red light. When the light turned green, they waited at least fifteen seconds before moving. With the low-status car, 84 percent of the time the car behind it honked to get the driver's attention. The high-status car was honked at only 50 percent of the time.

Authority can be as simple as a type of dress, type of car, or a person's job title. It can also come from a person's knowledge or experience in the area of exploration.

As with many other Mindless Marketing persuasion tricks, the key dimension is that customers are influenced by authority when they assume that they don't know or are unable to make a decision by themselves. **When customers are confused or uncertain, they are most likely to follow the opinions and actions of those they perceive know more.**

PRACTICAL **IDEAS**

Gain Authority by Knowing More: When you know more, you have genuine authority. Collect data and opinions of people that matter to the lives of your target consumer. Be the go-to person when others are looking for direction.

The shady side of knowing more is using gossip and secrets as your knowledge currency. I don't doubt its potential as a tool for making connections with customers; however, I do have concerns about potential ethical conflicts.

Use Closed-Ended Questions: Consciously listening is critical in the early stages of selling. However, at the midpoint of the sales process, closed-ended questions can be more effective. Analysis of recordings of phone sales calls found that when the seller asked closed-ended questions—"Would you like option A or B?" "Is option C or D more important to you?"—they were significantly more likely to close a sale. When you present fixed options, you provide a voice of authority as you have distilled the key issues into a simple choice.

Publish: The power of the written word as a source of authority is immense. When your writing becomes an academic paper, trade publication article, or even a book, it takes on a new level of significance. Even in today's multimedia world, the written word is king!

Make Your Brand the Expert: Sponsor research. Fund educational programs. Make your brand the perceived expert when it comes to knowledge in your field.

{ 7 }
SCIENTIFIC
ADVICE

BE LIKABLE. WHEN CUSTOMERS LIKE YOU, THEY ARE THREE TIMES MORE LIKELY TO PURCHASE

We prefer to buy from people we like. And we really like people who are like us.

Being likable is as simple as helping customers feel happy, feel relaxed, or even just feel good about themselves.

When customers feel good, they're more likely to purchase. When students were shown commercials for nearly identical products, they were three times more likely to select the one that featured likable music.

All things being equal, we would rather do business with those we like. Unlikable people can be successful when they have a monopoly. However, when the natural cycles of the marketplace create competition, customers will buy from someone they like better.

A key element of likability is similarity. When customers view you as similar to them, they are more likely to cooperate. A study involving 450 students found average attraction to a stranger rose from 6.4 to 11.9 when they were paired with someone who had higher similarity based on personality tests.

In another study, when asked to borrow money to make a phone call, over two-thirds of the time participants said yes when the requester was dressed like them and less than half the time when he was dressed differently. Connecting with customers based on common hobbies, feelings, or attitudes is one of the oldest sales tactics on earth.

Amazingly, studies have found that even when customers know you are complimenting them on purpose or are wrong in your compliment, they still feel better about you. As Ben Franklin once said, "**A flatterer never seems absurd: The flatter'd always takes his word.**"

PRACTICAL IDEAS

Be Observant and Understanding: It's in the little details of your customer's office that connections can be made. Know the lives of your customers. The more you make a relevant yet unexpected connection with their lives, the greater your chance of gaining their interest.

Show Solidarity: Analysis of recordings of phone sales calls found that when the seller gave overt statements of solidarity—approving of a customer's choice, laughing at a customer's joke, acknowledging a customer's opinion as valid—they were significantly more likely to close a sale.

Connect Meaningfully: Speak genuinely. Discuss the weather and the state of the world or your small part in the world. Take the time to find out about your customers. Understand what brought them to your product or service. Understanding their true motivations can help you connect with them in a more personal manner.

Talk Less and Listen to Customers More: Encourage your customers to talk as much as possible. Few sounds are as appealing to adults as the sound of their own voice. Studies indicate that the average person speaks at about 150 words per minute, but the average person thinks at 600 words a minute. The more you talk, the more your customer has time to think of objections to your proposal.

Become a Master at Handwritten THANK-YOU Notes: In today's voice mail, e-mail world, the handwritten note is becoming a scarce commodity. A simple handwritten note THANKING the customer for giving you her time reinforces that you value her and increases your chances that she will value you in return.

{ 8 }
SCIENTIFIC
ADVICE

THE EASY WAY FOR YOU TO GET CUSTOMERS TO "TRADE UP" IS TO OFFER THREE OPTIONS

In today's cost-conscious world, it's common for buyers to start from the "cheapest" as they see lower price as the best value. However, often this is not the right choice for them or for you.

In the interest of focus, many companies offer only a basic and deluxe version of their product or service. Academic research indicates that to get customers to "trade up," it's smarter for a company to offer three different options.

Research was conducted among 229 participants on the selection of various brands of watches. Three watches, a Casio at $29.99, a Citizen at $44.99, and a Seiko at $59.99, were reviewed.

In one test, the watches were shown in pairs, and the participants were asked to make choices on each set and then a final selection from the three. In the other test, customers were simply shown the three options and asked to select from the three. When the watches were compared as a set of three, the percentage of customers selecting the lowest-priced watch declined 36 percent versus when they were shown pairs.

Another study on pricing context found that customers judged a new product as less expensive when it was shown after viewing a higher-priced option than they did when first seeing the lower-priced option.

Context affects customers' price perception. They judge price relative to options. When provided with a choice of two, they naturally gravitate toward the cheapest offering. **When customers are provided three choices, they become more Meaningful in their decision-making and are more likely to avoid the lowest-priced option.**

PRACTICAL IDEAS

Package and Price Your Offering Portfolio Smartly: Use a set of three options to move customers from the lowest to the middle price range. The benefit of this is that you often realize a dramatic increase in profit margin. As you think about the three price options, define them clearly.

Lowest Cost: The absolute lowest-priced model. This offering is for those who consider price by itself to be the most important issue. They are open to trading off some ease of use and other features in order to get the lowest price. The profit margins are usually lower for this option, but the volume is usually larger.

Highest Performance: The most advanced and deluxe performance model. This product is for those who require or demand the highest level of performance. The profit margins are often very high; however, the volume is often low.

Smartest Price/Value Trade-Off: This offering is in the middle of the price range. It's about maximizing what customers receive relative to the price charged. Often this option provides higher profits relative to the lower-cost option and greater volume versus the highest-performance option.

Think beyond Your Set of Options: As you price and promote your offerings, think beyond your offerings to those of the competition. If your company cannot or does not want to offer the lowest price or highest performance, but your competitors do, then use them as a point of comparison and as one of the three options. This has the advantage of helping you focus on doing one or two things great as opposed to trying to cover the entire price range.

{ 9 }
SCIENTIFIC
ADVICE

BY LEVERAGING YOUR CUSTOMERS' NATURAL RHYTHMS, YOU WILL ENHANCE THEIR ATTENTION TO YOUR MESSAGE

Customers have natural circadian rhythms. Some people are morning people. Some people are evening people.

Research indicates that when approached about making a decision during their "off time," humans are less likely to make an independent and Meaningful decision. Instead of thinking for themselves, they take the path of least resistance and decide based on preexisting stereotypes. For example, if they have a prior perception that your brand is expensive, they are more likely to assume that your new offering is expensive before even learning its cost versus benefits.

This finding is based on two studies involving a total of 248 participants. Participants were tested either early in the morning or later in the evening.

In the first study they were asked to choose which of two descriptions (one stereotypical, the other not) were most likely to be true of a person whose picture and name they were shown. When morning people were tested in the evening, 32 percent more chose the stereotypical response than those tested in the morning. When evening people were tested in the morning, some 31 percent more chose the stereotypical response than those tested in the evening.

In the second study, participants read descriptions of various defendants in criminal cases. Again, when outside of their best time, participants were more likely to judge defendants described in stereotypical ways as guilty than participants who made the same evaluations during their best time of day.

Bottom line: To make a Meaningful connection with your customers, be sensitive to their personal rhythms.

PRACTICAL **IDEAS**

Be Polite and Respectful: First and foremost, be polite and respectful of customers' time and schedules. Ask them directly about the best time to connect with them to discuss new opportunities. Be honest and upfront about how much time it will take you to review what you have to say. The more respectful you are to customers, the more respectful they will be to you in honoring commitments to meet.

Ride Ahead of the Wave: Customers have natural buying and planning cycles. Retailers make purchases in advance of the holiday season, consumers make summer-vacation plans in the spring, and industrial buyers make commitments as part of annual budget-planning processes. By planning your marketing push to begin ahead of natural purchasing times, you are able to steal a greater share of your customers' minds by influencing their thinking early.

Create Your Own Rituals and Sales Rhythms: Industrial and business-to-business salespeople seek to establish regular traditions with customers—from medical sales reps bringing doughnuts when they arrive at the doctor's clinic the first Monday of every month, to winter slide shows of last year's children's summer camp as a tool for signing up new and repeat customers. Look to your business dynamics to find ways to create unique opportunities to make Meaningful connections with customers.

Collect and Document Funky Habits: Be observant of customer rituals. Most adults are creatures of habit. By observing when they place orders and how they deal with the stress inherent in corporate cultures, you can start to identify the right times to make new pitches and close significant sales.

{ 10 }
SCIENTIFIC
ADVICE

IF YOU LEVERAGE YOUR CUSTOMERS' PAST DECISIONS, YOU CAN MOTIVATE FUTURE PURCHASES

Customers are creatures of habit. They are most likely to follow previous behaviors even when there is no demand or cause for doing so.

A study of young adults found that in the four years after they left home, more than 50 percent of their purchases of a set of eight household products (common products like pain reliever, detergent, tissue, and toothpaste) were the same as what their parents bought.

Rather than think for themselves, youths carry their parents' choices for products with them. They do so because the path of consistency requires less mental effort. This simple fact is why it is so important that you make Meaningful connections with customers early in their lives—before mindless patterns set in.

Decisions made in the past tend to become amplified in consumers' minds in the present. Racetrack bettors were asked, on a seven-point scale, what they thought their chances of winning the next race were. Before placing a bet, the average rating was 3.5. After placing their bet, their rating rose to 4.8. The simple aspect of making a firm decision, by placing a bet, had amplified their confidence.

Customers have a natural gravitational pull toward repeating past actions. The sooner you can make a Meaningful connection regarding how your offering can make a real difference in their lives, the greater your chances of creating a long-term customer. Conversely, the longer they've been committed to another brand, the greater your challenge in getting them to switch.

PRACTICAL IDEAS

Make Connections with Past Precedents: Find ways to connect what you are selling with past precedents of customers' habits. Do this no matter how dramatically different your offer. Find points of connection to existing beliefs: "If you liked shopping at X for your Y needs, then you'll love shopping at Z."

Connect to Past Habits: "You've always valued greater X. Here's an offering that takes X to a higher level."

Connect to Past Requests: "You've always asked for a way for us to X. We've listened, and here's an opportunity that directly delivers on your request."

Connect to Previous Purchasing: "You loved the original as a teenager. Here's a version for your adult needs."

Leverage Transition Points: Transition points of any kind—graduations, marriages, or new jobs—offer an opportunity to break the mindless purchasing consistency that is inherent in life.

Evoke a Memory that Connects Family and Friends: The past can be a great trigger point for retrying a product long forgotten. Connections to familiar times and faces can bring strong points of consumer attraction: the "good-old days" or "Your mom used this, the same thing that has been improved for the demands of your life."

{ 11 }
SCIENTIFIC
ADVICE

YOU WILL BUILD YOUR SALES MOMENTUM IF YOU LEVERAGE THE MOMENTUM OF MASS POPULARITY

Monkey see, monkey do. This truth is powerful and frankly a little scary. Research has confirmed that **most of us will voluntarily give up our judgment and follow the masses.**

A set of classic studies conducted in New York City showed how the size of a group had direct impact on the behavior of others. When one person stopped on the sidewalk and looked upward, 4 percent of those passing by looked up also. When five test subjects stopped and looked up at the same time, 18 percent of passersby looked up. And when a group of fifteen looked up, some 40 percent of those walking on the sidewalk looked up.

The most disturbing evidence of imitation is a series of large-scale research studies that has documented the impact of news stories on increasing suicides, murders, and even crashes of airplanes or cars. Analysis has found that the bigger the news coverage, the greater the impact on numbers of imitative incidences.

Leveraging mass acceptance as a marketing tool is especially valuable when customers are uncertain. The greater their uncertainty, the more likely they are to follow the path trodden by the masses.

In effect, customers run on autopilot, giving up Meaningful thinking and instead mindlessly following.

The social proof set can be a broad-based mass of people or a more focused set. Teenagers act different from their parents yet in near total alignment with fellow teens.

Following the crowd is a means of reducing the perception of risk. It guarantees that "you won't lose. You won't do worse than most people." Given the risk-averse nature of the masses, this approach has some definite advantages as a trial method.

PRACTICAL IDEAS

Leverage Testimonials: Leverage testimonials from satisfied customers who share similarities. Testimonials reinforce that others were willing to take risks so that your customer doesn't have to. Make it easier to accept your product by finding those testimonials from people who overcame the major hurdles your target audience most identifies with.

Build Momentum: Take advantage of momentum. Traders on Wall Street know that a fast-moving stock, whether up or down, means it's possible that someone knows something that they don't. Create your own sense of "buzz" by drawing attention to the growing popularity. Overtly declare your growth in customers. Directly draw attention to how many customers have switched to you from the competition.

Avoid Negative Opinions: Negative opinions have been found to cause customers to back off making decisions. Analysis of recordings of phone sales calls found that when sellers stated negative opinions—"I think that might be a problem and you should consider . . ."—they were significantly less likely to close a sale.

See Themselves in the Action: Emulation is a standard human trait. Endorsements by celebrities your target audience emulates can bring new consumers. We may not be able to jump as high, run as fast, or drive like our heroes, but we love to wear, eat, and do those normal things they do.

Tell a Story: Develop case studies that show the human side of your consumers' experiences with your product or service. Use these case studies of personal stories to reduce fear.

{ 12 }
SCIENTIFIC
ADVICE

THE SIMPLE WAY TO INCREASE YOUR PERSUASION POWER IS TO SERVE AND ENJOY GOOD FOOD AND DRINK

Breaking bread and sharing a meal has a significant impact on customers' attitudes. This finding reinforces the merits of expense-account meals.

Studies were conducted asking participants to rate various people or marketing slogans. In the test cases, participants rated the stimuli while having a free lunch. In the test controls, the evaluations were made while not eating. In each case, significantly more positive attitudes were recorded when participants were eating.

Sharing a meal creates a sense of community among participants. It also softens the we/they barrier that can be created in classic buyer/seller interactions. When we have a meal together, we are forced to slow down and connect to others.

The positive impact of food has elements of the famous experiments conducted by Russian psychologist Ivan Pavlov. As you know, Pavlov found that it was possible to connect the ringing of a bell to a dog's salivation response. By always connecting the bell to food, Pavlov conditioned the dog to act in a preconditioned manner.

So, too, when customers are hungry, they are more likely to digest and politely accept what you're selling when you feed them. The roots of this may well go back to our childhood. The dinner table is often the center stage for teaching children politeness and manners. This teaching carries forward to our adult lives.

Another psychological driver of positive feelings during meals is related to the need for reciprocation. When we are given food or drinks, we feel thankful and develop a feeling of "owing" the giver.

Author Note: How cheesy can you get? Buying off a customer with food! Then again, I can understand if it's a glass of the water of life (that would be **Scotch whisky**)—or some of **Prince Edward Island's famous Island Blue Mussels or Malpeque Oysters!**

PRACTICAL **IDEAS**

Dine Like Europeans: Dine, listen, talk, and connect with your customers in a more leisurely manner.

Make Dining Unexpectedly Wonderful: Look for ways to make the dining a particularly memorable experience. Dining at a restaurant where you are well known by the chef and wait staff can make a positive impression. When the chef brings special appetizers for your table alone, it makes your customers know that you consider them special.

Even more effective, you cook and serve—either at your home or simply bring home-baked muffins to your breakfast meeting. Your grandmother's blueberry muffin recipe can be a powerful sales tool.

Make the Everyday Special: We all live in a busy, time-compressed world. Taking the time to make even a casual meeting or a hurriedly scheduled meeting special doesn't have to be difficult. Simple attention to details and the little things can speak volumes for you. For example, making sure the bread is fresh, the ice cubes are not melted, and the coffee is hot and freshly brewed are small but noticeable efforts that build connections.

Show Your Human Side: Certainly, if it is an important day in the life of a customer, celebrate it. We all have times when a birthday, anniversary, or other important date lands on a business day. Everyone enjoys a certain amount of attention. Also, learning about small yet important eating habits of a customer can be just as powerful. Be aware of special needs, such as a vegetarian diet or food allergies, or even simple food no-no's, like, "No brussels sprouts, please!"

{ 13 }
SCIENTIFIC
ADVICE

WHEN YOU GET CUSTOMERS TO GIVE THEIR WORD YOU INCREASE THE ODDS OF THEM FOLLOWING THROUGH ON WHAT THEY SAID BY A FACTOR OF FOUR!

When people give you their personal commitment, they are far more likely to follow through.

A series of studies was conducted to measure the number of times bystanders took action when they observed what they perceived was a theft. In one set of experiments bystanders on a beach were asked to keep an eye on a radio and other valuables while the owner went for a swim. While the owner was away, an accomplice came by and "stole" the radio. The reaction of the bystander was then observed.

Bystanders who had made a commitment to help stopped the thief 95 percent of the time. Only 20 percent of the time did bystanders stop the thief when a prior commitment had not been made.

The inherent human desire for consistency sets up a conflict within the bystanders. When they say yes, they'll keep an eye on the radio, they create a bond. It's difficult to follow through and intervene when the theft occurs; it's even more difficult to face the owner of the radio who would return to find it missing.

A restaurant reduced its no shows for reservations from 30 percent to 10 percent by simply asking, "Will you please call if you have to change your plans?" instead of stating, "Please call if you have to change your plans."

In your sales and marketing efforts, asking for and receiving a commitment can be a powerful tool when setting up meetings or gaining customer commitment.

PRACTICAL IDEAS

Gain Approval One Small Step at a Time: Selling is a step-by-step process. At each step along the way, we move closer to a sale. Break your purchase sequence into a series of steps that are small and unthreatening. Ask customers for thirty minutes to provide a presentation of your capabilities. Follow the meeting with a request to conduct a product demonstration. Offer to do a free survey of the company's situation to quantify the benefit of using your services. Each small step moves the client closer to buying.

Nurture a Skeptical Client: When you give your word to a skeptical client who has yet to commit to you, it signals your willingness to commit to them. People instinctively know that it is human nature to rise to meet the expectations of those closest to them. Giving your word—and then keeping it—signals a change in the customer/supplier relationship that can be the difference in winning future sales.

Ask Them to Tell You about Opportunities: Directly ask your customers to tell you when there is a significant change in the company's needs. Directly ask customers to call you when an opportunity to bid on new business occurs. Ask them to send you an e-mail when they hear of anyone who needs your product or service.

Give with No Strings Attached: You cannot lead customers where they do not want to go. Reinforce your overt benefit of your product or service together with your word and make sure to reinforce that no strings are attached. This signals that you are giving a customer-focused benefit without hidden expectations in return.

{ 14 }
SCIENTIFIC
ADVICE

TAKE THE SHORT CUT TO SUCCESS—
ASK FOR THE SALE!

This may be the simplest way to increase persuasion. Simply ask for the sale! When a customer is asked to make a purchase, it sets off a chain reaction of thinking and consideration.

This finding comes from a study of 40,000 households. A portion of the panel was asked about their likelihood of purchasing an automobile or a personal computer in the next six months. Subsequently, the actual purchasing of a car or computer by those who were surveyed was compared with those who had not been surveyed. Analysis found a 37 percent increase in automobile purchasing and an 18 percent increase in computer purchasing among those who had simply been asked their likelihood of purchasing.

The affect of the question is clearly small. However, the huge size of the study makes clear the power of suggestion. The simple act of asking customers whether they would like to purchase increases their odds of doing so.

When asked to make a purchase, customers are required to think more deeply about their actual needs. It also results in a greater awareness of the meaningfulness of your offering.

When customers think more meaningfully, they become more aware of their situational needs and desires.

A related study found that merely asking consumers to consider a scenario in which they would become cable television subscribers significantly increased the rate at which they subscribed to cable TV.

When we ask customers to think about or to purchase our offering, it sets off a mental discussion that lights a spark, resulting in a significant increase in actual purchasing, even among those who are not planning to purchase.

PRACTICAL **IDEAS**

Ask Customers if They Ever Expect to Make a Purchase: Once they agree that they will be in the market sometime for your product or service, you're halfway to a sale. Once they make a commitment to buying sometime, they set off a chain reaction toward an eventual sale. The only issue remaining then is timing.

Timing can be accelerated by increasing their dissatisfaction with their current purchasing option and by increasing their perception of your value. The more they see your offering as solving a Meaningful need they have, the more they will accelerate their decision.

Use Market Research as a Sales Tool: Survey attitudes about purchase interest as part of the sales process. When customers browse, they provide live market research as they consider their choices. Motivate browsing customers to buy by simply asking them which product is the most interesting to them. Overtly getting customers to display likability will increase the probability that they will purchase.

Consumers Run in Packs: While most people say they want to stand out from the pack, the real behavior is that consumers follow a herd instinct. Another way to ask them to buy is to reinforce that others like them are buying, too. This signals to them that they are indeed looking at the right product or service.

Assume Success: Start your conversations in marketing materials and live presentations with the presumption of success. Take the perspective that the customers have already made the purchase. Discuss how happy they will be with their decision. Talk about how they will never regret their purchase. Detail how, as they get used to the benefit of what you offer, they'll find it hard to ever go back to the competition.

{ 15 }
SCIENTIFIC
ADVICE

TO WIN YOUR CUSTOMER'S LOYALTY, INVITE THEM TO BASK IN GLORY

Everyone loves to be on the side of the winner. When we are associated with the best, the brightest, the winner, it enhances our feelings of self-worth and personal pride.

When you are associated with an organization that wins, that becomes part of you and what you are. When an athlete from your hometown wins an Olympic medal, you bask in the glory. When your company wins an award, you savor the victory.

In one study the number of students wearing school logo clothing on the Monday following a weekend win or loss in football was measured. Following a win, some 43 percent more students wore school logo clothing than following a loss.

These results were further confirmed in a phone survey of students asking them the results of the weekend's football game. When describing the results, students used the term we twice as often after a win than a loss.

Spark a sense of belonging between your customers and your organization—and you will celebrate victories together.

PRACTICAL IDEAS

Build a Sense of Belonging: Create a sense of belonging among your customers by enrolling them as members of a club. Use regular newsletters, special events, imprinted sportswear, and other premiums to reinforce customers' special membership status with your company.

Celebrate Wins: Invite customers to celebrate your milestones as victories that they made possible. Celebrate "one million cars sold" or "twenty-five years of service" as a broad statement of quality and performance. Think beyond the business dynamics and celebrate your people. Celebrate the winning of trade association awards, celebrate the hiring of your hundredth Ph.D. researcher, and celebrate your appearances on national television.

Build "Winner" Momentum: The perception of success can be achieved from major victories such as discovering patented breakthroughs, achieving market share leadership, or winning an award for outstanding quality. "Winner" momentum can also be achieved through a perpetual series of announcements of minor victories that together give the perception of a product or service brand that is successful. The management of Walt Disney World in Florida leverages this concept. Every year they identify something to celebrate, from the anniversary of Mickey Mouse's debut to the anniversary of one of the company's legendary animated movies.

Celebrate the Extremes: Victories can be identified in the extremes. When a customer has an outrageous request and your company succeeds, celebrate it as a case study. Stories of customer service success in outrageously difficult, torture-test conditions can be motivating. Though customers may never face similar situations, they feel good knowing that if they did, you would be there to help them.

CHAPTER FOUR

SELLING

I think of sales and marketing as variations on the same task— the art and science of communicating to customers the GOOD NEWS about what makes our product or service so dramatically different—and better for them.

Selling is about sparking an exchange of goods or services for monetary value. It involves knocking on doors and making phone calls, pitches, and presentations.

Marketing is about mass selling. It's about providing the sales staff with ammunition that enhances their effectiveness.

At their foundation, both sales and marketing are about communication. They're about communicating the story of the great product or service that your company's research, development, and production groups have created.

Some of you may see selling differently. You may see the word "SELL" as a four-letter word. Which it is. But please don't think of it as a nasty word.

By selling, I don't mean the stereotype of the high-pressure, fast-talking salesperson. In my view, **selling is about serving others**. It's about sharing the good news about how your product or service can make a meaningful difference in customers' lives.

Research reported by Gerald Zaltman, of Harvard Business School, in his book *How Customers Think* finds that **one of the best predictors of a salesperson's success was his or her CONFIDENCE IN THE PRODUCT being sold**. Zaltman writes, "The representative's confidence conveys in subtle, nonverbal ways a sense of authenticity that adds great persuasive power. Confidence contrived does not work. The unconscious expression of belief by sales personnel is a powerful cue that customers process both consciously and unconsciously. Thus, the first 'sale' must be to the sales representative."

The key to successful selling is to have something worth selling. When you really believe in what you're offering, then the selling task is more than half done.

In today's world everyone is in sales. Salespeople sell customers. Marketing managers sell salespeople. Engineers sell marketing managers on supporting their ideas for developing new products and services.

At every company the most important members of the sales staff are the CEO and president of the company. **It's only by being the company's chief salesperson that the leaders of an organization can gain the wisdom necessary to predict the future and set the company's vision.**

By sales, I mean real selling, not simply processing orders. Many confuse the task of responding to customer requests as selling. It's not. Selling is about helping connect customer needs with the appropriate company offering.

In a simple sense, selling is about making connections. Connections between customer needs and company benefits. Connections between customer aspirations and company offerings. Selling is about more than simply solving customer problems. **Selling is about helping customers see the future.** It's about showing them how through your offering can make their life better.

This chapter provides a broad portfolio of Scientific Advice and Practical Ideas to improve your sales results.

{ 1 }
SCIENTIFIC
ADVICE

YOUR SINGLE MOST IMPORTANT SALES MISSION IS TO GET CUSTOMERS TO EXPERIENCE A DEMO!

If we can assume that you have a GREAT offering, then your singular mission should be to DEMO. **Nothing is more persuasive than having customers gain first-person experience with your meaningful difference.**

In fact, research finds that marketing presentations that offer a first-person demonstration as proof of effectiveness are nearly 50 percent more effective than simply relying on your reputation. This comes from research of original marketing messages for nine hundred products. They were divided into four sets based on the type of credibility strategy used.

The baseline, or lowest, success credibility tactic was using the established brand's or parent company's *name and reputation*. The next best strategy was the new product's *development pedigree* (21 percent more effective). The next best strategy was the use of testimonials (29 percent more effective than the baseline).

The best strategy was the demonstration of the product or service itself (47 percent more effective) or a sensory cue (sight, sound, taste, touch) that provides first-person credibility of delivery of the benefit.

Today's mega-brands, from Black & Decker tools to Kellogg's cereal, were originally built through intensive investment in sampling. When beauty products entrepreneur Estée Lauder was turned down by advertising agencies because her budget was too small, she invested all $50,000 in samples. The quality of her products then set off a chain reaction of growth.

No amount of words comes close to the impact of firsthand experience with a Meaningful new product or service benefit. Don't blame your customer for not believing what you say. Prove it. Imagine Thomas Edison or the Wright brothers trying to "sell" a movie camera or airplane without a demo—impossible.

PRACTICAL **IDEAS**

Get the Customer to Test-Drive: Go to whatever length necessary to help your customers test-drive your product or service. Have them get inside and truly feel, experience, and enjoy the wonder of what you offer. If you want even more motivation to give your customers a GREAT EXPERIENCE, researchers from the University of Colorado and Cornell University found that among adults, experiences—unlike possessions—get better with time.

One of the country's most successful car dealers told me that it has a weekend test-drive program that provides qualified customers with a car for the weekend. Once a customer has test-driven a car for a weekend, the dealer has a 90 percent close rate. The use of an extended demo to create change fits with theories of what drives cultural Revolutions. Revolutions rarely happen when people are under oppression as they're so focused on surviving that they don't have the energy to revolt. Rather, Revolutions occur after a loosening of the oppression. When people have experienced something better—even for a short time—and are then faced with the prospect of GIVING UP WHAT FEELS GOOD, they are most likely to revolt. So, too, after customers have had an extended experience with your offering, they are most likely to revolt—from their old ways of doing things and move to your offering.

Show and Tell Your Demo: If you can't get customers to take a test-drive, then bring your point of difference alive through show-and-tell demos. Let them see, feel, and/or touch the point of difference to make it come to life in their minds. If your product has more of a special ingredient, bring samples of both your product and your competitor's. If your service time is faster, have the customer call your customer-service line and a competitor's. Clock response times on a stopwatch.

Use Technology to Bring the Demo to Life: If you can't bring the *real thing* to life as a demo, then bring photos and video that *show* the points of difference. Let customer see for themselves how the Meaningful difference fits into their lives.

{ 2 }
SCIENTIFIC
ADVICE

YOUR SECOND MISSION IS TO LEARN AND COMMUNICATE THE VIRTUES OF YOUR OFFERING

When you KNOW MORE—more about your offering, more about your competition's offering, and more about your customers' needs—you SELL MORE.

You sell more because you have knowledge.

You sell more because you have more confidence.

The importance of communicating the quality of your product or service offering was confirmed in a study of 1,209 industrial goods manufacturers. The research found that even in industrial markets, known for their focus on price, product quality was 9.2 times more important in explaining market share than relative price or spending on sales support.

Quality has long been known to be important. However, the relative magnitude of its importance is surprising.

It's the responsibility of company owners or management to lead the development of great products and services. It's your job to ensure that your company realizes a full, profitable return on its Meaningful advantages by communicating them to customers.

When you know more, you have more confidence. Confidence that is felt by customers. Confidence that creates a virtually unstoppable force.

Alternatively, if, as you learn more, you find that your company doesn't offer a really great product or service, then scream loud! If you're not heard, get up, get out, and take your selling talents to a company that makes a product or service worthy of your talents.

PRACTICAL **IDEAS**

Become an Encyclopedia of Brand Knowledge: Become an absolute expert on the quality advantages of your product or service. Learn everything you can about what makes your offering meaningfully great. Then focus your thinking and the decision process of the customers on what makes your offering really great!

Use Your Product or Service Exactly as Recommended Side by Side with Your Competition's: Directly compare and contrast your offering with your competition's offering. Call your company and your competition with a question or complaint to experience the difference in quality of customer service. Use your offering as not recommended. Abuse your product and the competition's to test your product's durability.

Learn the Purpose of Every Item Listed in Your Ingredient Statement or Service Specifications: Take your offering apart and examine everything that goes into it. Learn why your company does what it does to make the product or deliver the service. Examine every item on your ingredient list or on your service-delivery process and learn its purpose.

Be an Expert on Your Company's Comparative Quality: Understand fully the quality that your company's offering delivers relative to key competitors. Having absolute knowledge of quality is critical for those times when a customer looks you in the eye for assurance that he will really receive what you are promising.

Scream Loud When Quality Declines: It is the responsibility of the sales and marketing staffs to be the first-alert systems for quality issues. Your ongoing customer communications should give you news of quality problems long before they become a major issue.

{ 3 }
SCIENTIFIC
ADVICE

THE FUNDAMENTALS OF GREAT SELLING ARE SIMPLE: PASSION, PLANNING, PERSISTENCE, PEOPLE SKILLS, AND PRODUCT KNOWLEDGE

The five Ps of successful selling are a whole-brain blend of left-brain discipline—planning, persistence, product knowledge—with the right-brain emotional dimensions of passion and people skills.

These results come from a quantitative study of ninety-one sales managers on forty-six different aspects of sales success, sales failure, and the root causes of success versus failure.

Respondents had an average of thirteen years experience in sales management. Prior to being a part of sales management, the respondents had spent an average of eight years working as field salespeople.

The top five drivers of success were passion/ambition (3.8 out of 4.0), good planning/organizational skills (3.6), people skills (3.4), persistence (3.3), and product knowledge (3.3).

Focusing on a Meaningful benefit difference energizes all five dimensions.

A Meaningful difference fuels a natural *passion to help other people*. You will now concentrate on how you can make a real difference in your customers' lives instead of how to use Mindless Marketing sales trickery.

A Meaningful difference fuels your personal persistence and your natural curiosity to gain *product knowledge* and *plan your efforts*. You will have a level of depth and caring that is driven by integrity and authenticity.

PRACTICAL **IDEAS**

Passion: Seek passion in your heart, not your mind. Passion can't be faked. It comes from a deep belief that your offering will make a real difference in customers' lives. Passion comes from a spark of rational thought that has been swept up in emotional faith. Live and breathe your offering. Become fully immersed in your offering's merits.

Planning: Set clear and specific objectives. Then create a Meaningful plan for accomplishing those objectives. When you don't know what to do, then say so. Don't lie to yourself with false objectives. Instead of acting blindly, make learning and testing be the objectives you pursue. You fuel your passion when you are confident that your objectives are real and sustainable.

Persistence: Anything that is new creates tension and uncertainty for customers. This is not a reflection of your offering's merits, just a marketing fact. Persistence is easy to access when you genuinely believe in the merits of your offering.

People Skills: People skills are the natural outcome of an attitude of service. When your focus is on fulfilling your customers' true needs, your people skills are genuine and long-lasting. Alternatively, when your focus is on simply being a "buddy" to your clients, the relationship is often shallow and short-lasting.

Product Knowledge: Sales is about knowledge transfer. Each month, every month, commit yourself to at least one significant learning experience. Learn more about your customers' needs and your company's offerings.

{ 4 }
SCIENTIFIC
ADVICE

COMPETITION IS A VALUABLE "SPICE" FOR FUELING A PASSION THAT CAN HELP YOU WIN MORE SALES

The importance of business competition is highly controversial. Some see competition as an evil, a force that disrupts interpersonal teamwork and creates negative energy. Deming said, "Competition leads to loss. People pulling in opposite directions on a rope only exhaust themselves: they go nowhere. What we need is cooperation."

Others see competition as a fundamental fuel of a free marketplace economy where winners and losers are clearly identified. Research was conducted with 158 business-to-business salespeople. As expected, it found a direct relationship between those who set high personal goals and those with the greatest sales success.

The research also sought to understand the compelling reasons for a salesperson to set higher personal sales goals. Modeling of goals found that the following variables were the most predictive.

1. *Self-Confidence:* This is the confidence a salesperson has in his personal skills and abilities.
2. *Personal Competitiveness:* This is a love of interpersonal competition and a passion for winning and being better than others.
3. *Organizational Competitiveness:* This is a culture that encourages and rewards interpersonal competition.

The research found that all three dimensions were significant and interrelated reasons when it came to setting high personal goals.

Interestingly, when one component is missing, it directly affects the others. For example, a confident and personally competitive salesperson will tend to set lower goals if the work culture is not perceived to be competitive.

When it comes to making a Meaningful difference, competition on both the individual and organizational level can be an effective motivational "spice."

PRACTICAL IDEAS

Leverage the Rhythms of Sports Teams: Sports teams have a rhythm. They practice and prepare for a season that builds to a championship. Then they take a little time off and start the cycle again. You can create a similar momentum for your sales and marketing team. Develop a rhythm of rest, preparation, competition, and going for the championship.

Recruit Competitive People: Look for competitiveness in the backgrounds of prospective salespeople. Examples include participation in competitive sports, events, and activities. Overtly ask prospective employees if they consider themselves to be highly competitive. Ask what fuels their competitiveness. Ask for examples of times when they tried and failed. Then ask how they felt about losing. Look for a healthy level of competitive frustration with the loss. It's highly probable that those with no problem losing will have no problem not winning for you, as well.

Overtly Develop a Competitive Organization: Empower healthy competition between divisions, departments, and regions. Direct the competition toward the one thing that matters most—satisfying customers. Make sure everyone understands the rules of competition and that everyone plays fair. Recognize those who assist by bestowing "best supporting actor" awards to encourage full participation.

{ 5 }
SCIENTIFIC
ADVICE

INCREASE YOUR SALES TOOL KIT BY UNDERSTANDING BOTH THE EMOTIONAL AND RATIONAL DIMENSIONS OF YOUR OFFERING

Logical versus Emotional. Head versus Heart. Process versus Visionary. The frames of reference that managers use to make decisions vary.

Of all the different thinking styles, probably the broadest and most meaningful difference is between rational and emotional. It's important to note that research finds that both rational and emotional approaches are EQUALLY EFFECTIVE.

In your dealings with customers, you will find both styles. If you increase your sales "tool kit" by understanding both, you increase your odds of success.

Nine hundred new products were divided into two sets based on whether the customer benefit communicated was primarily rational (save money, solve a problem, cure a pain) or emotional (enhance peace of mind, feel better, feel sexier, gain more personal confidence). The data indicated no significant difference: 33.1 percent of brands with a primarily rational benefit survived, and 32.8 percent of brands with a primarily emotional benefit survived.

As you make your sales pitch, keep in mind that as you move through the chain of command, odds are that you will meet people with a logical left-brain style as well as those with a more emotional right-brain style. When you reach the top of the chain of command, the general manager or CEO will likely be one of the 28 percent of the population with a whole-brain orientation—those with the ability to see both the rational and emotional perspective simultaneously.

Meaningful Marketing means connecting with customers based on their preferred communications style. When you speak to customers based on their preferred approach, you show respect for them as individuals.

Every product and service contains emotional and rational dimensions. When you open your mind to both aspects, you add richness to your mission and will be able to sell to more types of people with less effort.

PRACTICAL **IDEAS**

Express the Feeling to Find the Facts: To identify emotional benefits, think "before" and "after." How do customers feel after using your product or service? Do they feel proud, happy, excited, or intelligent? What is the moment that a customer understands the real benefit of your product or service?

After defining the "feel" of the benefit, turn your attention to quantifying the source of the change in feelings. What, specifically, is the driver that sparked change? Rationally, what does your product offer? Search for the source of the feelings to identify the rationale for purchasing.

Define the Facts to Find the Feelings: Gather the charts, the data, the test results, and the economic projections that define your benefit. Define clearly the logical, rational benefit that your brand offers. What truly sets you apart from your competition?

Having defined the facts, think about how they make you feel. When you step back from the facts, how do you feel? How does the tangible benefit impact the experiences and feelings of the buyer?

Develop the Skill to Flip Between Rational and Emotional Thinking Styles: Practice the ability to flip between a rational and emotional perspective. This will help greatly when dealing with a multitude of customers and with ever-changing perspectives. Challenge yourself when you make a purchase: "I'm buying this because logically it will deliver X." Also, challenge yourself to define the emotional aspects: "I'm buying this because I hope it will make me feel more X."

{ 6 }
SCIENTIFIC
ADVICE

FUEL YOUR SALES TOOL KIT WITH TRUTH AND KNOWLEDGE TO EXCITE LOGICAL LEFT-BRAIN CUSTOMERS

Logical and Rational "Left-Brain" customers are the largest group. A study some years ago found that 44 percent of ALL ADULTS had a logical, rational orientation. Left-Brainers can be identified by their focus on logic, facts, discipline, and organization.

At the Eureka! Ranch our measurement of business executives attending inventing sessions reveals that about 75 percent of corporate executives are left-brained—or at least that's their self-perception and their behavioral approach.

Researchers at Hermann International concluded that **logical left-brainers are best sold with facts, data, and logical arguments.**

Additional research of business executives found that left-brain people respond best to presentations where the salesperson was more serious, very knowledgeable, and highly organized, with clear command of the facts and specific recommendations.

The greatest challenge with left-brain types is they are slow to change. By nature, they are highly conservative and skeptical. It can be particularly difficult to get left-brain types to stop and even consider new offerings.

The good news is that logical managers respond to factual truths. When they have made a commitment, they are more likely to remain loyal and are less likely to make a change based on an emotional impulse.

To find out where they stand, directly ask, "What do you think of our product compared to what you are using now?"

PRACTICAL **IDEAS**

Chart Your Differences Side by Side: Logical types love a side-by-side comparison. Chart what you do versus the alternatives. List the strengths and weaknesses. Be honest and straightforward. Left-brainers hate being hustled.

Stress Truth and Recognition of Your Client's Smarts: Logical types love being seen as smarter than others. Overtly praise them for the smart things they already do. Stress your search for truth and facts. Let them feel that they have intelligently discovered and deduced the right course of action.

Be Prepared, on Time, and Well-Rehearsed: Make your presentation with professionalism, directness, and as little "fluff" as possible. Left-brainers make their first evaluation based on details. Spelling mistakes and math errors in presentations are to them evidence of weak thinking and lack of intelligence.

Stand Strong—and Never Duck a Punch: Logical types have a machismo that requires them to challenge your thinking. Confront their questions straight on. When you don't know, say so. Don't bluff. And don't allow them to make inaccurate statements. If you stand strong, you win their respect. If you are evasive or cowardly, you are dead.

Be Specific about What You'll Do, and Do That: End your meeting with a summary of the overt and specific next steps. Summarize with clarity what you will do—what information you will get them, what questions you will get answers for, when you will set up a test-drive, etc. Then do exactly what you promised.

{ 7 }
SCIENTIFIC
ADVICE

FUEL YOUR SALES TOOL KIT WITH ENERGY AND ENTHUSIASM TO EXCITE EMOTIONAL RIGHT-BRAIN CUSTOMERS

Emotional and people-focused "Right-Brain" customers are A CLEAR MINORITY. A study some years ago found that 28 percent of ALL ADULTS had an emotional, visionary orientation. Right-Brainers can be identified by their emotional, spontaneous, people-oriented approach.

At the Eureka! Ranch our measurement of business executives reveals that something like 25 percent of corporate executives are right-brained—or at least that's their self perception and their behavioral approach. Researchers at Hermann International find that **emotional right-brainers are best sold with energy, personal relationships, and vision.**

Additional research of business executives showed that right-brain people responded best to sales approaches in which the salesperson was more humorous, animated, relationship-oriented, and focused on their personal needs more than their own company's needs.

The great challenge with right-brain types is that they are sometimes slow to make decisions. They love to "shop and talk," so closing the sale can be a challenge. The good news is that when they're committed to you, they tend to be vocal advocates, telling everyone they meet how great and wonderful you and your offering are.

To find where they stand, directly ask, "How do you feel about what I'm offering?" It is nearly impossible for right-brain people not to open up and tell you what's on their minds when asked.

PRACTICAL IDEAS

Trust Your Intuition: Emotional types continuously send out clues about their needs. Unlike left-brainers, who play their cards close to the vest, right-brainers are open with their feelings and fears. Listen closely; they are telling you what you need to know to succeed.

Build a Personal Relationship: Emotional types must like you before they can purchase your offering. They often don't trust their analytical skills when evaluating data, so instead they rely on their feelings about you as a person. When they connect with you, they connect with your brand.

Be Emotional and Passionate: Make your presentation with energy and enthusiasm. Right-brainers listen more to how you say it than to what you say. They have personal radar that searches your soul for genuine conviction.

Talk for as Long as They Want: Emotional types need to feel a sense of belonging and a sense that they are connected with others. This means they like to talk and talk and talk. Don't give them the slightest feeling that you are rushing them. Focus 100 percent of your attention on them. Be genuine. If you are shallow or deceitful, they will know, and you are dead.

Make Frequent Personal Contacts: End your meeting by telling them how good you feel about the possibility of working with them. After the meeting, follow up with handwritten notes and personal contact. Keep in-depth records of their interests, and refresh your memory before each contact to maximize the personal nature of your interactions.

{ 8 }
SCIENTIFIC
ADVICE

FUEL YOUR SALES TOOL KIT WITH BALANCE TO EXCITE WHOLE-BRAIN CUSTOMERS

The last thinking style is what is known as whole-brain. A study some years ago found that 28 percent of ALL ADULTS had the ability to access the perspective of both the Left- and Right-Brain styles.

However, at the Eureka! Ranch we find few managers who lead in a whole-brain fashion. In today's world to have a duality of focus is seen as a sign of weakness. To survive in today's corporate jungle, most Whole-Brain managers, like many Right-Brain types, live a Left-Brain existence and hide their Right Brain.

Genuine Whole-Brainers have a natural ability to see both the emotional and the logical side of each situation. The great difficulty with whole-brain types is determining their perspective at a particular moment. One moment they can be delving into the nitty-gritty factual details; the next they can be thinking in what-if visionary dimensions. They love to look at both sides nearly simultaneously.

Whole-brain types see nothing wrong with switching from details to dreams in the middle of a conversation. In many respects they view thinking as a natural extension of the scientific method: Define the dream (visionary hypothesis) with the right side of their brain, then test the practicality (analytical experimentation) using the left side of their brain.

Whole-brain customers are the easiest to sell your new offering to, because they're not scared by change, facts, or thinking big. They are comfortable assessing multiple variables simultaneously.

PRACTICAL **IDEAS**

Be Flexible: Be flexible in your sales and marketing presentation. Be ready to move and change in an instant from discussing the factual minutia to the long-term vision. As Ralph Waldo Emerson said, "A foolish consistency is the hobgoblin of little minds." With whole-brain customers, rapid change of direction is seen as a virtue, not a curse.

Nurture a Personal Passion for Facts and Emotions: Whole-brain customers have a natural passion for looking at the world from multiple dimensions. To them, a singular rational or emotional focus is limiting and one-dimensional. The more excited they get, the more likely they are to rapidly switch between the two perspectives. To make a Meaningful connection with them, nurture within yourself a genuine love for both facts and emotions.

Be Honest with Your Facts: When selling to whole-brain individuals, you need to fully understand the level of truth inherent in your claims. Do not overhype; be honest and factual. When you are certain, stand strong. When you're not, be open and honest. Whole-brain types are comfortable with uncertainty. They are not comfortable with those who attempt to declare truths as absolute. When you don't know, say so; don't try to trick them. They will see through you.

Be Genuine: Most important, be genuine in your presentation. Don't overhype or overthink. Rather, have a sense of balance and genuineness. Whole-brain customers respect those who are real and authentic in their presentations.

{ 9 }
SCIENTIFIC
ADVICE

WHEN YOU HAVE A REALLY DIFFERENT IDEA, YOU WILL WIN MORE IF YOU HAVE EXTRA PATIENCE AND A THICK SKIN

In today's technology-laden world, advanced products and services are often highly complex and not easily grasped in a simple sound bite. When you have a product or service that truly changes the world, it can be very frustrating when customers don't immediately see it as you see it.

Fortunately, research indicates that the challenge of **selling complex products becomes easier with patience and repeated exposures.** This is based on a series of studies. In one example, researchers showed 381 participants advertisements for dresses that ranged from the very simple to the very complex. They were shown the designs once, twice, three times, four times. They were then asked to rate how well they liked each on a set of three scales ranging from good to bad, pleasant to unpleasant, and likable to not likable. The average liking for COMPLEX designs rose steadily from 3.4 with one viewing to 4.3 after four viewings. Net: The more often customers came in contact with a complex concept, the more they started to like it.

Conversely, the very SIMPLE dress designs started with higher likability ratings, 4.2 with one viewing, and declined to 3.4 after four viewings. In effect, what started out as intriguing became less interesting or boring with each successive viewing.

At the Eureka! Ranch, we've noticed that initially clients tend to gravitate toward ideas that are the most familiar and/or easiest to execute. To combat this, we force clients to suspend judgment for a period of time while they review the ideas multiple times. The net effect is that what seemed a good idea at the start of a two- or three-day project often is considered boring at the end. What was unthinkable at the start becomes the chosen path at the end of the session.

PRACTICAL IDEAS

Plan for Repeated Exposures: Design your sales and marketing efforts such that they deliver multiple exposures. Define the big picture (dramatic difference) in the initial presentation or advertisement. Provide demonstrations, Web sites, and other sources of experiential learning. Provide follow-up information about the multitude of details that support your promise.

Compartmentalize Your Presentations: When presenting something that is highly technical, clearly state how you're not going to describe it in detail. Resist the temptation to explain everything. Instead, offer a "white paper" that defines your technology or method for later reading. Offer a Web site that has the complete details. Provide a video that tours the factory production process.

Be Open with Customers' Feelings of Fear: When what you offer is really new, be open about customers' feelings of fear. Instead of hard-selling, be patient and acknowledge that in some cultures and for some managers, it may take more time for them to accept the "new and different." Give customers an opportunity to "test-drive" for an extended period of time.

Reduce Fear by Making a Pedigree Connection: Reassure customers by providing an analogy of how, even though your offering is dramatically different, it has a pedigree in another category. For example, "Our new engine system is based on the same technology used in race cars." Or, "Our new type of beer is number one in Germany."

Help Ease the Transition: Reassure customers that the change will not be difficult. Detail clearly how easy the transition will be from where they are now and overtly address their specific fears.

{ 10 }
SCIENTIFIC
ADVICE

USE INCENTIVES TO MOTIVATE, BUT DON'T TRY TO "BUY" A CUSTOMER

At the risk of being criticized for being repetitive, **I want to reinforce the importance of not resorting to financial incentives to drive sales**.

Research shows that offering customers a modest financial incentive to try your product or service can have a dramatic impact on trial rates. Incentives can take the form of free samples, coupons, or straightforward discounts on initial purchases. However, more money is not always the smart choice. The return you realize from additional money has clear limits.

Researchers mailed a survey on group health insurance to 1,200 members of an industry trade association. They offered incentives varying from $1 to $40 to complete the survey. The results indicate that compared with the no-incentive control group, a $1 or $5 incentive doubled the response rates; however, higher incentives had minimal additional impact.

Survey Response Rate

No Incentive/Control	21 percent
$1 Incentive	41 percent
$5 Incentive	51 percent
$10 Incentive	44 percent
$20 Incentive	54 percent
$40 Incentive	54 percent

The control group grew to a 52 percent response rate, a rate similar to the incentive rate, after three additional mailings to those not responding previously. Similarly, you can achieve higher trial rates without the use of incentives. Of course, additional contacts and sales efforts will be required.

When introducing a new product or service, a modest incentive to early customers can be a wise investment. But as you'll learn later in this book, accelerating early trial rates through discounts may not be the smartest long-term action.

Net: A financial incentive can stir a customer to action. However, more money won't turn a non-customer into a customer.

PRACTICAL IDEAS

Provide an Incentive to Try, but Don't Give It All Away:
An incentive to try can be effective. However, giving everything away
at the start establishes that your product or service is worthless. Giving
an early-buy discount for a limited time establishes the value of your
offering.

Offer Limited-Use Samples: When possible, give a trial-size sample
of your offering—a taste, a test-drive, a sample financial plan. Don't
be surprised if even when your sample is free, you have a hard time
getting takers. Studies tracking usage of free product samples have
found that even with targeted mailing lists, it's not uncommon for only
50 percent of free samples to ever be used by customers.

Offer an Incentive for Sales Demonstrations: Create a value from
the sales presentation itself. Incorporate real learning value into your
marketing. When customers experience genuine learning during the
sales process, they develop confidence in your skills and abilities.

Stand Strong and Confident: Price discounting is often driven by
a lack of confidence. Salespeople who don't believe in the merits of
their offering will resort to discounts and incentives to make up the
difference. Sadly, the discounting can backfire, as it signals to customers
that the offering must not be worth the price. And when customers
start to doubt, no amount of discounts can motivate them to purchase.
When you have a Meaningful offering, establish a no-discount policy.
Stand strong, and when pushed for discounts, reply that the money
that would have been available for discounts has been invested in
higher product/service quality.

{ 11 }
SCIENTIFIC
ADVICE

SPARK NEW SALES BY FOCUSING YOUR ENERGY ON SELLING FUNDAMENTALS

New ideas for how to sell are discovered every year. However, in our desire to pursue the new, we must not lose sight of the time-tested fundamentals.

Selling to a consumer is considered to be different from selling to an industrial customer. Yet research indicates both types of salespeople agree that certain fundamentals are critical to their success.

Researchers surveyed 170 consumer and industrial salespeople about a list of eighty-four different sales strategies and tactics. Both groups identified the following tactics as being most important in their sales efforts:

1. *Personal Observation:* Look and listen.
2. *Ask Questions to Learn:* Ask prospects direct questions to learn about their situation and needs.
3. *Benefit-Focused:* Overtly state the benefit of your offering.
4. *Keep It Understandable:* Use short non-technical words in sales presentations.
5. *Direct Answers:* Provide specific responses to exact questions from prospects.
6. *Direct Close:* Ask for the order in a straightforward manner.
7. *Follow Up after the Sale:* Check with the customer after the sale to ensure satisfaction. Where necessary, provide training on how to best use the product.

The top-rated selling methods are simple. They all focus on understanding your customers' genuine needs and then fulfilling them with integrity.

Importantly, sophisticated closing gimmicks, dramatic showmanship, fear-focused sales tactics, and even the telling of jokes were not seen as important when it came to selling.

PRACTICAL **IDEAS**

Drive the Fundamentals: Get back to basics. Focus your energies on the fundamentals of successful sales and marketing.

1. *Personal Observation:* Get up, go out, and spend time observing real customers using your product or service. Watch for moments of delight and moments of frustration.
2. *Ask Questions to Learn:* Make a list of twenty-one things you think you know about how customers use and abuse your product. Then assess how absolutely certain you are of the factual nature of each statement. Rate them on a scale from 0 to 100, with 100 being absolute truth. Take the seven statements with the lowest certainty and ask your customers for their perspective.
3. *Benefit-Focused:* Challenge yourself to identify the benefits of each feature listed in your sales materials and advertisements.
4. *Keep It Understandable:* Explain your offering to a fifth-grader.
5. *Direct Answers:* List your customers' most frequently asked questions. Then challenge yourself to answer them in the most direct fashion possible.
6. *Direct Close:* Take three customers who are in the process of "thinking over" your offering and politely yet directly ask them to make a purchase.
7. *Follow Up after the Sale:* Call your last dozen customers and ask them how they're doing and what you can do to help them.

{ 12 }
SCIENTIFIC
ADVICE

YOU CAN SPARK NEW SALES BY LEVERAGING SELLING STRATEGIES OF OTHERS

Industrial and consumer salespeople have much in common, as stated in No. 11's Selling Advice. However, they also have some significant differences that hold potential for cross-leverage.

As mentioned before, 170 salespeople were surveyed on a list of 84 different sales strategies and tactics. Both consumer and industrial salespeople were researched, and their ratings of the importance of various approaches compared.

Industrial salespeople consider the following techniques significantly more important than consumer salespeople do.

1. *Propose Trial Use:* Industrial salespeople are more likely to overcome objections by suggesting the prospect use the product or service on a trial basis.
2. *Customize Sales Presentations:* Industrial salespeople are more likely to fully or partially customize their presentations to match each customer.

Consumer salespeople consider the following techniques significantly more important than industrial sales people do.

1. *Seek Referrals:* Consumer salespeople are more likely to ask customers for the names of other potential customers.
2. *Send Thank-You Notes:* Consumer salespeople are more likely to send a letter of appreciation to the customer.

PRACTICAL **IDEAS**

Leverage Industrial Techniques with Consumers: Find ways to get your customers to experience your product firsthand. If that's not possible, build simulations that you can take with you to help them experience your Meaningful difference. Leverage technological tools to customize your sales presentations. One-to-one database tools make it possible for you to mass customize your responses to consumer inquiries at a reasonable cost.

Leverage Consumer Techniques in Industrial Markets: By the nature of the business, an industrial salesperson's customers are often each other's competitors. Thus, there is a natural reluctance to overtly ask for referrals. However, in today's economy, movement between competitors by employees is frequent. Customers are therefore more open to providing referrals to salespeople, as the customers often view the salesperson as a tool for helping them network for new or better jobs.

In today's less personal, less connected world, a handwritten thank-you note can have a huge impact. A note from you to your customers conveys their importance to you.

Let Go of Ego and Become a Learning Sponge: A confident ego is valuable when presenting to skeptical customers. However, it's a negative when it comes to learning more about how to think quicker, smarter, and more creatively about your sales and marketing methods. Release your ego to learn. Challenge yourself to discover and apply at least one new method or idea each month.

{ 13 }
SCIENTIFIC
ADVICE

WHEN YOU TEACH YOUR CUSTOMERS, THEY WILL USUALLY BUY WHAT THEY LEARN

In simple terms, your job as a salesperson is to be a TEACHER.

The more customers are educated regarding your offering, the more likely they are to purchase. A research study found that customers' purchase-intent ratings, as well as their attitude toward a brand, were significantly higher when they experienced the product firsthand or watched an in-depth fifteen-minute commercial as opposed to a brief one-minute advertisement.

The more you educate and teach your customers about your true merits, the more likely they are to actually buy from you. This is in contrast with the accepted belief that customers don't have time to read or learn. The work of David Ogilvy and others in the field of direct marketing have shown clearly that, oftentimes, longer copy has more of an impact and is more persuasive than shorter copy.

A separate study of a technologically advanced product category found that customers with high category knowledge assessed options with double the accuracy of those with low category knowledge.

Customers with high levels of product understanding are able to translate product attributes into personal benefits. They have the ability to adapt what you claim into fulfillment of their needs.

Customers with little understanding see only your features and attributes. They mainly judge your product based on the direct application of what you describe.

Education was the secret to Home Depot's success. From the beginning, the company focused on teaching plumbing, electrical wiring, and construction. It gave free clinics, hired knowledgeable staff, and, most important, encouraged the staff to take time to answer even the most basic of home-improvement questions.

PRACTICAL **IDEAS**

Teach Differently to Different Target Audiences: One of the first rules of teaching is to understand the skill level and motivation of your students. Think deeply about your marketing message and sales approach. Force yourself to customize your communications to the most educated and the most novice customers. Having defined the two ends of the spectrum, you can now blend and adjust your message for those customers in between.

Education Starts with "Why Should I Care?": As stated previously, before any pitch or presentation can be made, your sales prospect must stop and listen. This means you must articulate your news in a simple, direct fashion. For maximum "stopping power," focus your headline statement on the Meaningful difference you offer. Be bold about how you can make a major difference for your customers.

The Second Question: "What's in It for Me?": Now that you have the customer's attention, overtly articulate what your customer will receive, experience, and enjoy from using your offering. Focus your communication on your customer's needs, not your personal preferences. In many cases this will be a restatement of "Why should I care?"

The Third Question: "Why Should I Believe You?": The last part of education is explaining how you will accomplish what you promise. The level of credibility required depends on the breadth of your promise. With a small promise, little doubt is created and thus little credibility is required.

Be Prepared for Honor Students: Some customers love to be challenged. Challenge these "honor students" by asking, "Is there anything else you'd like to know?" If you engage, challenge, and respect their thinking, honor students will become your brand's biggest fans.

{ 14 }
SCIENTIFIC
ADVICE

YOU WILL BUILD A GREAT CLIENT RELATIONSHIP IF YOUR FOUNDATION IS HONEST DEPENDABILITY

Cultivating personal trust among customers is of critical importance for sales success. The common stereotype is that of a salesperson seeking to become the most likable of friends with the customer.

Research indicates that while likability is the most often developed trait, it's also the least important when it comes to nurturing customer trust with you as a salesperson.

Researchers asked 187 industrial buyers to rate the most recent salesperson who had called on them. They provided eight different ratings of their trust in the salesperson, along with ratings on a series of diagnostic dimensions.

Results and importance versus likability were as follows.

1. *Dependability* (320 percent greater than likability): Following through on promises and being reliable.
2. *Honesty* (130 percent greater than likability): Telling the truth, not exaggerating, and being open about strengths and weaknesses of his offerings.
3. *Customer first* (80 percent greater than likability): The buyer's perception that the salesperson puts the buyer's true needs ahead of making a sale.
4. *Competence* (30 percent greater than likability): The salesperson's knowledge about his company's products or services.
5. *Likability* (control): How friendly and approachable the salesperson is. Likability was the least important trait and also the most likely trait, with nearly twice as many salespeople being rated highly on likability than the average for all trust traits.

The bottom line is simple: **Dependability and honesty are the foundations upon which a great relationship is built.**

PRACTICAL IDEAS

Dependability: As the classic saying goes, "Say what you do, and do what you say." Let everything else go crazed, but ensure that your word is good. Create a pattern of dependability through making small promises and over-delivering on results.

Honesty: Honesty is about being frank and truthful. It's about being real and genuine. Instead of being a "professional pitchman," be an honest adviser. Present both the strengths and the weaknesses of your offering. It's better for customers to learn about your weakness from you in advance than to discover it themselves later.

Customer First: You cannot serve two masters. And long-term, the way to best serve your company is by putting your customer first. You may lose the sale today, but long-term rewards are orders of magnitude greater.

Competence: No one should know more about your offering and your competitor's offering than you. Knowing more means an understanding of both the factual technology of your offering and the practical application of it. Continually test your mastery to build confidence.

Likability: Likability is about connecting to customers on a personal level through common interests and goals. It also means common courtesy—making efficient use of the buyer's time and being courteous and polite.

{ 15 }
SCIENTIFIC
ADVICE

THERE ARE FIVE FUNDAMENTAL REASONS THAT CUSTOMERS DELAY MAKING A DECISION, ALL OF WHICH YOU HAVE THE ABILITY TO INFLUENCE IF YOU TAKE RESPONSIBILITY

Few things are more maddening as a salesperson than to generate a sales lead, make the presentation, receive positive feedback, and then hear NOTHING about a final decision to purchase.

It can seem like a random event—an event not in your control—but in truth it's not. Research indicates that there are reproducible reasons that clients delay making a final purchase decision.

A series of research studies was conducted on why customers delay making purchase decisions. A total of eighty-one different reasons were identified. Mathematical modeling identified the following five factors as the critical causes of delays:

1. *Too Busy to Devote Time to Evaluating Options:* Customers don't feel they have the time to make a smart decision about what to purchase.
2. *The Buying Process Is Unpleasant:* Customers don't like the process of buying and making decisions.
3. *Fear of Making a Bad Decision:* Customers feel that the product might not work as advertised, based on the poor performance of similar products they've experienced in the past.
4. *Need More Information:* Customers feel a need for more information on other options and/or feel a need to get someone else's opinion.
5. *Pricing Concerns and Changes:* Customers are not only concerned about their ability to afford the item but that the price may drop soon after purchase.

Nothing can force clients to make instant decisions. However, by understanding why customers delay purchasing decisions, we can reduce our chances of getting stopped by delays.

PRACTICAL **IDEAS**

Make Your Benefit Personally Meaningful: When customers claim they don't have time to evaluate your offering, what they are really saying is that they don't anticipate a benefit worth investing in. Think DEEPLY about what you do and why it should matter to them. Think beyond the decision maker to the support staff and related departments. Key executives today often assign the task of making evaluations and recommendations to others.

Make the Process Painless for Customers: Review your buying process from start to finish. How can you make each step easier for your customers? Can you provide it on an audio CD that they can listen to in their car as they drive to work? Can you provide a simple SAMPLING PROCESS—experiential sampling at their office or yours?

Quantify Credibility: Fear of failure is reasonable. Provide measurable, tangible proof of how your product or service will deliver as promised. Show them your patent, your factory, and all the details of how you are able to fulfill your promise to them.

Make It Easy to Gather More Information: By overtly detailing the points of difference in your offering relative to a competitor's, you defuse issues about "needing more information." In addition, it allows you to determine the relevance and importance of various comparison criteria.

Give Customers Assurances of Long-Term Price Value: The biggest thing you can do to provide assurances of pricing stability is to have a firm policy. When a customer perceives that your pricing is open to discussion, they immediately assume that discounting is in the future. Stand strong regarding the value of your proposition.

{ 16 }
SCIENTIFIC
ADVICE

YOUR SALES PRESENTATIONS WILL BE MOST EFFECTIVE IF YOU FOCUS ON SUBSTANCE AND REDUCE THE FLASH AND FLUFF

When I was a teenager, I learned sales and marketing from an extraordinary promotion wizard named John MacDonald. John taught me the importance of knowing what I was selling. He would challenge me: "Doug are you selling the steak or the sizzle?" His goal was to make me conscious of what I was focusing my pitch on.

Academic research supports John's focus on "steak versus sizzle."

When you don't have substance, it's best to distract customers with flash and "sizzle." **When you do have a meaningful difference, it's best to reduce distractions.**

Customers have only so much ability to process information, and research indicates that when they are bombarded with engaging, exciting, or entertaining stimuli, they are less able to process, digest, and recall important sales messages.

Research was conducted with 324 adults to measure their ability to recall various advertising messages broadcast in three types of television program environments—extremely violent, sexually explicit or neutral.

Twenty-four hours after seeing one of the shows, participants were asked to recall what brands had advertised during the television show. Those in the neutral program control group were able to recall 4.7 of the 9 brands. Those watching the violent show recalled 3.0 brands. Those watching the sexual show recalled 2.8 brands.

A separate study in Italy found that about half as many men could remember a television news story reported by a very attractive female than could remember it if reported by an average-looking reporter.

It appears that the more customers direct their attention toward the television show, the less likely they are able to perceive and comprehend the marketing messages.

PRACTICAL **IDEAS**

Help Customers Focus on What's Meaningful: The more you have a Meaningful difference to communicate, the simpler your marketing communications should be. This was confirmed in a study of print advertisements. When the brand had a Meaningful message to communicate, it was more persuasive when the ad was shown in black and white, and color was used only to highlight the important differences.

Cut out meaningless distractions from your sales and marketing messages. Simplify your marketing presentations to make your Meaningful difference the "hero" of your message.

When You Have Nothing, Distract Customers: When you don't have anything Meaningful to communicate in your sales pitch, then your odds of success are greater if you turn up the flash, sizzle, and hype. But beware, in the long term, this is a losing strategy. At best, it can work for a short time. With today's access to public knowledge, it's just a matter of time before your trickery is exposed.

Slow Down Your Communication: We know our offering inside and out. Often customers do not. If we're not careful, we will talk too fast for customers to comprehend. Be sensitive to your customer's level of understanding. Offer to provide a step-by-step explanation or to provide documents or Web sites for teaching customers the same fundamentals that you know.

Show Your Product: Many advertising and sales presentations feature lots of talk and little product. If you have a meaningfully great product, show it. Make the product the center of every piece of customer communication. Stop reading now and check all your materials for photos of your product as the core of your marketing message.

{ 17 }
SCIENTIFIC
ADVICE

AT A MINIMUM, YOU SHOULD DELIVER THREE TO FIVE PITCHES BEFORE GIVING UP ON A POTENTIAL CUSTOMER

When first exposed to a new product or service, customers have an initial tendency to hesitate. They develop negative counterarguments because they do not fully understand how the new idea can make a difference to them.

Consumer research studies have found that it's during the third exposure that the number of positive thoughts outnumber the negative ones. By the third time people are presented with the marketing message, they are prepared to more fully and fairly assess the offering's merits. Another study found it takes an average of 4.6 face-to-face calls to close the typical industrial product sale.

A separate research study found that **customers' first opinion about a new product offering has a surprising amount of error in it**. Customers were shown pictures, descriptions, and pricing for new products and asked to rate each product on a scale from 0 to 10.

In 809 cases where customers voted 0 (i.e., there was no chance of them purchasing), some 144, or more than 1 in 6, actually did purchase the product in the following six months.

In 246 cases where customers voted 10 (i.e., that they were definitely likely to purchase), some 128, or a little over half, actually did not purchase the product in the following six months.

It appears that customers' first instincts are a directional yet not an absolute prediction of their ultimate purchasing behavior.

PRACTICAL IDEAS

Keep Pitching: While a good first impression is important, it is not a death sentence when a customer turns you down. With each customer interaction, be sure to leave yourself an opening for another presentation. Guide your prospect away from making firm and fixed "no" decisions. Define the gap between your customer's no and your Meaningful difference. Then address this gap with each additional presentation.

Don't Rest: Remember, when a customer gives you an absolute yes, there is still a 50 percent probability he will change his mind. When you get a yes, move rapidly to close the sale. Maintain excellent customer service and commitment to deliver a Meaningful difference after the customer has said yes—and after the purchase.

Stage Your Three Pitches: In some sales and marketing presentations, you can stage the three exposures. In this case, the first could be designed to provoke curiosity. The second is to develop understanding. The third encounter is to encourage a decision. Each stage can provide additional information.

* *Curiosity:* Articulate a "mind-opening thought" that causes customers to stop, listen, and think.
* *Understanding:* Confirm how the promise that was first communicated works and how you accomplish it.
* *Decision:* Reinforce the Meaningful difference, address any key concerns, and ask for the sale.

Let Follow-Up Correspondence Pitch for You: After each presentation, send follow-up notes thanking the customers for their time and feedback. Detail clearly what you are going to do to address their issues. Be clear and specific to demonstrate that you were really listening to them and value their opinions.

{ 18 }
SCIENTIFIC
ADVICE

YOU WILL INCREASE YOUR SUCCESS RATE IF YOU THINK DEEPER ABOUT YOUR BUSINESS BUYER'S DECISION STYLE

A two-year research project was conducted involving some 1,600 executives across a broad range of industries. The research identified five distinct types of business-to-business customers. By understanding who you are dealing with, you can modify your marketing approach to make it more Meaningful for the customer.

1. *Charismatics* (25 percent of executives): These are the visionaries who quickly grasp concepts and get excited about big ideas. When it comes to making a final decision, they often have a short attention span and need a balanced perspective.

2. *Thinkers* (11 percent of executives): These are the toughest executives to persuade. Thinkers are intellectual decision makers who dislike being forced into making decisions.

3. *Skeptics* (19 percent of executives): These are aggressive, instinctive executives. They distrust data, especially when it contradicts their beliefs and natural instincts.

4. *Followers* (36 percent of executives): These are the most conservative of executives. They live a life of fear. They trust precedent, previous experience, and the recommendations of other managers.

5. *Controllers* (9 percent of executives): These are the most fact-driven and fear-averse of all decision makers. They distrust ambiguity and uncertainty.

PRACTICAL **IDEAS**

Selling Charismatics: Focus on the most important and most dramatic "big picture" bottom-line benefits first. Use visual aids and minimize the use of catchwords and one-sided stereotypes. Keep your presentation fast and fluid. Be prepared to shift from the long-term vision to executional minutia and back to vision again in seconds. Be sure you really believe in what you're selling and have absolute knowledge of all details.

Selling Thinkers: Provide an open and honest presentation of all the data. Use market research, cost-benefit analysis, and details on precedents. Thinkers love a frame of reference, so provide tons of side-by-side comparisons. Focus on the facts and just the facts. Empower and guide, but don't force thinkers' decisions. Learn to pause and ask for their viewpoint before summarizing to build support.

Selling Skeptics: Prepare yourself emotionally for a demanding and disruptive presentation. Methodically build trust. Focus on why your offering is meaningfully different. When you're attacked, keep your cool and stay focused on your Meaningful difference to rise above skepticism.

Selling Followers: Show how what you have to offer reduces their chance of failure. Detail clearly the pedigree of all that you're recommending. Overtly explain how your recommendation is the path that many others are following. Detail clearly how large the potential gain is and how minimal the risk is.

Selling Controllers: Be the expert. Present your facts in a straightforward, linear fashion. Don't hesitate or show weakness of any kind. If you stand strong and confident, you'll reduce their fear.

{ 19 }
SCIENTIFIC
ADVICE

YOU WILL INCREASE YOUR SUCCESS RATE IF YOU THINK DEEPER ABOUT THE ORGANIZATIONAL CULTURE YOUR BUSINESS BUYER REPRESENTS

The organization that a buyer belongs to can have a direct impact on how he processes and proceeds with purchasing decisions. By understanding the different types of cultures, you improve your chances of making a Meaningful and successful connection.

A study of 109 business buyers identified three core types of large company decision cultures, along with a collection of methods for selling to them.

1. *Entrepreneurial:* These types of organizations often have no formal buying policies. Decisions are highly decentralized, with one or two people making decisions. Decision making is dependent on personal intuition and judgmental evaluation procedures. Entrepreneurial organizations can be easy to make a sale to but very difficult to maintain as they are just as likely to change vendors at any time for no good reason.

2. *Planning:* Planning organizations make decisions based on long-range considerations. Decisions are a result of a careful assessment of the organization's needs. Consensus across departments is a critical part of the decision process.

3. *Bureaucratic:* Decisions are based primarily on precedents and the official rules and regulations of the organization. Forms and procedures are critical. Buyers are more managers of the process than they are independent decision makers. Change is seen as an evil, as it disrupts the flow of mindless consistency. At first, sales can be difficult with bureaucratic organizations. However, the good news is, once sold, they are slow to change.

PRACTICAL IDEAS

Selling Entrepreneurial Cultures: Be simple and straightforward. The buyer is inclined to make independent decisions. Focus on building trust with the customer and yourself, your offering, your company. Empower the decision maker to just say yes. If your offering is complex or hard to understand, then you will lose the advantage of spontaneous decision making that entrepreneurial cultures love. Focus your presentation on the innovative nature of your offering and why it's such a smart decision. Stay in touch by asking what's new and build trust by keeping up with changes.

Selling Planning Cultures: Concentrate on the technical facts of your product's performance and compatibility. Leverage team selling by bringing a marketing and product technology expert with you to presentations. Match up your company's experts with their experts. Define clearly the strengths of your processes and quality-control systems. Focus your presentation on the systemic and "total solution" nature of your product or service. Stay in touch regularly to reinforce your commitment.

Selling Bureaucratic Cultures: These are the most mindless of all buyers. You need to make them aware of your services, but it's hard to sell them. Rather, the process usually involves your writing formal responses to your customer's requests for proposals in the exact manner as presented. Be as competitive as possible on price as there is a good chance that this will be the primary, if not the only, decision criteria. Focus your presentation on your flexibility in adapting to the customer's specifications and your systemic and long-term price advantages. Stay in touch by using testimonials from other users. Bureaucrats love to follow others.

{ 20 }
SCIENTIFIC
ADVICE

YOU WILL INCREASE YOUR SUCCESS RATE IF YOU THINK DEEPER ABOUT YOUR CONSUMER'S PERSONAL NEEDS.

A customer's state of mind has a direct impact on buying behavior. Psychologist Abraham Maslow defined a ladder hierarchy of human needs. At the bottom rung are the *physiological needs*—air, water, food, sex. Then come *safety needs*—security, stability; *social needs*—belonging, love, acceptance; and *ego needs*—self-esteem, self-confidence, respect. At the top of it all are the *self-actualization needs*—the need to fulfill oneself, to realize one's true potential. Maslow said we must feel secure on each rung before we can move up the ladder.

A study was conducted of 560 new-car consumers' values and perceptions of the sales process. The data identified three distinct sets of consumer attitudes toward the sales process.

1. *Low Self-Esteem and Self-Confidence:* These customers have a desire to be led. They prefer to purchase a vehicle that the salesperson recommends. They depend on the salesperson for help in making a decision. They even admit that they could be talked into making a purchase by a salesperson. NOTE: This dimension is REALLY IMPORTANT. Over the past 25 years we've created hundreds of market segmentation models. In more than 80 percent of the cases, customer self-esteem/self-confidence has emerged as a critical dimension.

2. *Low Sense of Belonging:* These customers consider themselves as outcasts and crave connections with salespeople. They prefer salespeople they can create a personal relationship with. Their primary focus is on the relationship that develops—not the product facts or salesperson's recommendation.

3. *Independent Decision Makers:* These are customers whose interaction with the salesperson is focused on learning information about the vehicles. They view themselves as not being directly influenced by a salesperson's recommendation.

PRACTICAL **IDEAS**

Ask Customers Their Opinions: Ask customers what they are looking for and what is most important to them. Be prepared to be amazed at how directly and honestly customers respond to direct and honest questions. Based on their responses, you will quickly understand the current state of their self-esteem with regard to the purchase decision at hand.

Leverage Preexisting Prejudices: Chameleons survive in nature because they developed the ability to change color to fit their surroundings. The same is true with your advertising message. Research subjects were asked to judge messages that either supported or contradicted their preexisting personal viewpoint. Subjects repeatedly rated arguments that aligned with their prejudices stronger even when they were in truth weaker than alternatives.

Leverage Others When Marketing Contradicts: New product or service breakthroughs that challenge existing ways of thinking can be particularly challenging to sell to low-self-esteem customers. Bold changes can be seen as risky and as having the potential to expose their lack of ability to assess and examine your strengths and potential issues. The result can be a reflexive "no" under the guise of "waiting to see what others do." To confront this, bring the testimonials of thought leaders to your presentation. With the support of industry leaders, the low-self-esteem manager now finds it riskier not to change than to change.

Use Color, Graphics, and Pictures to Reinforce Benefits: Research has found that people with low self-motivation have little ability to think through strengths and weaknesses. Often they base their attitudes on visual cues such as pretty ads and visually striking imagery.

{ 21 }
SCIENTIFIC
ADVICE

YOU WILL REALIZE DRAMATICALLY GREATER SUCCESS WITH YOUR PRICING CHANGES IF YOU'RE UPFRONT AND HONEST WITH CUSTOMERS

Setting price is part science, part art.

In a free market, **the price you set is a clear assessment of what you believe to be the value of your offering.** Cheap products are cheap products. Products that are of higher quality and that offer Meaningful advantages usually cost more.

When you can actually achieve a pricing premium compared with the competition, it can be one of the best measures of your brand because it is free-market testimony to the commitment of your customers.

The challenge is what to do when you need to increase your price due to changes in your product design or your costs. Research indicates that the key to successfully increasing your price is to provide customers with a real reason for the change. If you do, you can virtually eliminate pricing resistance.

A number of studies have shown that when customers perceive that you are simply seeking extra profits, they immediately perceive it to be UNFAIR. However, if you provide an explanation of the price increase, you can cut the perception of unfairness by 50 to 90 percent.

The most important dimension of pricing is profit margin. The greater your margin, the greater your ability to invest in R&D, pay shareholders a reasonable return, and have flexibility when competitors attempt to become more competitive with their pricing.

PRACTICAL IDEAS

Meaningful Pricing: Being open and honest about your pricing will win more sales than playing pricing games. Be direct about what value customers receive and what it costs. Give them confidence in the stability of your pricing.

One of the most important issues for customers is that they feel that they got the best price possible from you. If you have one price and only one price—with no price negotiations—customers might not like it, but they feel satisfied that they didn't overpay. Contrast this with situations where pricing is negotiated, causing customers to leave the transaction with a sense of apprehension that they paid too much.

Understand Volume vs. Price: As you set your prices, be sure that you understand how volume effects your cost structure. It could be that at higher volume, your cost of production drops dramatically as you move to lower-cost production methods. However, it's just as possible that higher volume will not have much of an effect. By understanding the effect of volume on pricing, you can better manage customers' pricing expectations and your own in the future.

Where Are Prices Going?: Price changes represent significant sales opportunities. When inflation is imminent, special sales opportunities exist prior to increases. In technology products, where raw costs are regularly decreasing, sales opportunities exist around each decline. By understanding the momentum and timing of pricing changes, you are better able to meaningfully advise your customers.

Look Different to Get Different Pricing: Research shows that when comparing prices between options, customers look for "cues" to assess the reasonableness of making comparison. The more you look the same, sound the same, or feel the same, the more likely they are to make the comparison. To break the tendency, do everything you can to make your offering look and feel different, such as bundle your options in a luxury package, as car companies do, or bundle an extended warranty or free installation with your offering.

{ 22 }
SCIENTIFIC
ADVICE

BY ADAPTING YOUR SELLING STYLE TO YOUR CUSTOMERS' LIFE STAGES, YOU CAN JOLT YOUR PRODUCTIVITY

It's been reported that a **1 percent increase in sales force productivity is capable of generating a 6.7 percent increase in revenue**. A powerful way to increase productivity is to understand and adapt to the needs of customers based on what life stage they are in with regard to their relationship with you and your company.

Research with approximately 1,400 customers of an industrial-products company showed that the effect of a salesperson varies with customer life stage. The four life stages and salesperson's roles are as follows:

1. *Exploration:* During this search-compare-and-trial phase, the customer reviews the costs, benefits, and trade-offs of doing business. The salesperson's primary role is to efficiently provide information and make connections between the customer's needs and the company's capabilities.

2. *Buildup:* The relationship deepens in this time of growth, and both sides share information. The salesperson's role is to nurture trust through mutual understanding of business goals and building a common vision for growth.

3. *Maturity:* The firms have made a pledge to continue collaborating on a regular basis. The customer believes that pricing ups and downs will even out over the long term and no longer aggressively looks at alternatives. The salesperson's role is to direct and configure the relationship to best leverage joint investments.

4. *Decline:* One or both firms experience dissatisfaction and consider ending the relationship. Through honest communication and flexibility, a trusted salesperson may be able to repackage the relationship to restore satisfaction.

PRACTICAL IDEAS

Enhancing Exploration Efficiency: Energy should be focused on clear communication of how your company can meaningfully fulfill the customer's needs. Lay the foundation for future trust by going above and beyond what is expected with regard to sharing information and assistance.

Enhancing Buildup Efficiency: Create a trusting relationship. Make a major investment in actions that help reduce your customer's risks and uncertainties about you and your company's motives and intentions. Outline actions for creating a long-term, mutually beneficial relationship.

Enhancing Maturity Efficiency: At this point the relationship goes on autopilot. Trust building has been replaced by long-term contracts. Your primary role as salesperson is to continue delivering on the existing promises. Be on the outlook for ways to make Meaningful adjustments in the relationship whenever challenges arise.

Enhancing Decline Efficiency: At this stage the relationship is nearing an end. As the sales rep you can make the end process orderly or take aggressive action to repair customer perceptions or past mistakes. As with the exploration stage, it's best that actions be focused on Meaningful, tangible changes in the relationship rather than trying to simply exploit emotional trust.

Restage Sales Relationships: Use the introduction of major new products or services as an opportunity to freshen and revitalize your sales relationship. Consider changes to established rituals and routines. Consider rotating sales coverage to connect the customer with a new person. Use changes to freshen and lengthen the relationship.

{ 23 }
SCIENTIFIC
ADVICE

YOU CAN PREVENT CUSTOMERS FROM MAKING MISTAKES IN JUDGMENT

Customers often think they know more than they do. Fortunately, sources of error are not totally random. In particular, customers often overestimate the effectiveness of their current choice.

A portfolio of studies on the accuracy of customer knowledge finds that the errors adults make tend to follow predictable patterns. By understanding the patterns of errors, you are better able to make a Meaningful sales and marketing connection.

In general, adults overstate their knowledge level. They think they are smarter than they actually are. This is a natural tendency that has been shown in dozens of studies. This is why with a new product or service you must meaningfully exceed, not just meet, the performance of competitive offerings.

The harder the task, the greater the overstatement. Studies have found that when given a more difficult task, adults' overstatement is significantly greater than with easy tasks. Thus, the greater the difficulty of objectively assessing performance dimensions in your category, the more likely customers are to overstate the performance of their existing choice—in effect creating an artificially high standard that you need to exceed to win their business.

Over time, adults' confidence in their knowledge grows, when in fact the accuracy of their knowledge declines. This means that the longer customers have been using a certain product or service, the more difficult it will be to get a fair comparison between your new offering and the truth about their current choice. A classic example of this is adults' perception of how well they've done with their financial investments. Research shows that it's common for investors to remember the gains and to minimize the losses.

Successful sales and marketing requires that you be respectful of the fact that customers believe that their current product or service choice is significantly better than it is.

PRACTICAL IDEAS

Ask for Confidence Levels: To probe for truth, ask customers to define on a scale from 0 to 100 how confident they are on various conclusions or facts before them. The research indicates greater accuracy when confidence levels are added to judgments. In addition, the act of thinking consciously about confidence levels can cause a shift from mindlessness to mindfulness. And the more you get customers to stop and think, the greater the likelihood they'll respond to your more Meaningful message.

Ask How They Measure and Assess Performance: To encourage conscious thinking by customers, ask them to define their performance criteria. By defining the clear-decision criteria, you are then able to compare and contrast your superiority on objective dimensions. When you ask for performance criteria, you help organize the existing decision process to give yourself higher odds of success.

Show Respect for History: The longer a customer has used an established process, the greater his commitment to it, even when today's reality does not match his memory. To confront this situation, prepare a presentation that respectfully details the wisdom of the past yet articulates the natural progression of improvement that your offering represents. Use the customer's established thinking patterns as the fuel to move to your offering.

Shock Customers into Awareness: Amplify the total cost of continuing on the current path. For example, multiply the amount of extra time required to write checks by hand versus using electronic bill paying times the number of times checks are written in a ten-year period to quantify the advantage. Further, quantify the average number of mistakes through each system.

{ 24 }
SCIENTIFIC
ADVICE

YOU CAN TANGIBLY REDUCE CUSTOMERS' PERCEPTIONS OF RISK

Buyers often want to make a purchase, but they hesitate because it involves risk: risk of potential loss, risk of looking foolish, risk of losing money. Fortunately, researchers have identified the kinds of risk and specific tools for reducing risk perceptions.

Research was conducted with 472 customers on how effective various methods were in reducing the risk associated with new purchases. In the survey, risk was articulated in four manners: risk of *time loss* (wasting time with poor product), *hazard loss* (danger to health or safety), *ego loss* (feeling foolish for buying), and *money loss* (the bottom-line cost of failure).

The average effectiveness of each risk reduction method is shown below on a 0 to 200 scale.

Brand Loyalty: Bought and used before	194
Major Brand: Large, well-known brand	156
Free Sample: Trial size	113
Word of Mouth: From friends or family	106
Endorsements: By expert or celebrity	85
Money-Back Guarantee	81

The data show that real, first-person experience from having purchased and used a product before is orders of magnitude more credible than manufactured marketing methods like endorsements and money-back guarantees.

We end this chapter where we started it—cheerleading the value of FIRST-PERSON DEMONSTRATION. Nothing beats first-person experience to reduce risk and quantify the reward of purchasing your offering.

PRACTICAL IDEAS

Demo or Die: Do whatever it takes to get customers to see, feel, and touch your offering. Bring the demo to them. Bring them to the demo.

Validate Customers' Real Fears: Openly acknowledge and validate customers' fears. Don't belittle them as unimportant. Fears are deeply personal. What customers perceive as a fear is real to them. It's also a real barrier to you if you wish to make a sale. Validate the fear, then show how your company has thought through the issue and dealt with it. Show how your offering is designed to reduce the fear, risk, and uncertainty.

Empower Greed: Fear is emotional. The only business emotion stronger than fear is greed. You can often defeat customers' fear by evoking greed through defining the Meaningful, quantitative, and substantial benefit that they will receive. The bigger the promised benefit, the less likely customers are to worry about potential fears or losses.

Provide Overt Reasons to Address Real Issues: Review the four types of risk to identify fears that may exist but that are not articulated by customers. Address these issues directly.

> ★ *Hazard Loss:* Safety testing results and expert endorsements.
> ★ *Time Loss:* Testimonials that it was worth the effort to change.
> ★ *Money Loss:* A side-by-side balance sheet of the advantage.
> ★ *Ego Loss:* Documentation of popularity with key customers.

CHAPTER FIVE

LEADERSHIP
&
TEAMWORK

★ ★ ★ ★ ★

This chapter starts with advice regarding personal leadership and then provides ideas and advice regarding how to better focus your team. It ends with a "call to take action" on what you've learned on these pages.

By team, I mean sales and marketing staff. I also mean the finance, engineering, production, design, and even legal departments. As Ben Franklin said more than 200 years ago, **"We must all hang together or most assuredly we will all hang separately."**

As you've probably come to realize, great Marketing is about much more than creating advertising or sales pitches. Great Marketing is about serving as the ambassador between the customers and your product development, finance, and production teams.

Small-business owners have a big advantage in linking "what's possible to produce" with "what customers wish to purchase." As the chief of technology, sales, marketing, production, and finance, you need only talk to yourself.

Historically, corporate departments have worked in isolated silos. Today many companies have broken down the walls and enjoy the benefits of the whole company—whole-brain thinking.

Success in business, as in life, requires the expenditure of energy. If we're not careful, we can waste more energy in conflict with one another than on inventing, marketing, and selling ideas that can fulfill customer needs.

I'll be blunt—it takes courage to lead sales and marketing. To be successful, you must make absolute decisions about what you want your business to stand for, and just as important, what you don't want to be known for.

Your odds of success are tied directly to your ability to assemble the right team.

Steve Jobs, CEO of Apple Computer and Pixar Animation Studios, described what he looks for in people this way: "What's needed is people who have a sense of adventure. People who firmly believe in their product and mission. People who, win or lose, are all in it together with great enthusiasm."

The right people aren't clones of you. The right people have a range of skills and strengths different from your own. Your team should reflect a wide portfolio of talents. But everyone on it should have the same basic values structure.

I look for people with eclectic, eccentric backgrounds. I'm more likely to hire a rebel with a cause: people who distrust systems and established methods, people who are dissatisfied with the status quo and unearned authority, people who appreciate the option to lead. And don't be overly concerned when war breaks out between them. It's not necessary that your team always work together in peace, as long as there is mutual respect and a shared sense of purpose.

On the flip side, I don't want people who need to be told what to do. I look for people with initiative. I look, too, for people who yearn for adventure. I tell my newly hired to expect thrills and chills, spiced with plenty of highs and lows. I tell them we'll make up the rules as we go and that what exists today will look a lot different tomorrow. I tell them they'll be expected not only to do their job, but to look for ways to make it faster, smarter, quicker, and, yes, more fun.

Most of all, I look for huge reservoirs of enthusiasm. At one point during my stretch at Procter & Gamble, I was looking to add a manager to the Procter & Gamble Invention Team that I led. My strategy for interviewing was simple: I asked each potential candidate for advice and feedback on a couple of new-to-the-world ideas (some would say crazed ideas) I was working on.

Among the folks I interviewed was a bright, buttoned-down business major with impeccable credentials who explained in a logical fashion the flaws in my thinking. "Logic man's" reasoning was sound, his thinking totally rational. I got the impression that he felt he was doing me a favor by pointing out why I was wasting my time with the ideas.

Next!

Then I interviewed a guy with far less impressive credentials who introduced himself as Eric Schulz. When challenged with the ideas, his eyes got big. He sat on the edge of his chair. He embellished on my original ideas and, in fact, made them better. He identified many of the same flaws as Logic Man, but instead of seeing the problems as an end point, Eric saw them as a launch pad for new ideas. He figured that if we broke enough rules and attacked the mission with enough energy, it could be accomplished.

Halfway through the interview, I hired him. Eric went on to create a wide range of breakthrough products as part of the Procter & Gamble Invention Team. Later he made history at Coca-Cola and the Walt Disney Company transforming everything from Coke's Olympic Marketing approach to how Walt Disney packaged home videos.

{ 1 }
SCIENTIFIC
ADVICE

YOUR MOST POWERFUL MANAGEMENT TOOL
IS WHERE YOU PHYSICALLY SPEND YOUR TIME

Nothing sends a more powerful message about what is really important to your team than WHERE you spend your time. If your time is spent on the FRONT LINES with customers, then customers are MOST important. If your time is spent FACE TO FACE with your R&D team, then R&D is what is most important.

Today's world makes it possible for us to more easily connect to many people, in many places, quickly, whether by mail, e-mail, cell phone, conference call, or videoconference.

In this time of electronic communication, don't forget the impact of old-fashioned face-to-face conversation. When you take the time to drive or fly to a customer's office, you are telling him that you value him and his business.

A study of response rates from 497 independent research surveys found that in-person requests were successful 82 percent of the time versus 47 percent for surveys sent by mail.

Another study was conducted to measure the effectiveness of various methods of encouraging households to recycle. One group had a marketing message left on its front doorstep. The other group had them personally delivered by a neighborhood block leader. The weekly average recycling rates over ten weeks were 12 percent for those who had the materials left at their door versus 28 percent for those who had been personally contacted.

Clearly, making a personal contact makes a Meaningful difference.

Research also finds that increasing customer contact time can pay dividends with employees. Specifically, when employees spend more time with customers, it's been shown to increase their job satisfaction and commitment to their company.

PRACTICAL IDEAS

Examine Your Calendar to Assess Your Priorities: Review your calendar for the past six months. What percentage of your days did you spend face to face with customers? What percent was spent with existing customers? Looking even deeper, ask yourself what percentage of your days was spent learning about your marketing craft, your brand, or your industry?

As a rule of thumb, we feel that sales and marketing executives should spend 25 percent to 50 percent of their time either connecting with current or prospective customers or learning more about their craft. To marketing managers who see this as unrealistic, we challenge them to show us their success rate with business-development initiatives. The first step toward reducing failure is to know more—and nothing beats personal contact for increasing knowledge.

Jolt Your Business Success with a Traveling Blitz: Spark positive sales momentum by hitting the road and visiting twenty current or potential customers. The more concentrated the period of time, the more impact it will have on your wisdom, perspective, and results. An alternative approach is to work the front lines of a trade show or the front of your retail store.

As you visit with customers, listen naively. Instead of defending and debating, listen with awareness and empathy. Seek to identify opportunities for growth. In fact, ask customers and potential customers directly what you can do to win more of their business.

Invite Them to Visit You: Create and host events for your customers. Events can include user conferences, technology demonstrations, or even educational seminars. By planning and hosting an event that is Meaningful for your customers, you demonstrate your knowledge and commitment.

{ 2 }
SCIENTIFIC
ADVICE

DO'S AND DON'TS TO HELP YOUR TEAM THRIVE IN TODAY'S FAST-CHANGING MARKETPLACE

Research indicates that when it comes to creating a culture that embraces change, growth, and innovation, there are some very clear do's and don'ts.

Organizations are MUCH MORE SUCCESSFUL embracing change if the culture:

> ★ Values flexibility and risk taking
> ★ Is more focused on "what could be" as opposed to "preventing loss"
> ★ Likes to experiment, change, and learn new things
> ★ Encourages independent decision making by everyone

Organizations are MUCH LESS SUCESSFUL embracing change if the culture:

> ★ Values order, efficiency, stability, and "not making a mistake"
> ★ Has a rigid hierarchy and strong departmentalization
> ★ Doesn't encourage free flow of information
> ★ Uses a strong "central command-and-control" decision system

There is no doubt about the research. There is also no doubt about which kind of organization is the better place to work.

PRACTICAL IDEAS

Fish Stink from the Head Down: If you desire to change from a DON'T to a DO culture, it must come from the top. As Ben Franklin said, "Fish stink from the head down." Similarly, Dr. Deming said, "94 percent of errors are caused by the system—and only MANAGEMENT can change the system."

Read and Learn: These four books articulate better than I ever could what needs to be done to create a winning organization in the future. The books are listed in the order that I recommend reading them.

1. Peters, Tom. *Re-imagine!*
   (London: Dorling Kindersley, 2003)
2. Deming, W. Edwards. *The New Economics*, 2nd ed.
   (Cambridge, Mass.: MIT Press, 2000)
3. Florida, Richard. *The Rise of the Creative Class*
   (New York: Basic Books, 2002)
4. Enriquez, Juan. *As the Future Catches You*
   (New York: Crown Business, 2001)

{ 3 }
SCIENTIFIC
ADVICE

A THREE-SIDED "ATTACK" ON DISTRUST IS YOUR BEST BET WHEN IT COMES TO WINNING CUSTOMERS' TRUST, COMMITMENT, AND PURCHASING

Trust is a belief that the benefit being promised will be reliably delivered. Building the trust required to spark a purchase is a never-ending challenge.

Through thousands of disappointments, customers have developed high levels of distrust for new offerings. A primary job of sales and marketing is to build bonds of trust with new customers.

Research was conducted with 568 purchasing managers to quantify the core source of customer trust. Computer modeling identified that trust was dependent on three factors: 1.) trust of the company, 2.) trust of the salesperson, and 3.) trust of the product's performance.

On a relative basis, Trust in the company was 1.9 times more important than trust in the product. Trust in the salesperson was 1.7 times more important than trust in the product. Buyers understand that products come and products go. Consequently, they judge trust based on the more sustainable nature—their perception of the level that the company and the salesperson will stand behind the product in the event of problems.

While companies and salespeople were more important, trust in the product also correlated with overall sales success. Thus, the SMART ADVICE is a three-sided attack on distrust.

Challenge your sales and marketing team to leverage the corporate pedigree, their personal pedigree and the pedigree of the new product or service in presentations. Be relentless in articulating real reasons that customers should give you their trust, commitment, and purchasing.

PRACTICAL **IDEAS**

Build the Corporate Brand: Leverage your company's historical pedigree of success. Articulate the corporate culture, people, and processes that stand behind everything you do. Clearly and overtly explain how your new offering builds on your company's commitment to making a Meaningful difference for customers. Literally wear your brand on your sleeve. Embroider and imprint your corporate logo everywhere.

Provide Leadership to Your Industry: Participate in your industry trade association on key committees. At industry-wide trade shows, make a major statement about your commitment to the industry and your customers. At industry conferences, provide keynote speakers and seminar leaders and publicly release research that helps the industry grow.

Build Personal Trust by Being a Raving Company Fan: Be open and overt about your absolute trust in your corporation and its offering. Be a raving fan for your corporation. Stand solidly behind the virtues and meaningfulness of what your company offers. Customers observe your attitude toward your company. The more you believe in your company, the more they will, too.

As a New Company, Confront Your Disadvantage: As a new company, your lack of corporate pedigree is an immediate and considerable disadvantage. Confront this directly by linking your company's credibility with the credibility of your company founders or leadership. Offer introductory extended warranties, on-site technical assistance, or free samples.

Let Your Product Do the Talking: Let your product do the talking: Challenge customers to participate in real-world product demonstrations.

{ 4 }
SCIENTIFIC
ADVICE

WHEN YOU STATE YOUR PURPOSE WITH ABSOLUTE CLARITY, YOU CREATE A PERPETUAL ENERGY MACHINE OF MOTIVATION

The selling process involves high levels of self-confidence and self-awareness, which are eroded away when the salesperson's energy is distracted. Like a car that's running low on oil, a salesperson who is running on or near emotional exhaustion delivers significantly lower performance.

A study of 203 field salespeople was conducted to determine what dimensions correlated with emotional exhaustion or burnout. The research found that when it came to defining the potential for performance burnout, role clarity was 2.4 times more important than the simple question, "Are you satisfied/happy with your job?"

Successful sales and marketing requires more than simply calling on customers and closing sales to achieve a numerical goal. For full satisfaction and continued motivation, it must also involve a cause greater than commercial success—helping make customers' lives better.

Money can motivate in the short term. However, **for sustained success, there needs to be a sense of serving others, of helping make customers' lives better**. And that means a clear understanding of the Meaningful difference that your offering will make in customers' lives.

When people are uncertain of an offering's true impact, or don't believe in their offering, they waste energy chasing fears, doubts, and imaginary concerns. Over time they lose confidence and effectiveness.

PRACTICAL **IDEAS**

Define Your Meaningful Mission in Writing: In simple words, clearly define how your brand makes a Meaningful difference for customers. Be sure that everyone understands and agrees on this as the core reason for your brand's existence.

Be Clear about Whom You Serve: As Ben Franklin once said, "A man with one watch knows what time it is; a man with two watches is never sure." So, too, is the uncertainty, conflict, and ambiguity that a salesperson faces when serving multiple masters—customers, manufacturing, marketing, shareholders, etc.

The primary focus of sales should always be on the one with the money: the customer. It is the salesperson's job to match the company's offerings with the customer's needs. Everyone else within the organization should be aligned in support of the sales department.

Break Your Mission into Smaller Goals: Define your sales mission as a set of specific goals to accomplish. Alan Chambers, the first Englishman to walk to the North Pole without resupply, defined it to us this way: "Instead of focusing on the hundreds of miles, I focused on each day, each week's goal. With each accomplishment, my mental confidence grew despite the weakening of my physical condition."

When Change Is Needed, Be Quick and Overt: There will be times when a change in the sales mission is necessary due to competitive reactions or new strategies. When the change is inevitable, be quick, direct, and overt about it. Make it clear that "today our sales mission is different." Mean it and stick to it. This approach will help reduce the potential for uncertainty, ambiguity, and burnout of the sales staff.

{ 5 }
SCIENTIFIC
ADVICE

WHEN YOU'RE THE "EASIEST COMPANY TO DO BUSINESS WITH," YOU CREATE DIFFICULTIES FOR YOUR COMPETITION

A key detail to "sweat" with your team is how easy it is to do business with your company. When a customer calls, are they helped INSTANTLY? When they have a question, is it answered on the first call, or does it take a series of calls to gain resolution?

A study of 463 retail shoppers found that customers' intentions to shop a store again are based on the merchandise value they will receive minus the stress, time, and effort costs they perceive. Merchandise value (what you're selling) was the primary driver of intentions to revisit. However, as the customer's perception of shopping stress, time, and effort increased, the net intentions to shop there again decreased.

Challenge your team to drive out customer stress!

Stress has a direct impact on decision quality. Frozen in fear is a truth. Fear-focused stress reduces the ability to think rationally. College students were challenged to solve fifty word problems. The test group was put under stress as they had one hand wired to an electronic device that they were told would deliver a mild and harmless shock sometime randomly during the test.

After participants had answered fifteen questions the test was stopped and their results checked. Stopping early made it possible to conduct the test without delivering shocks to any of the students. Participants who were under no stress were significantly more accurate in their responses to the word problems. Overall, those under no stress had an accuracy rate of 59 percent, compared with 36 percent for those under any type of stress.

PRACTICAL **IDEAS**

Total Value Equals Value Received Minus Hassles: To maximize total value, focus your energy on improving what customers receive as well as decreasing the cost and hassles involved with purchase and usage. The easier it is for customers to do business with you—to see, select, and purchase your goods and services—the greater their likelihood of repurchasing.

Help Customers Consider All Information: Stress has been found to cause people to make a decision before reviewing all the important information. Develop sales materials that lay out the options in simple side-by-side comparisons. Seek ways to make it nearly impossible for your customers to make a mistake when evaluating your offering versus competition.

Help Customers Think in a More Organized Fashion: Stress has been found to cause people to review alternatives in a disorganized and ineffective fashion. Make your retail store, your brochure, your Web site easy to understand, easy to search, and easy to find what your customers are looking for.

Help Customers Reduce Impulsive Decisions: Stress has been found to cause people to make short-term impulsive decisions without considering longer-term consequences. When your offering has long-term advantages, make that clear to customers at the start of the conversation. Explain that your company's mission is to "reduce total cost" or to "reduce long-term cost." It's important to provide data that confirm what you promise.

Use a Phased Approach to Reduce Stress and Conflict: A phased approach to big changes can help reduce customers' stress and internal corporate conflict. Develop programs of step-by-step tests and validations of the Meaningful difference that your product or service offers. Then, when broad-scale change occurs, it's already been validated as reliable in your customers' situation.

{ 6 }
SCIENTIFIC
ADVICE

BE BRAVE AND BE BOLD, BUT BE SENSITIVE TO THE STRESS ON YOUR TEAM

Just as stress causes your customers to make bad decisions, **change of any kind can create stress within your team**.

In life, events such as marriage or a new house are seen as creating positive stress. Events such as death in the family or loss of job create negative stress. The accumulation of stress, even positive stress, has been found to predict vulnerability to heart attacks or other health problems.

A research study of 526 sales representatives found that critical sales stresses follow a similar pattern. Critical sales stressors were defined as winning or losing a major customer, assignment to a different sales territory, new product introductions, major pricing changes, major change in the company's management team, or the entry of a major new competitor.

The study showed a direct link between the stresses a salesperson had faced in the previous three months and his level of role conflict and role ambiguity. Recall that research has found that role conflict and ambiguity have a direct, negative impact on sales success.

Encouragingly, the research also showed that training interventions can have a dramatic impact on reducing salesperson stresses. With education, role-playing, sales meetings, and individual one-on-one coaching, salespeople's confidence can be enhanced and stress reduced.

A growing business is one that changes to exploit new technological and customer opportunities. However, our success at exploiting the opportunities may well lie in how well we help our team handle the inevitable transitions.

PRACTICAL **IDEAS**

Teach Your People Why: Often we tell our people what to do but neglect to tell them why. By providing an in-depth explanation of why, you build a foundation of trust and commitment to your cause. Couple the why with the overt benefits that the change will bring about. It doesn't guarantee that everyone will agree; it simply means that you now have something to manage change against.

Explain the Consequences of Not Changing: The real workers in your organization likely have their heads down and eyes focused on accomplishing the specific assignment before them. To them, change is a disruption that reduces their daily routine. As the visionary, it's your job to clearly explain why continuing your current path of action is not sustainable.

Use Major Changes to Speed Meaningful Growth: It's human nature to dislike the uncertainty and chaos that come with change. However, when change does occur, for whatever reason, it provides an opportunity to make even more Meaningful changes. For example, the change associated with adding new products to your sales staff's responsibilities can be used as a time to add a more reliable customer-needs reporting system. Use change as an opportunity to realign or set new goals.

Stay in Touch with Everyone: When major change happens to a group, a department, or an entire organization, the old adage "no news is good news" just doesn't apply. The best way to unleash employees' strengths is to empower them with knowledge. Everyone is affected by critical events; use communication to keep everyone on track.

{ 7 }
SCIENTIFIC
ADVICE

MISTAKES ARE YOUR BEST OPPORTUNITY TO SHOW CUSTOMERS YOUR GREATNESS

Mistakes or customer complaints are a great opportunity for you to showcase your genuine commitment to service. Your attitude, attention, and commitment to resolving customer complaints can have a huge impact on customer satisfaction and increase the likelihood of their recommending your company to others.

A study was conducted of some 1,356 bank customers over twenty months. Customers were asked a series of questions regarding their overall satisfaction and their intentions to recommend the bank to their friends.

Analysis found that when customers had a problem and it was handled in a positive manner, their overall satisfaction ratings increased by 22 percent and their attitude ratings on giving positive word-of-mouth recommendations increased by some 58 percent.

Conversely, when customers' problems were handled in an unsatisfactory manner, their overall satisfaction ratings declined by 31 percent and their attitude ratings on giving positive word-of-mouth recommendations declined by some 16 percent.

Importantly, customers have a limited tolerance for repeated failures. Customers who complained twice about the same problem rated the bank very low despite two successful handlings of the same problem. (Overall satisfaction ratings declined 51 percent and word-of-mouth ratings declined by 47 percent versus the ratings provided before either problem occurred.) **Net: A customer respects you when you satisfactorily address a problem, but they have no tolerance for repeated incompetence.**

PRACTICAL **IDEAS**

Make Customer Service a Prime Marketing Tool: Align your team to thinking of customers who complain as a prime marketing opportunity. Explore their needs and issues. Resolving their problems with excellence lays the groundwork for future business from them. Listening closely to the problems they articulate also helps you identify product design and quality issues that others may also be experiencing yet are too timid to say anything about.

Encourage Complaints: Encourage your team to encourage customers to tell you about anything and everything that might not have been as good as they expected. Research indicates that nearly 70 percent of customers who experience problems with products do not complain to the seller.

Empower everyone to gather, record, and communicate customer impressions. Often customers will informally vent their concerns with receptionists or product delivery or installation staff and yet not make formal complaints.

Search for Root Causes of Failure: When a failure happens, identify whether it's a one-time honest mistake or a systemic flaw of your system or product. The only way to accomplish this analysis is to have a written record of customer issues and impressions. Create a system that signals an alarm when a repeated failure occurs.

Reward Speed of Recovery: Track speed of resolution. The faster your team can resolve a little problem, the less chance it will become a big problem.

{ 8 }
SCIENTIFIC
ADVICE

GLASS, CHINA, AND YOUR BRAND'S REPUTATION ARE EASILY BROKEN AND NEVER WELL MENDED

Reviews by movie critics and publications like *Consumer Reports* have long had an impact on customer purchasing behavior. The Internet has exploded the quantity of reviewers. Anyone with a Web site or a blog can post his opinion about a product or service for all to see.

The impact of negative reviews on your reputation is much greater than you would expect.

Research was conducted on customers' perceptions of a pair of reviews for a consumer electronics device tested by an "independent consumer-testing laboratory." For half of the subjects, the evaluation reported favorably on the product. For the other half, a negative review was provided.

As expected, a negative review caused customers' pre-use product expectations and purchase intent to decline significantly.

Customers were then provided with an opportunity to personally try the product. After usage of the same product, consumers gave lower purchase intention ratings (1.7 versus 2.4) when they had viewed the negative review, even though the product performed satisfactorily. The negative review by an independent third party was trusted more than the consumer's own personal experience with the product.

A second part of this same study documented how a positive marketing message couldn't help a bad product. The product was modified to purposely perform poorly. In this case it made no difference whether a positive or negative review was seen; purchase intent declined significantly.

The marketing messages and information customers receive have an impact that goes beyond simply persuading customers to purchase. **What customers perceive about a product or service directly impacts how they evaluate their product experience.**

PRACTICAL **IDEAS**

Fast Response: When a negative product review or customer service incident occurs, get your team to move quickly. Speed of response reduces the potential for damage to your brand and also communicates your concern and commitment to customers. The passage of time with no response is quickly elevated in customers' minds as justification of their growing dissatisfaction.

Teach Your Team to Admit Mistakes Quickly and Take Specific Action: In the course of normal business, mistakes will happen. Customers understand this. The key is how you react to them. When mistakes happen, admit them quickly and explain what you are going to do to make it right. If you don't know the cause of the mistake, say so. And explain clearly when you will get back to the disgruntled customer or the member of the media with additional information.

Manage Positive Momentum: Momentum is the elusive fuel for driving your sales and marketing. When your momentum is positive, everything you do has an extra boost of energy behind it. Momentum is built through a series of unexpected positives. The size of the positive news isn't as important as the frequency of the news. Manage for positive momentum by metering out the good news. But do not get tempted into a cycle of mindless news for news's sake. Your customers will soon tune you out.

Create Your Own Positive News: Positive news can create positive momentum. You can and should create your own positive news by entering contests, celebrating industry awards received by your staff, seeking endorsements, pitching the news media on feature stories, and applying for and receiving patents.

{ 9 }
SCIENTIFIC
ADVICE

NEVER, EVER, EVER GIVE UP!

Teach your team to follow the advice of Winston Churchill: "Never, ever, ever give up!" **When your offering can make a real difference for your customers, fight to the death for the righteousness of your cause.** This exhortation is not simply a cheerleading exercise; it's scientific advice.

The truth is that customers' opinions about purchasing are NOT absolute predictors of behavior

A sample of 4,707 customers' intentions versus actual purchases was tracked for a wide variety of products sold in grocery stores. Of those who indicated there was virtually NO CHANCE of their purchasing a product, nearly 1 out of 5 changed their mind and actually did purchase (19 percent). Of those stating they DEFINITELY WOULD purchase, only about 2 out of 5 actually did purchase (43 percent).

Customers' intentions have a clear relationship with behavior. Customers who are more interested are more likely to purchase. However, in the absolute, customers have a poor ability to predict their actual behavior. When asked to project their opinion, they don't appear to think deeply about the benefits and costs of the option presented to them.

This is good news. This research means that hope lives when you have a genuinely great offering. Just because you get a no doesn't mean you're destined to fail. Just because customers state that they are not likely to do something doesn't mean that with additional information or perspective they won't change their minds.

On the flip side, when a customer says yes, CLOSE THE SALE. **Don't do your victory dance until you have the order firm and the cash in hand.**

PRACTICAL IDEAS

Make the Unfamiliar Familiar: The more unique your offering, the more likely a customer is to give a stereotypical response to your request. However, as the research shows, a no is not necessarily a no. And the more times they consider your request, the more familiar it becomes and the more likely they are to feel comfortable saying yes. The key is to not create annoyance with your repeated presentations.

Delivering News: When you bring news, you open the door for reconsideration. Each time you present your offer, showcase another piece of news. Consumers respond to news. Leverage the revelation factor when communicating newness to capture attention.

The Power of Simplicity: When dealing with seemingly complex products or ideas, translate them into simple steps to circumvent a no. Often a no is a call for more information or clarity. The simpler and clearer the overt benefits of your offering, the easier it is for customers to say yes.

Manage Your Return on Investment: Measure the return you get on each presentation. Classify customers according to their current stage of sale—and quantify the cost and return on each subsequent marketing effort. You can also increase your profitability by learning how to eventually cut customers from your call list, database, and target marketing when the return no longer justifies expense.

Close the Sale: Turn positive momentum into a closed sale. When a customer indicates an inclination to purchase, make it as easy as possible for them to turn their intentions into reality.

{ 10 }
SCIENTIFIC
ADVICE

BRAND LOYALTY IS BUILT FROM PREDICTABILITY OF SATISFACTION AND EXPERTISE

The purchase and usage of a new brand either creates or destroys customer trust. Research among 280 customers found a significant correlation between level of brand trust and customer loyalty. Loyalty in this case is defined as agreement with statements such as, "I intend to keep buying this brand," "I often tell my friends how good this brand is," and "If this brand is not available when I'm shopping, I will wait to get it or search for it somewhere else."

Mathematical modeling of what drives customer trust identified three elements of trust to focus your team on:

1. *Brand Satisfaction* (importance score 0.46): The first and foremost stage of building trust is your performance versus expectations. No amount of marketing hype can overcome the importance of product performance.

2. *Brand Predictability* (importance score 0.21): The second stage of building brand trust is continuation of the satisfaction delivered during stage one. When customers experience reliable delivery of their initial satisfaction, they develop sustainable trust.

3. *Brand Expertise* (importance score 0.11) The third stage of building brand trust is the big-picture view of the brand's level of overall competence. It's about the brand's expertise relative to the offerings of competition. **When customers REALLY BELIEVE that you are best in class, their loyalty becomes Meaningful and unquestioning.**

PRACTICAL **IDEAS**

Consider Your Stage of Trust with Each Customer: Organize your customers based on what stage of trust they have in you and your brand. Develop sales and marketing programs that help each customer move to the next level of Meaningful trust.

Ensure Brand Satisfaction: Brand satisfaction is about having a healthy balance between marketing promises and real performance. It's our opinion that the most successful marketing sets an expectation level that is about 80 percent of reality. This leaves 20 percent above and beyond the marketing promise for exceeding customer expectations.

Ensure Brand Predictability: Ship quality predictably. Maintain open and frequent communication with customers to ensure no surprises for the customer. Predictability means communication, not mindless consistency. When even the simplest improvements or changes are made, from packaging to formulation to performance, be overt in communicating the changes.

Ensure Brand Expertise: Communicate clearly the Meaningful skill your company has in discovering, developing, and delivering world-class products or services. Provide technical seminars and newsletters discussing ongoing research efforts. Proudly share reviews and endorsements by industry thought leaders and the media.

Consistency Builds Trust: Monitor all communications of the brand with respect to the three factors just described by focusing on consistency. Once Mindless Marketing tactics take root, they are hard habits to break. Adopt a quality-control mentality with regard to communications so that your brand's credibility doesn't erode with mindless inconsistencies.

{ 11 }
SCIENTIFIC
ADVICE

THE LESS YOUR TEAM BELIEVES THAT IT KNOWS, THE MORE IT WILL GROW

Wisdom comes from direct and experiential education. When we first start on the job or assemble our team, our wisdom resources grow rapidly with new knowledge and experiences.

The risk with stored wisdom is that if it's not continually refreshed and reviewed, it gets out of step with today's reality. Research shows that **the more educated and experienced you feel you are, the greater your chances of misunderstanding your customers**.

A study was conducted of 540 industrial product buyers along with the sales representatives who called on them. It found that those salespeople with the most accurate understanding of their customers' true expectations were significantly more successful salespeople.

However, the study also found a negative correlation between accuracy of knowledge and experience in the industry, age, and formal education level. This suggests that while younger and less experienced salespeople have less overall wisdom, what they do have is a more accurate perception of the marketplace.

A separate study by AT&T found that salespeople are often poor judges of their customers' opinions. The researchers showed four new product options to salespeople and their customers. The salespeople were instructed to respond the way they thought their customers would. The results varied widely. The collective opinion of the sales force was not at all predictive of its customers' true opinions.

We start out our careers as wide-eyed and innocent. We're sponges—sucking up knowledge and wisdom. If we're not careful, as we age, we end up arrogant and out of touch with the reality of our marketplace.

PRACTICAL **IDEAS**

Observe How Customers Really Use Your Offering: Get your team up, out, and with customers. Observe firsthand the usage of your offering. Follow your offering from the moment of purchase to end consumption. Do this on a real-time, first-person basis. Ignore findings that confirm your perceptions. Look instead for knowledge that contradicts them.

Set Up Annual Vision Meetings with Customers: Set up annual reviews with customers to discuss their situation with your team. Review where they are now and where they see their business going. Listen closely to what they say and, more important, what they don't say. Often it's what customers don't say that's revealing about their challenges and opportunities.

Before these meetings, use the Internet to read the latest news stories about your customer's company. Read closely what senior management is saying in their briefings with financial markets. The more aware you are of these issues, the more freely your customers will help you "connect the dots" and understand how the broader company's vision may or may not affect you and your company.

Share with customers your company's long-term vision, as well. In particular, paint a picture of hope. Define clearly your long-term commitment to growth and development.

Stop Assuming: When your company's management has questions on the impact a new initiative will have with customers, don't automatically answer in your usual way. Rather, have your team hit the phones and the street to ask customers. Ask clearly and listen openly to what the real experts, your customers, think and believe.

{ 12 }
SCIENTIFIC
ADVICE

THE THIRTEEN VIRTUES OF MEANINGFUL MARKETING

Ben Franklin developed a program for personal improvement. He distilled all he knew about life into thirteen core virtues. So too, I've synthesized the wisdom on these pages into what we believe are the Thirteen Virtues of Meaningful Marketing. I recommend that, as Franklin suggested, you focus your attention and the attention of your team on one virtue each week seeking to live it to its fullest. Within a year, you and your team will have completed four cycles and Meaningfully changed your approach to sales and marketing.

All thirteen virtues are important for improving marketing and sales results. However, I've highlighted five that I believe are the most important for you personally. To be very OVERT, these are the five secrets to my personal success in life and business.

The Thirteen Virtues of Meaningful Marketing

1. *Learn:* Get smarter EVERY WEEK regarding your customers and your vocational craft.
2. *Pioneer:* Lead your marketplace and leave copying to those without the brains or courage to be original.
3. *Overtness:* Let a customer say no because what you offer doesn't apply to him. But never let a customer say no because he doesn't understand what overt benefit you're offering.
4. *Clarity:* Strive for self-evident clarity in all communications.
5. *Focus:* Eliminate the irrelevant.
6. *Credibility:* Continuously enhance customer trust in you, your company, and your brand.
7. **Authenticity: Communicate with honesty and integrity who and what you REALLY are.**
8. *Demonstrate:* Let your product, service, or idea talk for itself.
9. *Persistence:* Never, ever, ever give up when you are pursuing the right thing in the right way.
10. **Measurement: Use measurement to guide improvement of your SYSTEMS of thinking and doing.**
11. *Service:* Dedicate yourself to serving the genuine needs of your customers.
12. **Write, Write, Write: Use the WRITTEN WORD to define and refine your thinking.**
13. *Courage:* **Be BOLD. Be BRAVE. Leave a legacy.**

{ 13 }
SCIENTIFIC
ADVICE

YOUR SUCCESS COMES FROM SKILL MULTIPLIED BY EFFORT

The advice and ideas on these pages are designed to help you KNOW MORE. However, the success you realize comes from skill multiplied by effort. To make a Meaningful difference, you must run advertisements, knock on doors, or make sales calls. You must get yourself actively involved and take conscious action.

The rules of basic multiplication indicate that no matter how effective the truths in this book are in improving your skills, if you exert zero effort in applying them, the net result is still zero. **No action guarantees no result.**

The greater the change you act on, the greater your chances of realizing a Meaningful improvement in your sales and marketing results. In theory this is easy. In reality it's not. It's not because fear holds us back. The greater the change, the greater your fear will be. And research finds a direct negative correlation between fear level and productive creativity.

Fear is rational and fear is emotional. Fear is social and fear is personal. Fear is conscious and fear is subconscious.

Paradoxically, when our sales and marketing results are their absolute worst and our fear is at its highest is exactly the time when we have the greatest need for boldness and courage.

To make a difference in the world, you must get up, get out, read, listen, learn, and take action. And that takes courage. The following quote from Winston Churchill puts courage in perspective: **"Courage is rightly esteemed the first of human qualities, because . . . it is the quality which guarantees all others."**

PRACTICAL **IDEAS**

Make the Unknown Known: The unknown is one of the primary sources of fear. What we don't see or don't know scares us. Reducing this fear is as simple as opening ourselves to learning. Reading this book has taught you about the root causes of sales and marketing failure. Beyond this book, you can learn more by talking to others, by analyzing data trends, and by speaking with customers directly.

Fail Fast and Fail Cheap: We can reduce our fear by first prototyping and testing our thinking in small-scale, low-cost environments. Test a new sales pitch with your next ten sales calls, in person, via the phone, at trade shows, or through your next direct mail campaign. Continuously seek opportunities to test, try, and learn.

Do the Right Thing: There is no more powerful way to find courage than when you focus your energies on making a *Meaningful* difference for your customers. When we serve others *meaningfully*, we find the sort of authentic and genuine courage that helps us confront and defeat the biggest fears.

NOW Would Be the Right Time to Start: Right now. This instant. This moment would be the perfect time to take a blank piece of paper and identify three concrete things you will do over the next seven days. Don't know what to do? Look at what you've written in the white spaces of the book. Don't have anything written? Then look at the pages you turned down. Something sparked you to turn them down. Look back to create ideas to leap your marketing forward. I'm consciously keeping the time short to build momentum. By setting some simple goals and achieving success—week by week, like water eroding stone—you will find your way to Meaningful Marketing success.

CHAPTER SIX

MEANINGFUL MARKETING VS. MINDLESS MARKETING

★ ★ ★ ★ ★ ★ ★

Meaningful Marketing is about honesty.

Meaningful Marketing is about respecting your customers' intelligence.

Meaningful Marketing is about having the courage to focus your energies and resources on developing offerings that make a real difference in your customers' lives. And because you are trying to make money, it also means having the courage to offer a product or service that is meaningfully different from what your competition offers.

Meaningful Marketing's focus is on the acquisition of new customers. This is because the acquisition of new customers has been found to be the key driver of long-term growth.

Mindless Marketing is the alternative to Meaningful Marketing. It's about using sales and marketing persuasion tricks as opposed to the actual merits and virtues of your offering to make the sale.

Mindless Marketing is often easier to execute, as it involves changes only to your sales and marketing promotional tactics. Meaningful Marketing is harder to execute, as it requires the support of your R&D, manufacturing, and operations departments in the design, development, and delivery of a product or service that provides a Meaningful difference versus competition.

Mindless Marketing is mass hypnotism. It is about getting customers to take the path of least resistance. It's also about coaxing entranced customers to follow your spell and do as you say. When under a trance, customers will do the unthinkable— so long as the trance is not broken.

For example, when a teenager buys a bizarre article of clothing because it's trendy, it's best that he not think about how it will look in his photo album years from now.

When parents pay too much for a hot Christmas toy, it's best that they not think about it rationally.

When you're buying a cool new car model—and paying above sticker price—it's best that you not make a rational evaluation of the price versus your resale value.

When we blindly follow the latest business fad without thorough evaluation of its relevance, we, too, are acting mindlessly.

With Mindless Marketing, customers are encouraged not to think. They are encouraged to simply follow the persuasive marketing path laid before them like pigs to a slaughterhouse, following only the tail of the pig in the lead, never looking up and asking whether the herd they follow is going to a place they really want to go.

Meaningful Marketing is about having an adult conversation. It's about a dialogue between you and your customers regarding what they will receive, enjoy, and experience as a result of committing their time, energy, and money.

Meaningful Marketing is about telling the story of your genuine patentable breakthroughs. Mindless Marketing is about exaggerating the performance of mediocre products or services.

Meaningful Marketing is a conscious choice. Mindless Marketing is about impulse purchasing.

Meaningful Marketing leads to customers who become your biggest cheerleaders. Mindless Marketing–driven purchases often lead to buyer's remorse.

A MEASURABLE DIFFERENCE

A singular focus on Meaningful or Mindless Marketing can be successful in the short term. The difference between the two lies in longer-term success rates and profitability. A study of 901 new products found that when an offering was sold with a thoughtful, Meaningful approach, it was successful (as defined by five-year-plus survival in the marketplace) some 53 percent of the time versus only 24 percent when a Mindless Marketing approach was used.

Even more significant, the data indicate that when customers make thoughtful purchases, they are more loyal and less demanding of pricing discounts. The research found that 18 percent of brands sold using a primarily Meaningful message were vulnerable to pricing pressures versus 90 percent of those sold using a primarily Mindless Marketing approach.

Research also indicates that on average, **new products that primarily leverage Meaningful Marketing realize first-year sales results that are more than 50 percent higher** than for new products sold without Meaningful differences.

Rarely are marketing efforts singularly Meaningful or Mindless. Most are a blend. When I work with innovation teams, on new products and services, I encourage them to first focus their attention on the Meaningful aspects of the new offerings. After having defined their core brand story then they should add some Mindless Marketing promotional spin to speed awareness building.

TODAY'S CUSTOMERS ARE SHORT ON BANDWIDTH

The driving force for both Meaningful Marketing and Mindless Marketing is the overwhelming number of options today's customers have.

Today's customers are mentally overwhelmed. The average supermarket has more than 40,000 different items in it.

The total of all printed knowledge is estimated to double every five years.

In 1993 the *New York Times* estimated that humanity publishes as many words each week as it did in all of human history up to 1800.

Three times as many magazines exist today as did twenty years ago (5,500 consumer titles alone).

More than 120,000 new books are published every year!

A report by the 3M Company indicated the average adult is exposed to some 3,000 marketing messages a day! Recent news reports place the number as high as 4,000.

The American Academy of Pediatrics estimates that children take in more than 20,000 television commercials a year.

With increasing numbers comes massive fragmentation. According to Nielsen Media Research, the number one network television show is viewed by ever-shrinking audiences. In the 1950s, the top show reached 62 percent of the adult population; in the 1970s, 31 percent; in the 1990s, 21 percent.

The prestigious McKinsey & Company consulting firm reported recently, "There has been an explosion in consumer touch points fueled by the Internet and other technology-driven channels like call centers, ATMs, WebTV, and kiosks. This has created an array of options for building brand presence. At the same time, marketing space everywhere has experienced increased clutter, narrowed audiences, and escalating costs."

Potential customers have limited capacity to perceive and process your message. They have only so many channels of mental bandwidth. It's estimated that customers use only 2 percent of the available information that presents itself each day.

When your customers' craniums are occupied with real-life deadlines and stresses, your message can all too easily fail to get honest consideration. Customers ignore Meaningless Marketing messages and focus their attention on either substance-rich Meaningful messages or the path of least resistance offered by Mindless Marketing messages such as low price.

TRENDS DRIVING THE IMPORTANCE OF MEANINGFULNESS

Three mega-trends–*increasing education, population aging, and growing free-market access*–make it urgent that you include as much Meaningfulness in your marketing as possible.

Increasing Education: In 1960 barely four in ten Americans age twenty-five or older had graduated from high school. Today eight out of ten have high school diplomas. In 1960 fewer than one in ten Americans had graduated from college; today nearly three out of ten have.

With increasing education comes the ability and the desire to know more and to make more Meaningful purchasing decisions.

Population Aging: Between 1960 and 2000, the number of adults age sixty-five and over doubled from 18 million to 37 million. It's expected to double again by the year 2040.

With increasing age comes greater experience in separating factual marketing messages from mindless hype.

In the 1950s and 1960s, when television advertising was new, you could tell the youthful, uneducated American population to "buy this," and they would. Today, an older, wiser population is more discerning. They want to know precisely how your offering will make a Meaningful difference in their lives.

Growing Free-Market Access: The last mega-trend multiplying the importance of Meaningfulness is the true free-market knowledge network created by the World Wide Web. The Web makes it easy for everyone to research, compare, and contrast purchase options. And when customers have greater access to information, they make more Meaningful purchasing decisions.

In the past, an advertiser could use Mindless Marketing tricks to generate significant sales before he was found out. Today, **the Internet has improved customers' ability to quickly uncover the truth behind marketing hype and gimmicks.**

Today, people routinely search the Internet when they consider a major purchase like a new car. In the future, as advanced computer intelligence systems become available, computerized "alter egos" will be programmed to think through and make many Meaningful purchasing decisions that we don't have time for.

A similar explosion in free-market access occurred from 1870 to 1910 as 5.1 million phones were installed, the railroads developed into an efficient national network, and the concepts of "brands" and national advertising were born. In just four years, from 1871 to 1875, the number of brands with registered trademarks grew nearly tenfold, from 121 to 1,138.

The net effect of this growth in free-market access and the concurrent industrial revolution was a nearly 30 percent decrease in the consumer price index. As customers had more access to knowledge, manufacturers' prices went down.

Today, companies that don't offer a Meaningful difference are facing similar pressure on both their pricing and bottom-line profits.

Together, increased education, population aging, and growing free-market access mean good news for manufacturers of products or services that make a Meaningful difference for customers. The same factors are bad news for those seeking to live solely on Mindless Marketing trickery and gimmicks.

The business world is becoming aware of the size of the shift that is occurring. Sadly, recent business books have been focused primarily on finding methods for more effectively "tricking" customers into purchasing. Business people are encouraged to build "buzz" by such methods as giving free gifts to college students to order and "talk up" the virtues of various brands of alcohol. Marketers are being encouraged to trick customers into giving them "permission" to propagandize them—a modern version of the age-old "foot in the door" persuasion technique.

Mindless Marketing tricks can succeed for a short time. However, that period of time is getting shorter as knowledge access grows. The real return on investment with Mindless Marketing tricks is shrinking rapidly.

THE SEARCH FOR MINDLESS MARKETING TRICKS IS ENDLESS

The search for new Mindless Marketing techniques is never-ending. It's driven by the fundamental human desire to find a shortcut to success.

It's also driven by a lack of faith in a brand's fundamental value, quality, and virtues. In our experience, we've found a near one-to-one relationship between managers' faith in their brand and their pursuit of Meaningful Marketing communications.

A rich source of Mindless Marketing gimmicks is new advertising vehicles. The theory is that where you place your advertisement is more important than what you communicate. Common sense and academic research find this concept flawed. Direct mail, print advertising, and television advertising research have repeatedly shown that *what you say is more important than where you say it.*

THE EVOLUTION FROM MEANINGFUL MARKETING TO MINDLESS MARKETING

Virtually all businesses start out with a product or service concept that provides a Meaningful difference for customers. This difference is the basis for the creation of the new business venture.

If the difference in the product or service is sufficiently Meaningful and it is marketed with sufficient investment of time, energy, and money, the company thrives.

In a free market, as a company grows, it soon attracts opportunistic competitors with neither the imagination nor the courage to create a meaningfully different offering of their own. The clones attempt to replicate the wonder of the original at lower prices. As they succeed, what started out as a Meaningful marketplace quickly degenerates into a game of Mindless Marketing price maneuvering.

I'm an advocate for competition. However, I'd like that competition to be customer focused, and that means thinking deeply about discovering and developing ideas that make a Meaningful difference for customers.

Innovation clones can be beat through a continuous commitment to innovation. As your competition works its way through the technical, production, distribution, marketing, and patent challenges associated with your current innovation, you bravely invent even more Meaningful products and services.

It's a simple matter of grow or die. If your offering today is virtually the same as it was twenty-four or twelve months ago, your enterprise is dying. One day you will look up and discover the world has changed and your business has vanished.

If your marketplace is competitive, you will see the change first in your bottom line. Clones will first turn your Meaningful difference into a commodity and encroach on your profits. Later, when you can't go any lower in price, you will either 1.) go out of business, 2.) sell out to a competitor in hopes of "economies of scale," or 3.) reinvent yourself to restore your competitive advantage.

If you have a virtual monopoly in your marketplace, it will happen much more slowly, but it will be just as devastating. One day you will find that your monopoly in the world of buggy whips, stagecoaches, or even carburetors for cars has been made irrelevant by the train, automobile, or fuel injection.

To survive and thrive in the world of business requires a continuous commitment to inventing ideas that can make a Meaningful difference in our customers' lives.

MEANINGFUL LOYALTY

With Meaningful Marketing, customers consciously decide to purchase your offering. If their level of satisfaction with your actual product or service is equal to or exceeds their expectations, they develop trust.

With repeated satisfaction, further trust develops—until the customer arrives at a point of Meaningful loyalty. The customer has consciously made your offering her choice. She has meaningfully decided to forego future thinking and, from then on, as long as she's satisfied, continues to purchase your offering.

We often order a Coca-Cola, a Budweiser, ranch dressing on our salad, or cheesecake for dessert because we've made a Meaningful decision that they are our preferred choice.

We often stay at specific hotel chains, rent cars from a certain company, and fly specific airlines not by conscious choice; rather, we've made a Meaningful decision to commit our purchases to specific brands to grow our frequent-traveler accounts.

In the United States, we often visit mega-size stores like Wal-Mart and Home Depot because, through repeated experiences, we've proved to ourselves that "they're cheap" and/or "they'll have everything I'm looking for." One research study found that nearly 80 percent of consumer purchases of laundry detergent were based on a Meaningful loyalty decision process. In-store observations revealed that customers picked up and examined only one product option and spent only thirteen seconds from when they entered the laundry detergent aisle to when they made a purchase.

On one hand, meaningfully loyal customers are a major advantage for incumbents who enjoy it. It's an annuity that, as long as your quality is maintained and competition doesn't create a more Meaningful offering, pays dividends day after day, year after year.

On the other hand, meaningfully loyal customers are a major barrier to growth for new companies, products, or services.

ACHIEVING MEANINGFUL LOYALTY

How easy it is to achieve meaningfully loyal customer relationships varies depending on your category and marketplace competitive set.

When customers have made numerous purchases and been satisfied with results, they will develop Meaningful loyalty.

When the risk of making the wrong choice is not large—and price differences are minimal—customers will often commit to Meaningful loyalty based on historical brand choices without thinking further.

When customers believe your category of goods and services is stable and unchanging, they will allocate less of their mental processing ability to making decisions and will repeatedly purchase with Meaningful loyalty. Academic research has found that consumers exerted considerably less effort in choosing peanut butter than in choosing a pair of running shoes or an automobile.

When the risk of disappointment has a high cost, the consumer is making a decision for the first time in your category, or your industry is undergoing considerable change, then customers are less likely to give up their right to think. They are more likely to make purchases on a Meaningful basis.

STEALING YOUR COMPETITION'S MEANINGFULLY LOYAL CUSTOMERS

Meaningful loyalty is similar to Mindless Marketing buying in that customers are on autopilot. The difference between the two is their level of conscious choice.

To steal your competitors' meaningfully loyal customers, you have to THINK BIG. You have to offer a big and bold, Meaningful benefit difference.

Starbucks broke the hypnotic trance that Folgers and Maxwell House coffee enjoyed by delivering a superior, total-coffeehouse experience. Starbucks has thrived by changing the rules of coffee consumption.

Samuel Adams from the Boston Beer Company broke the trance that Budweiser, Miller, and Coors had by delivering a lager with richer taste and greater hops content. Today, they've transformed an industry and continue to lead the craft brewing segment of the market.

Southwest Airlines broke the trance of the larger airlines through a spirited delivery of greater value. They even created a meaningfully different frequent-flyer program. Instead of making customers collect and redeem miles, Southwest keeps its Rapid Rewards program customer-focused and simple.

> *Rapid Rewards is the frequent flyer program you can use. Rapid Rewards is the only major frequent-flyer program that doesn't limit the number of seats available for Award Ticket use. If a seat is available on the flight you want to take, it's yours!*
>
> *Fly just 8 roundtrips, and you receive a free ticket! Rapid Rewards counts credits, not long miles. If you take just eight (8) roundtrips (or receive 16 credits) within 12 consecutive months [you] receive a free Award Ticket on Southwest Airlines, no matter how far you fly or what fare you pay.*

MEANINGFUL MARKETING DRIVES YOUR SENSE OF MISSION

The purpose of most business enterprises is to realize profits for shareholders through the sale of a product or service that fulfills a need.

Thus, **the Meaningful difference that is your primary marketing message is also the mission of your company**. It's your reason for existence. It follows, then, that

- ★ Gaining awareness of your Meaningful difference is the purpose of your advertising, public relations, sales, and marketing departments.
- ★ Production and delivery of your brand's Meaningful difference is the purpose of your product supply operation.
- ★ Protecting your brand's Meaningful difference from illegal copying by competitors is the purpose of your legal department.
- ★ Identifying new dimensions of your Meaningful difference is the purpose of your brand's research and development department.

Research shows that when new products are meaningfully matched to customers' needs, a chain reaction of synergies occurs, from higher profit margins to greater cross-department synergy to faster development and delivery to the marketplace.

Srully Blotnick documented the opportunity for significant personal profits from the pursuit of meaningfulness. He studied the careers of 1,500 business-school graduates from 1960 to 1980. At graduation, 1,245 of the students were categorized as being focused on making money, while 255 of the graduates were focused on pursuing something that was personally Meaningful to them. Twenty years later, there were 101 millionaires. One came from the first group, one hundred from the second.

MINDLESS MARKETING TACTICS HAVE A VALUABLE ROLE

Mindless Marketing tricks are very effective in helping you get your customer's attention and to convert that attention into purchases. The key is that they be used as an ADDITION to your Meaningful Marketing tool kit as opposed to as a replacement.

When trying to get your direct mail piece opened, a deadline or personalization can be a powerful tactic.

When trying to get customers to stop at your tradeshow booth, being likable and stressing the mass popularity of your offering can be a valuable tactic.

When trying to sell teenagers, catching a popular music trend, clothing trend, or leveraging a celebrity can be a successful tactic.

Mindless Marketing tactics are fun to create and execute. In the spirit of P.T. Barnum they add excitement and entertainment. The challenge is that without a Meaningful satisfaction of customers' needs the "flash" excitement that attracted interest soon turns to boredom and you can see your sales evaporate likewise.

THE MINDLESS MARKETING DRUG ADDICTION

The most popular method of creating sales with Mindless Marketing is through pricing trickery. Academic research and real-world experience shows that selling at a lower price than competition generates sales.

A large price differential can be quite successful in breaking the trance of customers who are mindlessly purchasing competitive products. The challenge is that research also indicates that many

customers who make a mindless switch based on price stop purchasing when the price goes up.

A research study of major brands found that promotional events—price reductions, coupons, etc.—generated enough incremental profits to cover costs only 16 percent of the time.

Mindless Marketing price promotions are like a drug addiction. It's difficult to stop, and when you do, it's painful.

In a bold move in the 1990s, Procter & Gamble went to an everyday low pricing strategy and virtually eliminated temporary price reductions and coupons. The net effect was an effective increase in net price and an average 18 percent loss of market share across the twenty-four categories studied during a seven-year period.

Most grocery store packaged goods do not offer a Meaningful difference versus competition. Customers realize this. That's why, when the price of an item goes up and a less expensive alternative is available, a significant number of customers switch. In the case of Procter & Gamble, scanner data indicates this equaled 17 percent of its customers.

Interestingly, not all customers left at once. Customers kept purchasing P&G brands despite the effective price increase. These were the loyal customers that had been created over the years as a result of the Meaningful differences that the brands had historically provided. The decline that P&G experienced was temporary. Its enhanced focus on Meaningful Marketing, through elimination of discounting, a new commitment to product excellence, and Meaningful advertising, led to outstanding sales and profit growth by 2003.

It's even possible to use massive advertising awareness levels to create temporary Mindless Marketing success. Massive investments of advertising can spark impulse purchasing for a period of time. But the effect is temporary. A study of fifty-five successful advertising campaigns found that when media spending in support of the commercials stopped, the incremental sales also stopped. In the year after advertising was stopped, 31 percent of the sales gained from the advertising was lost. In the second year, 59 percent of the gain was lost. And remember—this is for the successful commercials. Studies indicate two-thirds of all commercials generate no significant growth in sales at all. Net: Sustainable success through out spending, out shouting, and out promoting your competition is a clear long shot.

By making your offering and your marketing message more Meaningful, a more genuine customer connection is established.

You dramatically increase your ability to realize a sustainable return on your investment.

THE MEANINGFUL MARKETING IDEAL DEVELOPMENT CYCLE

In an ideal world, your offering will continuously offer a Meaningful difference versus competition. That's nice, but in the real world, customers, technologies, and markets are dynamic and ever-changing. The reality is that you'll experience a never-ending succession of peaks and valleys in the normal cycle of innovation and competitive introductions.

In the peak times, you will have superiority. In the valleys, you will have parity or, worse yet, a deficit versus competition. If you deliver a reliable pattern of Meaningful differences, most of your customers will remain loyal to you during the valley periods.

David Ogilvy neatly summed up the secret to new product success:

> **Most new products fail because they are not new enough. They do not offer any perceptible point of difference—like better quality, better flavor, better value, more convenience, or better solutions to problems.**

GET UP! GET OUT! GET GOING!

While some managers are addicted to pursuing Mindless Marketing persuasion, I'm optimistic that within every corporation there are independent thinkers with a passion for doing work that matters.

When he appeared as a guest on our *Brain Brew* radio program, Drayton Bird, former vice chairman of the Ogilvy & Mather Direct Agency, defined the purpose of business learning this way:

> Essentially what you want to do in business is to be able to go in every morning and say today I can do better than I did yesterday. And the only way you are going to do that is if you know more. And the only way you are going to know more is if somebody tells you more.

★ ★ ★ ★ ★ ★ ★ ★ ★ ★ ★

The book you've just read is a meaningful step toward KNOWING MORE. **Now it's up to you to get up, get out, and get going with applying your new knowledge!**

Benjamin Franklin said many things. There is, however, one Franklin quote that precisely captures the essence of Meaningful Marketing. It's how I lead my life. It's how I end every book and every lecture. It's so important to me that when I'm laid to rest on Prince Edward Island in the historic St. Thomas Church cemetery in Springbrook, it will be carved on my tombstone. It's my challenge to you as you go forth into the world of marketing. His command was this:

**"Up, Sluggard, and waste not life;
in the grave will be sleeping enough."**

TECHNICAL APPENDIX

The articles referenced are a combination of laboratory experiments, marketplace experiments, and secondary data analyses of real-world results. I prefer studies that are conducted in real-world situations. However, in some cases the noise and chaos of everyday life make laboratory studies the preferred research methodology.

Statistical data, impartially analyzed, allow us to separate illusions from reality. With statistics, we can quantify the likelihood that what we're observing is a reproducible and reliable truth versus a coincidental, one-time random event.

Casino gambling shows what can happen to our human decision-making abilities when random events become mixed up with long-term trends. When we win, we often draw cause-and-effect conclusions that lead us to false truths about the factors that put a few bucks in our pocket. In our excitement, we try to make it happen again—whether by using a certain slot machine, standing in a particular location at the roulette table, or wearing a certain pair of so-called lucky socks. But in chasing these false truths, we quickly lose what we've won and then some. The long-term statistical edge of the casinos is reproducible. Our short-term hunch is not.

Sir Isaac Newton once said, "If I have seen further it is by standing on the shoulders of Giants." In the case of *Jump Start Your MARKETING Brain*, this was literally true, as I used academic journals in the fields of sales, marketing, and psychology as the primary sources of data for this book.

I reviewed well over 2,000 academic articles as potential sources for Scientific Advice. Every month brilliant breakthroughs are published in peer-reviewed academic journals. Except for a lucky few that cross over to the popular press, awareness of these research findings never reaches the front-line business people who could really use them to grow their businesses.

A primary criterion in selecting research articles to reference was their practical application to front-line sales and marketing managers.

Secondarily, I screened articles for what I call "**elegance of design and data output.**" As this book is intended for a broad audience, I had a bias toward those studies that could be easily explained in layman's terms.

There are usually multiple studies that confirm each truth. To keep the text clean, I've chosen to highlight the one or two that I believe are the most representative of the academic literature and also the most easily understood.

I've supplemented the academic articles with the results of our own Eureka! Ranch research efforts. Original research efforts included analysis of commercially available data, like the panel data collected by IRI (Information Resources, Inc.) on the purchasing behavior of some 50,000 households on more than 9,000 products.

Original research also involved analysis of proprietary data sets. One such study involved the factors that separate new products that survive long term (for five-plus years) from those that fail and are killed (discontinued by the manufacturer). This study involved 901 new products and is called the Darwin 900 in honor of the famous naturalist Charles Darwin's theory of evolution by natural selection—that is, survival of the fittest.

PROPRIETARY DATA SETS

Darwin 900: The Darwin 900 is a study Chris Stormann and I conducted by tracking the survival rate of 901 products from their initial introduction over a period of five years.

In the development of this data set, Chris and I removed products that were seasonal, short-term promotions, or were potentially undercapitalized efforts from small or start-up companies. Thus, by their nature, products in the Darwin 900 were branded products from major consumer products companies. The products in this data set comprised a cross-section of the grocery category and included food and beverages, health and beauty aids, and cleaning products.

One of our greatest challenges in working with this data was agreeing to a reliable definition of success versus failure. In other studies I found that success was typically a self-reported response by the manufacturers (see Cooper and Kleinschmidt, 1993). However, as the old corollary warns, one company's definition of success is another's failure, and I desired a more objective definition.

After considering many options, we settled on a Darwinian survival definition. We defined success as still being in production and distribution after five years. I can't say for sure that all products that are still on the shelf are successful for their manufacturers. However, it is a reasonable assumption that those that were discontinued were unsuccessful.

To determine whether the products were alive or dead, Chris and I visited major chain grocery stores. If we didn't find the products, we then checked the brand or corporate Web site, or in cases where additional uncertainty existed, we called the corporation directly.

The general analysis method we used to score products for the Darwin 900 was a secondary variable and then "t-tests" to quantify significant differences between products that were still alive (on the shelf) and those that were dead (had been discontinued). Having determined statistical significance, we conducted a secondary sorting to provide the simplified description of results for this book. The process involved sorting the concepts into tertiles based on the secondary variable. Then the percentage surviving was calculated within each of the three groups, and the results from the top versus bottom tertile group were indexed. Thus, if 45 percent of the products in the top tertile survived and 30 percent in the bottom tertile survived, we reported that you had a 50 percent greater chance of success by following the researched approach.

The primary source of the secondary data was ratings of marketing materials content by multiple raters on more than two hundred archetype attributes related to Meaningful Marketing versus Mindless Marketing dimensions (for example, the number of benefits promised). The raters were validated for standardized accuracy and reliability.

Another source of secondary data was consumer research results. This data had been gathered among a nationally representative set of consumers within the first few weeks of introduction. Consumers rated the products in concept form based on the original marketing materials, package copy, point-of-sales copy, or print advertising on such variables as purchase interest, product uniqueness, and price sensitivity. We used these data to calculate the impact of Meaningful versus Mindless Marketing persuasion. Specifically, the difference was empirically derived as the combination of purchase interest and uniqueness perception scores from consumer ratings. We then looked at the significance of various levels of each archetype trait that comprised the top and bottom 10 percent of the Meaningful difference distribution. Concepts in the top 10 percent are defined as Meaningful, the bottom 10 percent as Mindless Marketing Tricks. In the case of the Mindless Marketing–focused concepts, the primary customer selling points were the classic Mindless Marketing approaches of "foot in the door" (low initial price) and "consistency and authority" (leveraging a major brand name).

Note to researchers: The Darwin 900 data set contains proprietary client data that is covered under confidentiality agreements. I am legally restricted from sharing it publicly. However, I am committed to continuing research and am interested in partnering on further academic studies as resources allow. Please e-mail me at Doug@DougHall.com with your proposal or area of interest in joint research.

Scanner 9000: The Scanner 9000 is a study by the Merwyn Technology division of the Eureka! Ranch. This data set used information from the 1999 marketing fact book *Consumer Knowledge Suite* produced by IRI (Information Resources, Inc., Chicago, Ill.). It contains annual purchasing data from some 50,000 households that are provided with an in-home UPC scanner. The analysis conducted here used 9,804 carefully screened products. The data were analyzed by subcategories, categories, and brand basis, then evaluated by multiple regression to compare the relative importance of standardized regression coefficients for various marketplace variables of interest.

Chapter 1. Marketing Strategy

Marketing Strategy—Advice & Ideas 1
Steenkamp, Jan-Benedict E. M., and Katrijn Gielens. "Consumer and Market Drivers of the Trial Probability of New Consumer Packaged Goods." *Journal of Consumer Research*, Volume 30 (December 2003): pp. 368–384.

Shorter, Frank. NPR *Morning Edition* commentary. 2004.

Marketing Strategy—Advice & Ideas 2
Hall, D. *Jump Start Your BUSINESS Brain.* Cincinnati: Brain Brew Books, 2001.

Kahle, L. R., D. B. Hall, and M. J. Kosinski. "The Real-Time Response Survey in New Product Research: It's About Time." *Journal of Consumer Marketing*, 14:3 (1997): pp. 234–248.

Im, Subin, and John P. Workman Jr. "Market Orientation, Creativity, and New Product Performance in High-Technology Firms." *Journal of Marketing*, Volume 68 (April 2004): pp.114–131.

Marketing Strategy—Advice & Ideas 3

Kim, W. Chan, and Renee Mauborgne. "Blue Ocean Strategy." *Harvard Business Review*, October 2004, p. 80.

Romaniuk, Jenni, Andrew Ehrenberg, and Byron Sharp. "Perceptions of Differentiation, Do Users See Their Brand as Different?" *Research & Development Initiative* Report 17 (October 2004).

Marketing Strategy—Advice & Ideas 4

Im, Subin, and John P. Workman Jr. "Market Orientation, Creativity, and New Product Performance in High-Technology Firms." *Journal of Marketing*, Volume 68 (April 2004): pp.114–131.

Narver, John C., Stanley F. Slater, and Douglas L. MacLachlan. "Responsive and Proactive Market Orientation and New-Product Success." *Journal of Product Innovation Management* (2004) 21: pp. 334–347.

Srinivasan, Raja, Gary L. Lilien, and Arvind Rangaswamy. "Technological Opportunism and Radical Technology Adoption: An Application to E-Business." *Journal of Marketing*, Volume 66 (July 2002): pp. 47–60.

Marketing Strategy—Advice & Ideas 5

Kalyanaram, G., W. T. Robinson, and G. L. Urban. "Order of Market Entry: Established Empirical Generalizations, Emerging Empirical Generalizations, and Future Research." *Marketing Science*, 14:3, Part 2 of 2 (1995): pp. G212–G221.

Robinson, W. T. "Sources of Market Pioneer Advantages: The Case of Industrial Goods Industries." *Journal of Marketing Research*, 25:1 (February 1988): pp. 87–94.

Robinson, W. T., and C. Fornell. "Sources of Market Pioneer Advantages in Consumer Goods Industries." *Journal of Marketing Research*, 22:3 (August 1985): pp. 305–317.

Urban, G. L., T. Carter, S. Gaskin, and Z. Mucha. "Market Share Rewards to Pioneering Brands: An Empirical Analysis and Strategic Implications." *Management Science*, 32:6 (June 1986): pp. 645–659.

Data Source: Information Resources, Inc. *Client Study: How Advertising Works for New Products.* (Chicago, 2001).

Marketing Strategy—Advice & Ideas 6
Boyd, T. C., and C. H. Mason. "The Link Between Attractiveness of 'Extrabrand' Attributes and the Adoption of Innovations." *Journal of the Academy of Marketing Science*, 27:3 (July 1999): pp. 306–319.

Golder, P. N., and G. J. Tellis. "Will It Ever Fly? Modeling the Takeoff of Really New Consumer Durables." *Marketing Science*, 16:3 (1997): pp. 256–270.

Hall, D. *Jump Start Your BUSINESS Brain.* Cincinnati: Brain Brew Books, 2001.

Marketing Strategy—Advice & Ideas 7
Hall, D. *Jump Start Your BUSINESS Brain.* Cincinnati: Brain Brew Books, 2001.

Kahle, L. R., D. B. Hall, and M. J. Kosinski. "The Real-Time Response Survey in New Product Research: It's About Time." *Journal of Consumer Marketing*, 14:3 (1997): pp. 234–248.

Marketing Strategy—Advice & Ideas 8
Supphellen, Magne, Oivind Eismann, and Leif E. Hem. "Can Advertisements for Brand Extensions Revitalize Flagship Products?" *International Journal of Advertising*, 23 (2004), pp.173–196.

Van Heerde, Harald J., Carl F. Mela, and Puneet Manchanda. "The Dynamic Effect of Innovation on Market Structure." *Journal of Marketing Research*, Volume XLI (May 2004): pp. 166–183.

Marketing Strategy—Advice & Ideas 9
Anschuetz, N. "Why a Brand's Most Valuable Consumer Is the Next One It Adds." *Journal of Advertising Research*, 42:1 (January–February 2002): pp. 15–22.

Jones, John Phillip. *When Ads Work.* New York: Lexington Books, 1995.

Lau, G. T., and S. H. Lee. "Consumers' Trust in a Brand and the Link to Brand Loyalty." *Journal of Market-Focused Management*, Volume 4 (1999): pp. 341–370.

Sharp, Byron, Erica Riebe, John Dawes, and Nick Danenberg. "A Marketing Economy of Scale—Big Brands Lose Less of their Customer Base than Small Brands." *Marketing Bulletin*, 13 (2002), Research Note 1.

Data Source: Eureka! Ranch. Based on marketplace scanner data analysis of 9,804 established brands: *Merwyn Technology Internal Data Set: Scanner 9000 Study* (Eureka! Ranch, 2001).

Marketing Strategy—Advice & Ideas 10

Ailawadi, K. L., and S. A. Neslin. "The Effect of Promotion on Consumption: Buying More and Consuming It Faster." *Journal of Marketing Research*, 35:3 (August 1998): pp. 390–398.

Kahle, L. R., D. B. Hall, and M. J. Kosinski. "The Real-Time Response Survey in New Product Research: It's About Time." *Journal of Consumer Marketing*, 14:3 (1997): pp. 234–248.

Mela, C. F., K. Jedidi, et al. "The Long-Term Impact of Promotions on Consumer Stockpiling Behavior." *Journal of Marketing Research*, 35:2 (May 1998): pp. 250–262.

Data Source: Eureka! Ranch. Based on marketplace scanner data analysis of 9,804 established brands: *Merwyn Technology Internal Data Set: Scanner 9000 Study* (Eureka! Ranch, 2001).

Marketing Strategy—Advice & Ideas 11

Boatwright, P., and J. C. Nunes. "Reducing Assortment: An Attribute-Based Approach." *Journal of Marketing*, 65:3 (July 2001): pp. 50–63.

Iyengar, S. S., and M. R. Lepper. "When Choice Is Demotivating: Can One Desire Too Much of a Good Thing?" *Journal of Personality and Social Psychology*, 79:6 (December 2000): pp. 995–1006.

Marketing Strategy—Advice & Ideas 12
Gartner, W. B., and R. J. Thomas. "Factors Affecting New Product Forecasting Accuracy in New Firms." *Journal of Product Innovation Management*, 10:1 (January 1993): pp. 35–52.

Marketing Strategy—Advice & Ideas 13
Calder, B. "Cognitive Consistency and Consumer Behavior." In *Perspectives in Consumer Behavior*, edited by H. H. Kassarjian and T. S. Robertson, 247–263. Glenview, Ill.: Scott, Foresman & Co., 1973.

Doob, A., J. M. Carlsmith, et al. "Effect of Initial Selling Price on Subsequent Sales." *Journal of Personality and Social Psychology*, 11:4 (1969): pp. 345–350.

Marketing Strategy—Advice & Ideas 14
Arndt, J. "A Test of the Two-Step Flow in Diffusion of a New Product." In *Perspectives in Consumer Behavior*, edited by H. H. Kassarjian and T. S. Robertson, 331–342. Glenview, Ill.: Scott, Foresman & Co., 1973.

Daghfous, N., J. V. Petrof, and F. Pons. "Values and Adoption of Innovations: A Cross-Cultural Study." *Journal of Consumer Marketing*, 16:4 (1999): pp. 314–331.

Dwyer, S., J. Hill, and W. Martin. "An Empirical Investigation of Critical Success Factors in the Personal Selling Process for Homogenous Goods." *Journal of Personal Selling and Sales Management*, 20:3 (Summer 2000): pp. 151–159.

Keller, E., and J. Berry. *The Influentials*. New York: The Free Press, 2003.

Marketing Strategy—Advice & Ideas 15
Kahle, L. R., D. B. Hall, and M. J. Kosinski. "The Real-Time Response Survey in New Product Research: It's About Time." *Journal of Consumer Marketing*, 14:3 (1997): pp. 234–248.

Reinartz, W. J., and V. Kumar. "On the Profitability of Long-Life Customers in a Noncontractual Setting: An Empirical Investigation and Implications for Marketing." *Journal of Marketing*, 64:4 (October 2000): pp.17–35.

Data Source: Eureka! Ranch. Based on marketplace scanner data analysis of 9,804 established brands: *Merwyn Technology Internal Data Set: Scanner 9000 Study* (Eureka! Ranch, 2001).

Marketing Strategy—Advice & Ideas 16
Gupta, S. "Impact of Sales Promotions on When, What, and How Much to Buy." *Journal of Marketing Research*, 25:4 (November 1988): pp. 342–355.

Kotler, P. "Mathematical Models of Individual Buyer Behavior." In *Perspectives in Consumer Behavior*, edited by H. H. Kassarjian and T. S. Robertson, 541–560. Glenview, Ill.: Scott, Foresman & Co., 1973.

Marketing Strategy—Advice & Ideas 17
Bettman, J. R., M. F. Luce, and J. W. Payne. "Constructive Consumer Choice Processes." *Journal of Consumer Research*, 25:3 (December 1998): pp. 187–217.

Drolet, A. "Inherent Rule Variability in Consumer Choice: Changing Rules for Change's Sake." *Journal of Consumer Research*, 29:3 (December 2002): pp. 293–305.

Marketing Strategy—Advice & Ideas 18
Alpert, F. H., M. A. Kamins, and J. L. Graham. "An Examination of Reseller Buyer Attitudes Toward Order of Brand Entry." *Journal of Marketing*, 56:3 (July 1992): pp. 25–37.

Marketing Strategy—Advice & Ideas 19
Keller, K. L., S. E. Heckler, et al. "The Effects of Brand Name Suggestiveness on Advertising Recall." *Journal of Marketing*, 62:1 (January 1998): pp. 42–51.

Data Source: Eureka! Ranch. Based on marketplace analysis of 900 new product launches: *Merwyn Technology Internal Data Set: Darwin 900 Study* (Eureka! Ranch, 2001).

Marketing Strategy—Advice & Ideas 20
Sullivan, M. "Brand Extension and Order of Entry." Report No. 91-105. Boston: Marketing Science Institute, 1991.

Data Source: Eureka! Ranch. Based on comparison of Merwyn marketplace predictive models for established brands versus new brands: *Merwyn Technology Internal Data Set: Merwyn Comparison Study* (Eureka! Ranch, 2001).

Marketing Strategy—Advice & Ideas 21
Clancy, K. J., and R. S. Shulman. *Marketing Myths That Are Killing Business: The Cure for Death Wish Marketing*, pp. 275–278. New York: McGraw-Hill, 1994.

Marketing Strategy—Advice & Ideas 22
Enriquez, Juan. *As the Future Catches You*. New York: Crown Business, 2001.

Rust, R. T., C. Moorman, and P. R. Dickson. "Getting Return on Quality: Revenue Expansion, Cost Reduction, or Both?" *Journal of Marketing*, 66:4 (Oct. 2002): pp. 7–24.

Marketing Strategy—Advice & Ideas 23
Hellofs, L. L., and R. Jacobson. "Market Share and Customers' Perceptions of Quality: When Can Firms Grow Their Way to Higher Versus Lower Quality?" *Journal of Marketing*, 63:1 (January 1999): pp. 16–25.

Marketing Strategy—Advice & Ideas 24
Pieters, Rik, and Michel Wedel. "Attention Capture and Transfer in Advertising: Brand, Pictoral, and Text-Size Effects," Volume 68 (April 2004): pp. 36–50.

Marketing Strategy—Advice & Ideas 25
Carpenter, G. S., and K. Nakamoto. "Consumer Preference Formation and Pioneering Advantage." *Journal of Marketing Research*, 26:3 (August 1989): pp. 285–298.

Kuester, S., C. Homburg, and T. S. Robertson. "Retaliatory Behavior to New Product Entry." *Journal of Marketing*, 63:4 (October 1999): pp. 90–106.

Marketing Strategy—Advice & Ideas 26
Dowling, G. R., and M. Uncles. "Do Customer Loyalty Programs Really Work?" *Sloan Management Review*, 38:4 (Summer 1997): pp. 71–82.

Estell, L. "Loyalty Lessons." *Incentive*, 176:11 (November 2002): pp. 38–41.

Kearney, T. J. "Frequent Flyer Programs: A Failure in Competitive Strategy, with Lessons for Management." *Journal of Consumer Marketing*, 7:1 (Winter 1990): pp. 31–40.

Timson, J. "Fliers, Airlines Love Their Point Programs." *The Toronto Globe and Mail*. February 1, 2003.

Marketing Strategy—Advice & Ideas 27
Wotruba, T. R. "The Effect of Goal-Setting on the Performance of Independent Sales Agents in Direct Selling." *Journal of Personal Selling and Sales Management*, 9:1 (Spring 1989): pp. 22–29.

Chapter 2: Marketing Message

Marketing Message—Advice & Ideas 1
Hall, D. *Jump Start Your BUSINESS Brain*. Cincinnati: Brain Brew Books, 2001.

Lau, G. T., and S. H. Lee. "Consumer's Trust in a Brand and the Link to Brand Loyalty." *Journal of Market-Focused Management*, Volume 4 (1999): pp. 341–370.

Data Source: Eureka! Ranch. Based on marketplace analysis of 900 new product launches: *Merwyn Technology Internal Data Set: Darwin 900 Study* (Eureka! Ranch, 2001).

Marketing Message—Advice & Ideas 2
Anderson, R. E. "Personal Selling and Sales Management in the New Millennium." *Journal of Personal Selling and Sales Management*, 16:4 (Fall 1996): pp. 17–32.

Hall, D. *Jump Start Your BUSINESS Brain*. Cincinnati: Brain Brew Books, 2001.

Liu, A. H., and M. P. Leach. "Developing Loyal Customers with a Value-Adding Sales Force: Examining Customer Satisfaction and the Perceived Credibility of Consultative Salespeople." *Journal of Personal Selling and Sales Management*, 21:2 (Spring 2001): pp. 147–156.

McLaughlin, K., and C. Halsall. "Marketing Spending Effectiveness: How to Win in a Complex Environment." *McKinsey Marketing Practice Working Paper*, June 2000.

Data Source: Eureka! Ranch. Based on marketplace analysis of 900 new product launches: *Merwyn Technology Internal Data Set: Darwin 900 Study* (Eureka! Ranch, 2001).

Marketing Message—Advice & Ideas 3

Hall, D. *Jump Start Your BUSINESS Brain*. Cincinnati: Brain Brew Books, 2001.

Data Source: Eureka! Ranch. Based on marketplace analysis of 900 new product launches: *Merwyn Technology Internal Data Set: Darwin 900 Study* (Eureka! Ranch, 2001).

Marketing Message—Advice & Ideas 4

Lau, G. T., and S. H. Lee. "Consumer's Trust in a Brand and the Link to Brand Loyalty." *Journal of Market-Focused Management*, Volume 4 (1999): pp. 341–370.

Trout, J. "Differentiate or Die." *Ad Age*, November 22, 1999.

Data Source: Eureka! Ranch. Based on marketplace analysis of 900 new product launches: *Merwyn Technology Internal Data Set: Darwin 900 Study* (Eureka! Ranch, 2001).

Marketing Message—Advice & Ideas 5

Lau, G. T., and S. H. Lee. "Consumer's Trust in a Brand and the Link to Brand Loyalty." *Journal of Market-Focused Management*, Volume 4 (1999): pp. 341–370.

Data Source: Eureka! Ranch. Based on marketplace analysis of 900 new product launches: *Merwyn Technology Internal Data Set: Darwin 900 Study* (Eureka! Ranch, 2001).

Marketing Message—Advice & Ideas 6

Kanouse, D. E. "Explaining Negativity Biases in Evaluation and Choice Behavior: Theory and Research." *Advances in Consumer Research,* Volume 11 (1984): pp. 703–708.

Data Source: Eureka! Ranch. Based on marketplace analysis of 900 new product launches: *Merwyn Technology Internal Data Set: Darwin 900 Study* (Eureka! Ranch, 2001).

Marketing Message—Advice & Ideas 7

Data Source: Eureka! Ranch. Based on marketplace analysis of 900 new product launches: *Merwyn Technology Internal Data Set: Darwin 900 Study* (Eureka! Ranch, 2001).

Marketing Message—Advice & Ideas 8

Vorhies, D. W., and M. Harker. "The Capabilities and Performance Advantages of Market-Driven Firms: An Empirical Investigation." *Australian Journal of Management*, 25:2 (September 2000): pp. 145–171.

Vorhies, D. W., M. Harker, and C. P. Rao. "The Capabilities and Performance Advantages of Market-Driven Firms." *European Journal of Marketing*, 33:11/12 (1999): pp. 1171–1202.

Data Source: Eureka! Ranch. Based on marketplace analysis of 900 new product launches: *Merwyn Technology Internal Data Set: Darwin 900 Study* (Eureka! Ranch, 2001).

Marketing Message—Advice & Ideas 9

Dwyer, S., J. Hill, and W. Martin. "An Empirical Investigation of Critical Success Factors in the Personal Selling Process for Homogenous Goods." *Journal of Personal Selling and Sales Management*, 20:3 (Summer 2000): pp. 151–159.

Edell, J. A., and R. Staelin. "The Information Processing of Pictures in Print Advertisements." *Journal of Consumer Research*, Volume 10 (June 1983): pp. 45–61.

Percy, L., and J. R. Rossiter. "Mediating Effects of Visual and Verbal Elements in Print Advertising Upon Belief, Attitude, and Intention Responses." In *Advertising and Consumer Psychology*, edited by L. Percy and A. G. Woodside, pp. 171–196. Lexington, Mass.: Lexington Books, 1983.

Marketing Message—Advice & Ideas 10
Anderson, R. E. "Consumer Dissatisfaction: The Effect of Disconfirmed Expectancy on Perceived Product Performance." *Journal of Marketing Research*, 10:1 (February 1973): pp. 38–44.

Marketing Message—Advice & Ideas 11
Cooper, R. G., and E. J. Kleinschmidt. "Major New Products: What Distinguishes the Winners in the Chemical Industry?" *Journal of Product Innovation Management*, 10:2 (March 1993): pp. 90–111.

Marketing Message — Advice & Ideas 12
Chandy, Rajesh K., Jaideep C. Prabhu, and Kersi D. Antia. "What Will the Future Bring? Dominance, Technology Expectations, and Radical Innovation." *Journal of Marketing*, Volume 67 (July 2003): pp.1–18.

Cox, D., and A. D. Cox. "Communicating the Consequences of Early Detection: The Role of Evidence and Framing." *Journal of Marketing*, 65:3 (July 2001): pp. 91–103.

Keller, P. A., and L. G. Block. "Increasing the Persuasiveness of Fear Appeals: The Effect of Arousal and Elaboration." *Journal of Consumer Research*, Volume 22 (March 1996): pp. 448–459.

Meyerowitz, B. E., and S. Chaiken. "The Effect of Message Framing on Breast Self-Examination Attitudes, Intentions, and Behavior." *Journal of Personality and Social Psychology*, 52:3 (1987): pp. 500–510.

Marketing Message — Advice & Ideas 13
Settle, R. B., and L. L. Golden. "Attribution Theory and Advertiser Credibility." *Journal of Marketing Research*, 11:2 (May 1974): pp. 181–185.

Smith, R. E., and S. D. Hunt. "Attributional Processes in Promotional Situations." *Journal of Consumer Research*, Volume 5 (December 1978): pp. 149–158.

Marketing Message—Advice & Ideas 14
Bedell, G. "Persuading People to Buy Your Product." *Incentive*, 175:2 (February 2001): pp. 70–71.

Meyvis, T., and C. Janiszewski. "Consumers' Beliefs about Product Benefits: The Effect of Obviously Irrelevant Product Information." *Journal of Consumer Research*, 28:4 (March 2002): pp. 618–635.

Marketing Message—Advice & Ideas 15
Keller, S. B., M. Landry, J. Olson, et al. "The Effects of Nutrition Package Claims, Nutrition Facts Panels, and Motivation to Process Nutrition Information on Consumer Product Evaluations." *Journal of Public Policy and Marketing*, 16:2 (Fall 1997): pp. 256–269.

Scammon, D. L. "Information Overload and Consumers." *Journal of Consumer Research*, 4:3 (1977): pp. 148–155.

Marketing Message—Advice & Ideas 16
Mukherjee, A., and W. D. Hoyer. "The Effect of Novel Attributes on Product Evaluation." *Journal of Consumer Research*, 28:3 (December 2001): pp. 462–472.

Marketing Message—Advice & Ideas 17
Alwitt, L. F. "What Do People Mean When They Talk About Advertising?" In *Advertising and Consumer Psychology*, edited by L. Percy and A. G. Woodside, pp. 273–286. Lexington, Mass.: Lexington Books, 1983.

Weitz, B. A., and K. D. Bradford. "Personal Selling and Sales Management: A Relationship Marketing Perspective." *Journal of the Academy of Marketing Science*, 27:2 (April 1999): pp. 241–254.

Marketing Message—Advice & Ideas 18
Shimp, T. A., and W. O. Bearden. "Warranty and Other Extrinsic Cue Effects on Consumers' Risk Perceptions." *Journal of Consumer Research*, Volume 9 (June 1982): pp. 38–46

Till, B. D., and M. Busler. "Matching Products with Endorsers: Attractiveness versus Expertise." *Journal of Consumer Marketing*, 15:6 (1998): pp. 576–586.

Marketing Message—Advice & Ideas 19
Davies, James C. "Toward A Theory of Revolution." *American Sociological Review*, Volume 27:1, Number 1, (February 1962): pp. 5–19.

Tuan Pham, Michel, and Tamar Avnet. "Ideals and Oughts and the Reliance on Affect versus Substance in Persuasion." *Journal of Consumer Research*, Volume 30 (March 2004): pp. 503–518.

Ziamou, Paschalina, S. Ratneshwar, "Innovations in Product Functionality: When and Why Are Explicit Comparisons Effective." *Journal of Marketing*, Volume 67 (April 2003): pp. 49–61.

Chapter 3: Mindless Marketing

Mindless Marketing—Advice & Ideas 1
Cialdini, R. B., and K. V. L. Rhoads. "Human Behavior and the Marketplace." *Marketing Research*, 13:3 (Fall 2001): pp. 9–13.

Howard, D. J. "The Influence of Verbal Responses to Common Greetings on Compliance Behavior: The Foot-in-the-Mouth Effect." *Journal of Applied Social Psychology*, 20:14 (1990): pp. 1185–1196.

Reingen, P. H. "On Inducing Compliance with Requests." *Journal of Consumer Research*, Volume 5 (September 1978): pp. 96–102.

Reingen, P. H., and J. B. Kernan. "Compliance with an Interview Request: A Foot-in-the-Door, Self-Perception Interpretation." *Journal of Marketing Research*, 14:3 (August 1977): pp. 365–369.

Sherman, S. J. "On the Self-Erasing Nature of Errors of Prediction." *Journal of Personality and Social Psychology*, Volume 39 (1980): pp. 211–221.

Mindless Marketing—Advice & Ideas 2
Aronson, E., and J. Mills. "The Effect of Severity of Initiation on Liking for a Group." *Journal of Abnormal and Social Psychology*, Volume 59 (1959): pp. 177–181.

Cialdini, R. B. *Influence: Science and Practice,* pp. 75–80, Boston: Allyn and Bacon, 2001.

Mindless Marketing—Advice & Ideas 3
Dwyer, S., J. Hill, and W. Martin. "An Empirical Investigation of Critical Success Factors in the Personal Selling Process for Homogenous Goods." *Journal of Personal Selling and Sales Management*, 20:3 (Summer 2000): pp. 151–159.

Tversky, A., and E. Shafir. "Choice Under Conflict: The Dynamics of Deferred Decision." *Psychological Science*, 3:6 (November 1992): pp. 358–361.

Mindless Marketing—Advice & Ideas 4
West, S. G. "Increasing the Attractiveness of College Cafeteria Food: A Reactance Theory Perspective." *Journal of Applied Psychology*, 60:5 (1975): pp. 656–658.

Worchel, S., J. Lee, and A. Adewole. "Effects of Supply and Demand on Ratings of Object Value." *Journal of Personality and Social Psychology*, 32:5 (1975): pp. 906–914.

Mindless Marketing—Advice & Ideas 5
Cialdini, R. B., J. E. Vincent, et al. "Reciprocal Concessions Procedure for Inducing Compliance: The Door-in-the-Face Technique." *Journal of Personality and Social Psychology*, 31:2 (1975): pp. 206–215.

Gruner, S. "Reward Good Customers." *Inc.* (November 1996): p. 84.

Mowen, J. C., and R. B. Cialdini. "On Implementing the Door-in the-Face Compliance Technique in a Business Context." *Journal of Marketing Research*, 17:2 (May 1980), pp. 253–258.

Reingen, P. H. "On Inducing Compliance with Requests." *Journal of Consumer Research*, Volume 5 (September 1978): pp. 96–102.

Mindless Marketing—Advice & Ideas 6

Bushman, B. J. "The Effects of Apparel on Compliance." *Personality and Social Psychology Bulletin*, 14:3 (September 1988): pp. 459–467.

Chaiken, S. "Communicator Physical Attractiveness and Persuasion." *Journal of Personality and Social Psychology*, 37:8 (1979): pp. 1387–1397.

Cialdini, R. B. *Influence: Science and Practice*, pp. 148–150. Boston: Allyn and Bacon, 2001.

Doob, A. N., and A. E. Gross. "Status of Frustrator as an Inhibitor of Horn-Honking Responses." *Journal of Social Psychology*, Volume 76 (1968): pp. 213–218.

Lefkowitz, M., R. R. Blake, and J. S. Mouton. "Status Factors in Pedestrian Violation of Traffic Signals." *Journal of Abnormal and Social Psychology*, Volume 51 (1955): pp. 704–706.

Mack, D., and D. Rainey. "Female Applicants' Grooming and Personnel Selection." *Journal of Social Behavior and Personality*, 5:5 (1990): pp. 399–407.

Schuster, C. P., and J. E. Danes. "Asking Questions: Some Characteristics of Successful Sales Encounters." *Journal of Personal Selling and Sales Management*, 6:1 (May 1986): pp. 17–27.

Stieg, B. "Facts of Life." *Men's Health*, March 2003, p. 52.

Mindless Marketing—Advice & Ideas 7

Cialdini, R. B. *Influence: Science and Practice*, p. 152. Boston: Allyn and Bacon, 2001.

Garrity, K., and D. Degelman. "Effects of Server Introduction on Restaurant Tipping." *Journal of Applied Social Psychology*, 20:2 (1990): pp. 168–172.

Gonzales, M. H., J. M. Davis, et al. "Interactional Approach to Interpersonal Attraction." *Journal of Personality and Social Psychology*, 44:6 (1983): pp. 1192–1197.

Gorn, G. J. "The Effects of Music in Advertising on Choice Behavior: A Classical Conditioning Approach." *Journal of Marketing*, 46:1 (Winter 1982): pp. 94–101.

Howard, D. J., C. Gengler, and A. Jain. "What's in a Name? A Complimentary Means of Persuasion." *Journal of Consumer Research*, 22 (September 1995): pp. 200–211.

Schuster, C. P., and J. E. Danes. "Asking Questions: Some Characteristics of Successful Sales Encounters." *Journal of Personal Selling and Sales Management*, 6:1 (May 1986): pp. 17–27.

Tracy, B. "Stop Talking . . . and Start Asking Questions." *Sales and Marketing Management*, 147:2 (February 1995): pp. 79–86.

<u>Mindless Marketing—Advice & Ideas 8</u>

Adaval, R., and K. B. Monroe. "Automatic Construction and Use of Contextual Information for Product and Price Evaluations." *Journal of Consumer Research*, 28:4 (March 2002): pp. 572–588.

Simonson, I., S. Nowlis, and K. Lemon. "The Effect of Local Consideration Sets on Global Choice Between Lower Price and Higher Quality." *Marketing Science*, 12:4 (Fall 1993): pp. 357–376.

<u>Mindless Marketing—Advice & Ideas 9</u>

Bodenhausen, G. V. "Stereotypes as Judgmental Heuristics: Evidence of Circadian Variations in Discrimination." *Psychological Science*, 1:5 (September 1990): pp. 319–322.

<u>Mindless Marketing—Advice & Ideas 10</u>

Feltham, T. S. "Leaving Home: Brand Purchase Influences on Young Adults." *Journal of Consumer Marketing*, 15:4 (1998): pp. 372–385.

Howard, J. A., and J. N. Sheth. "A Theory of Buyer Behavior." In *Perspectives in Consumer Behavior*, edited by H. H. Kassarjian and T. S. Robertson, pp. 519–540. Glenview, Ill.: Scott, Foresman & Co., 1973.

Knox, R. E., and J. A. Inkster. "Post Decision Dissonance at Post Time." *Journal of Personality and Social Psychology*, 8:4 (1968): pp. 319–323.

Mindless Marketing—Advice & Ideas 11

Milgram, S., L. Bickman, and L. Berkowitz. "Note on the Drawing Power of Crowds of Different Size." *Journal of Personality and Social Psychology*, 13:2 (1969): pp. 79–82.

Phillips, D. P. "Airplane Accidents, Murder, and the Mass Media: Towards a Theory of Imitation and Suggestion." *Social Forces*, 58:4 (June 1980): pp. 1001–1024.

Phillips, D. P. "Suicide, Motor Vehicle Fatalities, and the Mass Media: Evidence Toward a Theory of Suggestion." *American Journal of Sociology*, 84:5 (1979): pp. 1150–1174.

Schuster, C. P., and J. E. Danes. "Asking Questions: Some Characteristics of Successful Sales Encounters." *Journal of Personal Selling and Sales Management*, 6:1 (May 1986): pp. 17–27.

Whittler, T. E. "Eliciting Consumer Choice Heuristics: Sales Representatives' Persuasion Strategies." *Journal of Personal Selling and Sales Management*, 14:4 (Fall 1994): pp. 41–53.

Mindless Marketing—Advice & Ideas 12

Cialdini, R. B. *Influence: Science and Practice,* pp. 167–168, Boston: Allyn and Bacon, 2001.

Razran, G. H. S. "Conditioning Away Social Bias." *Psychological Bulletin*, Volume 35 (1938): p. 693.

Razran, G. H. S. "Conditioned Response Changes in Rating and Appraising Sociopolitical Slogans." *Psychological Bulletin*, Volume 37 (1940): p. 481.

Wyrwicka, W. "Classical Conditioned Reflexes." *Conditioning*, pp. 5–10. New Brunswick, N.J.: Transaction Publishers, 2000.

Mindless Marketing—Advice & Ideas 13
Cialdini, R. B. *Influence: Science and Practice,* p. 74, Boston: Allyn and Bacon, 2001.

Moriarity, T. "Crime, Commitment, and the Responsive Bystander: Two Field Experiments." *Journal of Personality and Social Psychology,* 31:2 (1975): pp. 370–376.

Mindless Marketing—Advice & Ideas 14
Morwitz, V. G., E. Johnson, and D. Schmittlein. "Does Measuring Intent Change Behavior?" *Journal of Consumer Research,* Volume 20 (June 1993): pp. 46–61.

Mindless Marketing—Advice & Ideas 15
Cialdini, R. B., R. J. Borden, et al. "Basking in Reflected Glory: Three (Football) Field Studies." *Journal of Personality and Social Psychology,* 34:3 (1976): pp. 366–375.

Chapter 4: Selling

Selling—Advice & Ideas 1
Cialdini, R. B. *Influence: Science and Practice,* pp. 147–148. Boston: Allyn and Bacon, 2001.

Dwyer, S., J. Hill, and W. Martin. "An Empirical Investigation of Critical Success Factors in the Personal Selling Process for Homogenous Goods." *Journal of Personal Selling and Sales Management,* 20:3 (Summer 2000): pp.151–159.

Data Source: Eureka! Ranch. Based on marketplace analysis of 900 new product launches: *Merwyn Technology Internal Data Set: Darwin 900 Study* (Eureka! Ranch, 2001).

Selling—Advice & Ideas 2
Liu, A. H., and M. P. Leach. "Developing Loyal Customers with a Value-Adding Sales Force: Examining Customer Satisfaction and the Perceived Credibility of Consultative Salespeople." *Journal of Personal Selling and Sales Management,* 21:2 (Spring 2001): pp. 147–156.

Robinson, W. T. "Sources of Market Pioneer Advantages: The Case of Industrial Goods Industries." *Journal of Marketing Research*, 25:1 (February 1988): pp. 87–94.

Selling—Advice & Ideas 3
Morris, M. H., R. W. LaForge, and J. A. Allen. "Salesperson Failure: Definition, Determinants, and Outcomes." *Journal of Personal Selling and Sales Management*, 14:1 (Winter 1994): pp. 1–15.

Selling—Advice & Ideas 4
Brown, S. P., W. L. Cron, and J. W. Slocum Jr. "Effects of Trait Competitiveness and Perceived Intraorganizational Competition on Salesperson Goal Setting and Performance." *Journal of Marketing*, 62:4 (October 1998): pp. 88–98.

Selling—Advice & Ideas 5
Sharma, A., and R. Pillai. "Customers' Decision-Making Styles and Their Preference for Sales Strategies: Conceptual Examination and an Empirical Study." *Journal of Personal Selling and Sales Management*, 16:1 (Winter 1996): pp. 21–33.

Thomas, R. W., G. N. Soutar, and M. M. Ryan. "The Selling Orientation–Customer Orientation (S.O.C.O.) Scale: A Proposed Short Form." *Journal of Personal Selling and Sales Management*, 21:1 (Winter 2001): pp. 63–69.

Data Source: Eureka! Ranch. Based on marketplace analysis of 900 new product launches: *Merwyn Technology Internal Data Set: Darwin 900 Study* (Eureka! Ranch, 2001).

Selling—Advice & Ideas 6
Hall, D. *Jump Start Your Business Brain* (Cincinnati: Brain Brew Books, 2001).

Herrmann, N. *The Whole Brain Business Book*. New York: McGraw-Hill, 1996.

Leonard, D., and S. Straus. "Putting Your Company's Whole Brain to Work." *Harvard Business Review*, 75:4 (July/August 1997): pp. 110–121.

Selling—Advice & Ideas 7

Hall, D. *Jump Start Your BUSINESS Brain.* Cincinnati: Brain Brew Books, 2001.

Herrmann, N. *The Whole Brain Business Book.* New York: McGraw-Hill, 1996.

Leonard, D., and S. Straus. "Putting Your Company's Whole Brain to Work." *Harvard Business Review,* 75:4 (July/August 1997): pp. 110–121.

Selling—Advice & Ideas 8

Hall, D. *Jump Start Your Business Brain* (Cincinnati: Brain Brew Books, 2001).

Herrmann, N. *The Whole Brain Business Book* (New York: McGraw-Hill, 1996).

Leonard, D., and S. Straus. "Putting Your Company's Whole Brain to Work." *Harvard Business Review,* 75:4 (July/August 1997), pp. 110–121.

Selling—Advice & Ideas 9

Cox, D., and A. D. Cox. "Beyond First Impressions: The Effects of Repeated Exposure on Consumer Liking of Visually Complex and Simple Product Designs." *Journal of the Academy of Marketing Science,* 30:2 (2002): pp. 119–130.

Selling—Advice & Ideas 10

Church, A. H. "Estimating the Effect of Incentives on Mail Survey Response Rates." *Public Opinion Quarterly,* Volume 57 (1993): pp. 62–79.

James, J. M., and R. Bolstein. "Large Monetary Incentives and Their Effect on Mail Survey Response Rates." *Public Opinion Quarterly,* Volume 56 (1992): pp. 442–453.

Marks, L. J., and M. A. Kamins. "The Use of Product Sampling and Advertising: Effects of Sequence of Exposure and Degree of Advertising

Claim Exaggeration on Consumers' Belief Strength, Belief Confidence, and Attitudes." *Journal of Marketing Research*, 25:3 (August 1988): pp. 266–281.

Selling—Advice & Ideas 11
Gouillart, F. J., and F. D. Sturdivant. "Spend a Day in the Life of Your Customers." *Harvard Business Review*, 72:1 (January/February 1994): pp. 116–125.

Hite, R. E., and J. A. Bellizzi. "Differences in the Importance of Selling Techniques Between Consumer and Industrial Salespeople." *Journal of Personal Selling and Sales Management*, 5:2 (November 1985): pp. 19–30.

Selling—Advice & Ideas 12
Hite, R. E., and J. A. Bellizzi. "Differences in the Importance of Selling Techniques Between Consumer and Industrial Salespeople." *Journal of Personal Selling and Sales Management*, 5:2 (November 1985): pp. 19–30.

Selling—Advice & Ideas 13
Schoormans, J. P. L., R. J. Ortt, and C. J. P. M. de Bont. "Enhancing Concept Test Validity by Using Expert Consumers." *Journal of Product Innovation Management*, 12:2 (March 1995): pp.153–162.

Singh, M., S. K. Balasubramanian, and G. Chakraborty. "A Comparative Analysis of Three Communication Formats: Advertising, Infomercial, and Direct Experience." *Journal of Advertising*, 29:4 (Winter 2000): pp. 59–75.

Selling—Advice & Ideas 14
Doyle, S. X., and G. T. Roth. "Selling and Sales Management in Action: The Use of Insight Coaching to Improve Relationship Selling." *Journal of Personal Selling and Sales Management*, 12:1 (Winter 1992): pp. 59–64.

Locke, K. D., and L. M. Horowitz. "Satisfaction in Interpersonal Interactions as a Function of Similarity in Level of Dysphoria." *Journal of Personality and Social Psychology*, 58:5 (May 1990): pp. 823–831.

Swan, J. E., and J. J. Nolan. "Gaining Customer Trust: A Conceptual Guide for the Salesperson." *Journal of Personal Selling and Sales Management*, 5:2 (November 1985): pp. 39–48.

Swan, J. E., I. F. Trawick Jr., D. R. Rink, and J. J. Roberts. "Measuring Dimensions of Purchaser Trust of Industrial Salespeople." *Journal of Personal Selling and Sales Management*, 8:1 (May 1988): pp. 1–9.

Selling—Advice & Ideas 15
Greenleaf, E. A., and D. R. Lehmann. "Reasons for Substantial Delay in Consumer Decision Making." *Journal of Consumer Research*, 22:2 (September 1995): pp.186–199.

Selling—Advice & Ideas 16
Bushman, B. J., and A. M. Bonacci. "Violence and Sex Impair Memory for Television Ads." *Journal of Applied Psychology*, 87:3 (June 2002): pp. 557–564.

Meyers-Levy, J., and L. A. Peracchio. "Understanding the Effects of Color: How the Correspondence Between Available and Required Resources Affects Attitudes." *Journal of Consumer Research*, Volume 22 (September 1995): pp. 121–138.

Stieg, B. "Facts of Life." *Men's Health*, March 2003, pp. 52.

Selling—Advice & Ideas 17
Anderson, R. E. "Personal Selling and Sales Management in the New Millennium." *Journal of Personal Selling and Sales Management*, 16:4 (Fall 1996): pp. 17–32.

Brock, T. C., and S. Shavitt. "Cognitive-Response Analysis in Advertising." In *Advertising and Consumer Psychology*, edited by L. Percy and A. G. Woodside, pp. 91–116. Lexington, Mass.: Lexington Books, 1983.

Dwyer, S., J. Hill, and W. Martin. "An Empirical Investigation of Critical Success Factors in the Personal Selling Process for Homogenous Goods." *Journal of Personal Selling and Sales Management*, 20:3 (Summer 2000): pp. 151–159.

Kahle, L. R., D. B. Hall, and M. J. Kosinski. "The Real-Time Response Survey in New Product Research: It's about Time." *Journal of Consumer Marketing*, 14:3 (1997): pp. 234–248.

Krugman, H. E. "Why Three Exposures May Be Enough." *Journal of Advertising Research*, 12:6 (December 1972): pp.11–14.

Pechmann, C., and D. W. Stewart. "Advertising Repetition: A Critical Review of Wearin and Wearout." *Current Issues and Research in Advertising*, Volume 12 (1988): pp. 285–330.

Vakratsas, D., and T. Ambler. "How Advertising Works: What Do We Really Know?" *Journal of Marketing*, 63:1 (January 1999): pp. 26–43.

Selling—Advice & Ideas 18
Williams, G. A., and R. B. Miller. "Change the Way You Persuade." *Harvard Business Review*, 80:5 (May 2002): pp. 65-73.

Selling—Advice & Ideas 19
Sharma, A., and R. Pillai. "Customers' Decision-Making Styles and Their Preference for Sales Strategies: Conceptual Examination and an Empirical Study." *Journal of Personal Selling and Sales Management*, 16:1 (Winter 1996): pp. 21–33.

Selling—Advice & Ideas 20
Goff, B. G., D. N. Bellenger, and C. Stojack. "Cues to Consumer Susceptibility to Salesperson Influence: Implications for Adaptive Retail Selling." *Journal of Personal Selling and Sales Management*, 14:2 (Spring 1994): pp. 25–39.

Selling—Advice & Ideas 21
Bolton, Lisa E., Luk Warlop, and Joseph W. Alba. "Consumer Perceptions of Price (Un)Fairness," *Journal of Consumer Research*, Volume 29, (March 2003): pp. 474–491.

Campbell, Margaret C. "Why Did You Do That? The Important Role of Inferred Motive in Perceptions of Price Fairness." *Journal of Product and Brand Management*, 8:2, (1999): pp.145–152.

Campbell, Margaret C. "Perceptions of Price Unfairness: Antecedents and Consequences." *Journal of Marketing Research*, Volume XXXVI (May 1999): pp.187–199.

Kahneman, Daniel, Jack L. Knetsch, and Richard Thaler. "Fairness as a Constraint on Profit Seeking: Entitlements in the Market." *The American Economic Review*, 76:4 (September 1986): pp.728–741.

Vorhies, D. W., M. Harker, and C. P. Rao. "The Capabilities and Performance Advantages of Market-Driven Firms." *European Journal of Marketing*, 33:11/12 (1999): pp.1171–1202.

Xia, Lan, Kent B. Monoe, and Jennifer L. Cox. "The Price is Unfair! A Conceptual Framework of Price Fairness Perceptions." *Journal of Marketing*, Volume 68 (October 2004): pp. 1–15.

Selling—Advice & Ideas 22
Jap, S. D. "The Strategic Role of the Salesforce in Developing Customer Satisfaction across the Relationship Lifecycle." *Journal of Personal Selling and Sales Management*, 21:2 (Spring 2001): pp. 95–108.

Selling—Advice & Ideas 23
Alba, J. W., and J. W. Hutchinson. "Knowledge Calibration: What Consumers Know and What They Think They Know." *Journal of Consumer Research*, 27:2 (September 2000): pp. 123–156.

Wood, S. L., and J. G. Lynch, Jr. "Prior Knowledge and Complacency in New Product Learning." *Journal of Consumer Research*, 29:3 (December 2002): pp. 416–426.

Selling—Advice & Ideas 24
Roselius, T. "Consumer Rankings of Risk Reduction Methods." In *Perspectives in Consumer Behavior*, edited by H. H. Kassarjian and T. S. Robertson, pp. 55–64. Glenview, Ill.: Scott, Foresman & Co., 1973.

Chapter 5: Leadership & Teamwork

Team—Advice & Ideas 1

Burn, S. W. "Social Psychology and the Stimulation of Recycling Behaviors: The Block Leader Approach." *Journal of Applied Social Psychology*, Volume 21 (1991): pp.611–629.

Donavan, D. Todd, Tom J. Brown, and John C. Mowen. "Internal Benefits of Service-Worker Customer Orientation: Job Satisfaction, Commitment, and Organizational Citizenship Behaviors." *Journal of Marketing*, Volume 68 (January 2004): pp. 25–146.

Yu, J., and H. Cooper. "A Quantitative Review of Research Design Effects on Response Rates to Questionnaires." *Journal of Marketing Research*, 20:1 (February 1983): pp. 36–44.

Team—Advice & Ideas 2

Srinivasan, Raja, Gary L. Lilien, and Arvind Rangaswamy. "Technological Opportunism and Radical Technology Adoption: An Application to E-Business." *Journal of Marketing*, Volume 66 (July 2002): pp. 47–60.

Matsuno, Ken, John T. Mentzer, and Aysegul Ozsomer. "The Effects of Entrepreneurial Proclivity and Market Orientation on Business Performance." *Journal of Marketing*, Volume 66 (July 2002): pp. 18–32.

Team—Advice & Ideas 3

Plank, R. E., D. A. Reid, and. E. B. Pullins. "Methods in Sales Research: Perceived Trust in Business-to-Business Sales: A New Measure." *Journal of Personal Selling and Sales Management*, 19:3 (Summer 1999): pp. 61–71.

Swan, J. E., and J. J. Nolan. "Gaining Customer Trust: A Conceptual Guide for the Salesperson." *Journal of Personal Selling and Sales Management*, 5:2 (November 1985): pp. 39–48.

Team—Advice & Ideas 4
Babakus, E., D. W. Cravens, M. Johnston, and W. C. Moncrief. "The Role of Emotional Exhaustion in Sales Force Attitude and Behavior Relationships." *Journal of the Academy of Marketing Science*, 27:1 (January 1999): pp.58–70.

Team—Advice & Ideas 5
Baker, J., A. Parasuraman, D. Grewal, and G. B. Voss. "The Influence of Multiple Store Environment Cues on Perceived Merchandise Value and Patronage Intentions." *Journal of Marketing*, 66:2 (April 2002): pp. 120–141.

Dwyer, S., J. Hill, and W. Martin. "An Empirical Investigation of Critical Success Factors in the Personal Selling Process for Homogenous Goods." *Journal of Personal Selling and Sales Management*, 20:3 (Summer 2000): pp.151–159.

Keinan, G. "Decision Making Under Stress: Scanning of Alternatives Under Controllable and Uncontrollable Threats." *Journal of Personality and Social Psychology*, 52:3 (1987): pp. 639–644.

Team—Advice & Ideas 6
Russ, F. A., K. M. McNeilly, et al. "Exploring the Impact of Critical Sales Events." *Journal of Personal Selling and Sales Management*, 18:2 (Spring 1998): pp. 19–34.

Team—Advice & Ideas 7
Charlett, D., R. Garland, and N. Marr. "How Damaging Is Negative Word of Mouth?" *Marketing Bulletin*, Volume 6 (May 1995): pp. 42–50.

Maxham III, J. G., and R. G. Netemeyer. "A Longitudinal Study of Complaining Customers' Evaluations of Multiple Service Failures and Recovery Efforts." *Journal of Marketing*, 66:4 (October 2002): pp. 57–71.

Team—Advice & Ideas 8
Wilton, P. C., and D. K. Tse. "A Model of Consumer Response to Communication and Product Experiences." Eds. L. Percy and A. G. Woodside. *Advertising and Consumer Psychology*, pp.315–322, Lexington, Mass.: Lexington Books, 1983.

Team—Advice & Ideas 9
Kahle, L. R., D. B. Hall, and M. J. Kosinski. "The Real-Time Response Survey in New Product Research: It's about Time." *Journal of Consumer Marketing*, 14:3 (1997): pp. 234–248.

Sherman, S. J. "On the Self-Erasing Nature of Errors of Prediction." *Journal of Personality and Social Psychology*, 39:2 (1980): pp. 211–221.

Team – Advice & Ideas 10
Lau, G. T., and S. H. Lee. "Consumers Trust in a Brand and the Link to Brand Loyalty." *Journal of Market-Focused Management*, Volume 4 (1999): pp. 341–370.

Team—Advice & Ideas 11
Lambert, D. M., H. Marmorstein, and A. Sharma. "The Accuracy of Salespersons' Perceptions of Their Customers: Conceptual Examination and an Empirical Study." *Journal of Personal Selling and Sales Management*, 10:1 (Winter 1990): pp. 1–9.

Strub, P., and S. Herman. "Can the Sales Force Speak for the Customer?" *Marketing Research*, 5:4 (Fall 1993): pp. 32–35.

Wood, S. L., and J. G. Lynch Jr. "Prior Knowledge and Complacency in New Product Learning." *Journal of Consumer Research*, 29:3 (December 2002): pp. 416–426.

Team—Advice & Ideas 12
Goodman, Nathan G., ed. *A Benjamin Franklin Reader*, pp. 118–131. New York: Thomas Y. Crowell Company, 1971.

Hall, D., and D. Wecker. *The Maverick Mindset*, pp. 207–210. New York: Simon & Schuster, 1997.

Team—Advice & Ideas 13
Hall, D. *Jump Start Your BUSINESS Brain*. Cincinnati: Brain Brew Books, 2001.

REFERENCES FROM THE INTRODUCTION AND APPENDIXES

Abraham, M. M., and L. M. Lodish. "Getting the Most out of Advertising and Promotion." *Harvard Business Review*, 30:3 (May–June 1990): pp. 50–60.

Ailawadi, K. L., D. R. Lehmann, and S. A. Neslin. "Market Response to a Major Policy Change in the Marketing Mix: Learning from Procter & Gamble's Value Pricing Strategy." *Journal of Marketing*, 65:1 (January 2001): pp. 44–61.

Albion, Mark. Making a Life, *Making a Living*, p.17. New York: Warner Books, 2000.

Anderson, R. E. "Personal Selling and Sales Management in the New Millennium." *Journal of Personal Selling and Sales Management*, 16:4 (Fall 1996): pp.17–32.

Bettman, J. R., M. F. Luce, and J. W. Payne. "Constructive Consumer Choice Processes." *Journal of Consumer Research*, 25:3 (December 1998): pp. 187–217.

Bettman, J. R., and C. W. Park. "Effects of Prior Knowledge and Experience and Phase of the Choice Process on Consumer Decision Processes: A Protocol Analysis." *Journal of Consumer Research*, Volume 7 (December 1980): pp. 234–248.

Goodman, Nathan G., ed. *A Benjamin Franklin Reader*, pp. 118–131. New York: Thomas Y. Crowell Company, 1971.

Hoyer, W. D. "An Examination of Consumer Decision Making for a Common Repeat Purchase Product." *Journal of Consumer Research*, Volume 11 (December 1984): pp. 822–829.

Lasn, K. "Ad Spending Predicted for Steady Decline." *Adbusters*, Volume 45 (January/February 2003), www.adbusters.org/magazine/45/articles/ad_spending_predicted_for.html.

Lodish, L. M., and M. M. Abraham. "How T.V. Advertising Works: A Meta-Analysis of 389 Real World Split Cable T.V. Advertising Experiments." *Journal of Marketing Research*, 32:2 (May 1995): pp. 125–139.

Lodish, L. M., M. M. Abraham, J. Livelsberger, et al. "A Summary of Fifty-Five In-Market Experimental Estimates of the Long-Term Effect of TV Advertising." *Marketing Science*, 14:3, Part 2 of 2 (1995), pp. G133–G140.

Maidique, M. A., and B. J. Zirger. "A Study of Success and Failure in Product Innovation: The Case of the U.S. Electronics Industry." *IEEE Transactions on Engineering Management*, EM 31:4 (November 1984): pp. 192–203.

Marton, B. A. "Mastering the Art of Persuasion." *Harvard Management Communication Letter*, 3:7 (July 2000): pp. 4–6.

Mela, C. F., and S. Gupta. "The Long-Term Impact of Promotion and Advertising on Consumer Brand Choice." *Journal of Marketing Research*, 34:2 (May 1997): pp. 248–261.

Petty, R. E., and J. T. Cacioppo. "Central and Peripheral Routes to Persuasion: Application to Advertising." In *Advertising and Consumer Psychology*, edited by L. Percy and A. G. Woodside, pp. 3–23. Lexington, Mass.: Lexington Books, 1983.

Data Source: Digital Scriptorium. "Emergence of Advertising in America: 1850–1920." http://scriptorium.lib.duke.edu/eaa/.

Data Source: Eureka! Ranch. Based on marketplace analysis of 900 new product launches: *Merwyn Technology Internal Data Set: Darwin 900 Study* (Eureka! Ranch, 2001).

Data Source: Information Resources, Inc. InFocus Report: New Product Trends 2002 Study (Chicago, 2002): pp. 6–7.

Data Source: Sahr, R. "Inflation Conversion Factors for Dollars 1665 to Estimated 2013." http://oregonstate.edu/dept/pol_sci/fac/sahr/sahr.htm.

ANSWERS TO THE
MARKETING
BRAIN IQ TEST

At the end of all but two of the questions, I've noted the percentage of managers who answered the question correctly as part of a World Wide Web audio conference. (Two of the questions are new ones.) As you review the percentages, recall that there are only two options to most of the questions, so random guessing should result in about 50 percent of the managers being correct.

1. The smartest way to significantly grow sales is ...
    a. Build Loyalty
    b. Find New Customers

    Contrary to popular belief, finding new customers is significantly more valuable than building loyalty. In fact, modeling of more than 9,000 brands found that number of customers was 2.8 times more important for generating SIGNIFICANT growth.

For further details, see Marketing Strategy #9
(9 percent of managers answered B).

2. To build greater annual loyalty it's smarter to ...
    a. Increase dollars purchased per purchase occasion
    b. Increase frequency of purchase

    A customer's annual purchase volume comprises two parts: the number of times she buys per year and the amount she buys each time. A statistical model on the same 9,000 brands found that the amount bought each time is 3.5 times more important than how often a customer buys. When a customer purchases twice as much as normal, not only do you receive 100 percent of her current purchase, but 100 percent of her next purchase as well.

For details, see Marketing Strategy #10
(39 percent of managers answered A).

3. Most new products or services fail because of ...
    a. Poor execution of sales and marketing
    b. Poor product or service performance
    c. **Not being a very good idea in the first place**

In-depth research on forty-eight new product introductions found that THE IDEA was 2.2 times more likely to be the source of failure versus the marketing plan and 1.5 times more likely versus product performance.

For details, see Marketing Strategy #7
(this question not asked in the Web conference).

4. When creating ideas for new products or services the smartest strategy is ...
    a. To create ideas based on listening to the "voice of the customer"
    b. **Create ideas that customers are not necessarily asking for**

In-depth analysis of 120 businesses found that a FUTURE FOCUS was 10 times more predictive of success than a "Voice of the Customer" approach.

For details, see Marketing Strategy #4
(this question not asked in the Web conference).

5. <u>When presenting data to a customer, you will be most effective if ...</u>
    a. You provide a clear and simple chart
    b. <u>You explain the data in clear and simple words</u>

This finding came from a study that presented the nutritional value of two food products to 250 consumers in various formats. The storytelling format proved twice as effective in communicating the nutritional values, prompting more consumers to accurately recall the information and three times as many of them to say they intended to purchase.

For details, see Marketing Message #15
(41 percent of managers answered B).

6. <u>A customer letter or a print ad has the best chances of success if ...</u>
    a. You respect their intelligence and write at a high school level
    b. <u>You dumb it down and write so a 10-year-old can understand it</u>

Using the Flesch-Kincaid reading complexity measure, the marketing messages of 901 new brands that survived or failed five years after market introduction were analyzed. There was significantly higher probability for those brands whose message was written with the clarity of a fifth-grade level or less (10 year old).

For details, see Marketing Message #8
(46 percent of managers answered B).

7. Significant overall sales growth can be realized if ...
    a. You cut your product line by as much as 50 percent
    b. You expand your product line to service all customers

This may be the easiest way to increase sales and profits according to the results of three separate studies. One study showed that when twenty-four flavor samples of jam were offered, only 2 percent of customers purchased. When six samples were offered, 12 percent of customers purchased. Thus, the more options presented, the more uncertain customers become, and the longer they delay buying.

For details, see Marketing Strategy #11
(36 percent of managers answered A).

8. When selling a customer it is best to ...
    a. Be blunt and direct about what you offer
    b. Use a softer, relationship-focused approach

In today's world of advertising bombardment, customers have little time to compare, contrast, or even consider each message they receive. To break through the barrier, you must be direct and obvious about the benefit that you offer to them. A study of more than 10,000 concepts found that when you communicated an OVERT benefit, you were over three times more likely to succeed.

For details, see Marketing Message #1
(40 percent of managers answered A).

9. Building customer credibility is most effective if you offer ...
    a. A product demonstration
    b. Testimonials from satisfied customers

There is never enough time to present everything you know about your wonderful product. So how does a customer know your product is as wonderful as you claim it to be? According to a study about the credibility strategy used on 900 new products, a product demonstration was 47 percent more effective than any other approach.

For details, see Selling #1
(26 percent of managers answered A).

10. <u>Forced to choose, buyers prefer salespeople who are . . .</u>
    a. **Highly dependable**
    b. Highly competent

The foundation of all sales relationships is dependability. Brilliance without dependability is meaningless. This comes from a study of industrial buyers that found that dependability was actually a step change more important than competence or even basic "likability."

For details, see Selling #14
(43 percent of managers answered A).

11. <u>The smartest way to introduce a new consumer product or service is to ...</u>
    a. Introduce at a lower price to generate trial
    b. **Keep your price at list price from the beginning**

Oftentimes, new products or services are offered at a low introductory price. The problem with this practice is that it lowers the value of the product in the customer's mind and once the price goes up to its regular level, the customer stops buying it. Five new products studied in two sets of identical stores showed that long-term volume was higher when the brand was sold at the regular price from the onset.

For details, see Marketing Strategy #13
(33 percent of managers answered B).

12. In industrial marketing it's nine times more important to focus on ...
    a. Price advantages
    b. Performance and quality advantages

    The quality of a product was found to be the most important factor in explaining market share according to a study conducted on more than 1,200 industrial goods manufacturers. Another study of 186 corporations found that a strategy of focusing quality improvements on improved customer satisfaction is much more effective than a cost-focused one.

For details, see Marketing Strategy #22 & Selling #2
(25 percent of managers answered B).

13. With a major breakthrough product or service, you can usually tell ...
    a. You have a winner within twelve months
    b. It usually takes as much as six years before you can tell

    It takes time to change the world. The more genuinely unique your offering the longer it may take to realize significant success. A long-term study of thirty-one major innovations like automobiles, color televisions, camcorders, etc., found that, on average, it took six years before sales "took off."

For details, see Marketing Strategy #6
(28 percent of managers answered B).

Compare Your Results

11 to 13 Correct	You're a Sales & Marketing Superstar!
7 to 10 Correct	You're significantly above average
3 to 6 Correct	You're average (four is the average).
0 to 2 Correct	You have made a wise investment in purchasing this book.

★ ★ ★ ★ ★ ★ ★ ★ ★ ★ ★

DOUG HALL'S CURRENT & FUTURE BOOKS

The Jump Start Your BUSINESS Brain Series: Just as each of my children are unique interpretations of the same family pedigree, so too each book in the Jump Start series is a unique articulation of my fundamental philosophy on life and business. Each book shares scientific ideas and advice proven in quantitative research to dramatically improve your odds of success. Each book also shares a healthy dose of caffeinated energy and optimism designed to nudge you to Get Up! Get Out! Get Going!

Doug Hall

Jump Start Your BUSINESS Brain (Brain Brew Books, 2001), by Doug Hall. Foreword by Tom Peters. The first book in the series articulated the three Laws of Marketing Physics and the three Laws of Capitalist Creativity. This national best-seller is based on analysis of more than 10,000 new products, services, and marketing messages—some 6,000 innovation teams and thirty years of front-line experience. The wisdom comes to life in case studies of real-world entrepreneurs from Prince Edward Island, Canada.

Jump Start Your MARKETING Brain (Brain Brew Books, 2003), by Doug Hall. Foreword by Sergio Zyman. This book is a DEEP DIVE into the complex world of sales and marketing. It's for those with a genuine commitment to measurably improving their success rate. It was originally published in hardcover as *Meaningful Marketing*. The book won critical acclaim, but its "academic style" prevented it from reaching the mass audience of *Jump Start Your BUSINESS Brain*. A comprehensive redesign and rewrite has added caffeinated energy as well as even more meaningful advice and ideas for improving your sales and marketing success rates.

Jump Start Your CREATIVE Brain (Brain Brew Books, PLANNED for fall 2006), by Doug Hall. The ultimate guide to the leading Scientific Systems for thinking quicker, smarter, and more creatively. Each of the major systems will be explained in simple STEP-BY-STEP fashion along with their advantages and disadvantages. The book will detail the world's most powerful and proven creative systems from Alex Osborn's original four rules of Brainstorming, defined fifty years ago, to the Eureka! Ranch's newest patent-pending system: The Three Dimensions of Creativity™.

Jump Start Your AMERICAN DREAM (Brain Brew Books, PLANNED for fall 2007), by Doug Hall and David Wecker. The only guide you'll ever need to Find, Develop and Start your own small business. The book is in three acts. Act I details how to find the right idea for the right business for you, Act II helps you refine and develop your concept, and Act III helps you launch your business more successfully by avoiding the pitfalls and problems common with small-business start-ups. The book's advice comes to life in real-world stories from callers to the Brain Brew radio program hosted by Doug and David. It's one part inspiration mixed with one part science-based ideas blended with a healthy dose of caffeinated energy and enthusiasm.

OTHER BOOKS
BY DOUG HALL

Maverick Mindset (hc, Simon & Schuster, 1997) and **Making the Courage Connection** (pb, Fireside, 1998), both with David Wecker. A GREAT BOOK and one of Doug's and David's personal favorites. It features motivational stories and ideas for helping you find the courage to journey from fear to freedom.

Jump Start Your Brain (Warner Books, 1995), by Doug Hall with David Wecker. Doug's first book is ideal for inspiring artists, teachers, and children. Later research has found that many of the teachings and techniques don't work especially well in today's high-stress business world. Sorry! *Jump Start Your CREATIVE Brain* is intended as the newest and most up-to-date version on what drives innovation success in today's marketplace.

North Pole Tenderfoot: 20 Dogs, 40 Below, 200 Miles. (Brain Brew Books, PLANNED for early 2006), by Doug Hall. The true story of Doug's re-creation of Admiral Peary's 1906 "Last Dash to the Pole." It's a tale of adventure and leadership that will inspire you to Get Up! Get Out! and Get Going! with your life, your business, your dreams, and aspirations.

I Love to Receive E-mail and PICTURE POSTCARDS from Readers

And, YES, I do respond.

Thank you for letting me into your life for this short time.

I'd like to know your thoughts, reactions, and comments about *Jump Start Your MARKETING Brain*.

I'd also like to know the Advice and Ideas you like the most, which you didn't, and what effect, if any, this book has had on your sales and marketing success.

Please e-mail me at:

Doug@DougHall.com

I promise to make every effort to personally respond to each message.

I also love to receive Picture Postcards. They're so much more fun and exciting than e-mails. If you send me one with your return address on it, I'll do my best to send one back to you. Mail Picture Postcards to:

Doug Hall
3849 Edwards Road
Cincinnati, Ohio 45244

Scientific Advice & Ideas for Immediately Doubling Your Marketing or Innovation Success Rate

Jump Start Your Business Coaching Programs help leaders of small and medium-sized businesses with under $50 million (US) in annual sales double the effectiveness of their marketing messages, new products, and services. Programs are led by licensed experts in Scotland, Canada, and the United States. For information about attending a program or becoming a *Jump Start Your Business* licensee, e-mail **Doug@DougHall.com** or visit **www.JSYB.com**.

Brain Brew Idea Factory

If you liked this book, you'll love listening to *Brain Brew*. It's a weekly show of ideas and encouragement from the Coffee House Studio at the Eureka! Ranch. It's hosted by Ranch founder Doug Hall and David Wecker, chief writer at the Eureka! Ranch. Brain Brew is nationally distributed by PRI (Public Radio International). If your public radio station doesn't carry the show, visit **www.800BrainBrew.com** to listen to this week's show as well as a twenty-four-hour channel of archived shows.

EUREKA！RANCH
INVENTING

The World's Only SCIENTIFIC SYSTEM
for Inventing BIG IDEAS at Corporate Meetings!

Eureka! Ranch founder Doug Hall will turn your ordinary department off-site, sales meeting, or executive event into an EXTRAORDINARY idea machine! All programs incorporate the same caffeinated energy and excitement that has made the Eureka! Ranch *America's No. 1 Innovation Team*. To learn more, visit **www.DougHall.com**, e-mail **Doug@DougHall.com**, or call **(513) 271-9911**.

THANK YOU

My name appears on the cover as the creator of this book. However, in truth, the book is the result of thousands of pieces of advice and ideas provided by my family, friends, and business associates.

Thank you, **Debbie Hall**—my High School Sweetheart, Wife, and Best Friend.

Thank you, **Kristyn**, **Tori** and **Brad Hall**—The three greatest teenagers on earth! Each a unique individual. Each with special gifts. I love you all, just the way you are.

Thank you, **Richard Hunt**—Publisher and Chief Cheerleader for my books and independent booksellers.

Thank you, **Jack Heffron**, Editor. If the reading is worthwhile, it's because of Jack. If it's not, it's because I was too stubborn to listen.

Thank you, **Kari McNamara**—President of the Eureka! Ranch and the Smartest Business Partner I've ever had.

Thank you, **Kevin McNamara**—The world's greatest graphics guru.

Thank you, **Corie Roudebush**—my Executive Assistant and the Master of Managing my Universe.

Thank you to Jeffrey Stamp for technical assistance and promotional appearances for the first edition of this book. Thank you to Rose Randolph for research help. Thank you to Chris Stormann for your usual outstanding statistical analysis.

Thanks to the thousands of Eureka! Ranch clients over the past nineteen years who have challenged me to think quicker, smarter, and more creatively about the SYSTEMS that drive marketing success.

Thanks to the Eureka! Ranch staff and the Trained Brain Posse: Bruce Hall, Matt Kirk, Lorrie Paulus, Hannah Buchanan, Anne Badanes, Tracy Duckworth, Scott Dunkle, Juliann Gardner, Benjamin Franklin, Colleen

Harris, Sarah Hawkins, Craig Kurz, Sondra Kurz, Mike Katz, Jane Portman, Matthew Fenton, Laura Rolfes, David Wecker, Tod Gentile, Sam Wecker, Scott Wells, Tom Wilson, Billay Brooks, Pam Twist, Mark Twist, Julie Phillipi, Kara Stumph, Bruce Forsee, Margaret Henson, Negia York. Thanks to Les Moermand—gone but not forgotten.

Thanks to the friends of the Ranch whose never-ending support helped make this book possible: Tom Ackerman, John Altman, David Cassady, Steve and Mary Friedberg, Ann Herrmann, Patty Hogan, Chris Hylen, Kip Knight, Copthorne MacDonald, Thane Maynard, Austin McNamara, Jerry McNellis, Dave Owens, Tim Riker, Eric Schulz, Renee Steele, Dick Steuerwald, Chic Thompson, Tracie Tighe, and Andy Timmerman.

Special thanks to the world-class team at EMMIS BOOKS: Richard Hunt, Jack Heffron, Ann Comello, Steve Sullivan, Matthew DeRhodes, Howard Cohen, Amy Fogelson, Mary Schutz, and Andrea Kupper.

Thanks to the *Brain Brew* radio team at WGUC: Mark Perzel, Robin Gehl, Bruce Ellis, Rich Eiswerth, Gordon Bayliss, Don Danko, Tim Lanter, Andrew Lucyzyn, Sherri Mancini, Coleen Tracey, Chris Phelps.

Thank you to the people of Prince Edward Island, Canada, who continuously teach me how to live life meaningfully. Special thanks to those who provided good food and never-ending support to nourish me when I was hidden away at our farmhouse in Springbrook: Mike and Margaret England, Cop MacDonald and Bev Stetson, Scott MacAulay, Don Groom, and Mary and Mel Crane.

INDEX

★ ★ ★ ★ ★ ★ ★ ★ ★ ★

DOUG HALL
{inventor, author, revolutionary}

Doug Hall is founder and CEO of the Eureka! Ranch. You may not know him, but the odds are you know of his work. A national survey found that the average home in the USA utilizes eighteen products or services Doug and his Eureka! Ranch team have helped withgrow. And that's just the beginning, over half his work is for industrial, business-to-business and international brands.

Doug began his entrepreneurial career at age twelve, later earned a degree as a chemical engineer from the University of Maine and then worked for Proctor & Gamble, where he rose to the rank of Master Marketing Inventor and set a corporate record developing and introducing nine new business initiatives in a twelve-month period.

After 10 years, Doug retired from corporate life to found what is now known as the Eureka! Ranch, a corporate think tank that has won accolades from some of the biggest corporations in the world including American Express, Procter & Gamble, The Ford Motor Company, Nike and Walt Disney.

Known for his plain talk, energetic style and bold approach Doug has been named by *Inc. Magazine*, *The Wall Street Journal*, *A&E top 10* and *Dateline NBC* as "One of America's Top Innovation Experts."

Beyond his corporate work, Doug's Eureka! Institute helps small businesses, colleges, governments and non-profits leverage the Eureka! Ranch innovation systems. Doug also co-hosts the weekly radio program *Brain Brew Idea Factory* nationally distributed by PRI, Public Radio International.

Doug is a citizen of both the USA and Canada. In recognition of his original research in the fields of Marketing marketing and Innovationinnovation, he was awarded an honorary doctorate degree by the University of Prince Edward Island in Canada.

To contact Doug e-mail **Doug@DougHall.com** or call **(513) 271-9911**.